I0817563

Additional Praise for *Rough House*

"I could not love a book more. As I think about *Rough House*, I think what Alison Lyn Miller has done here is portraiture—Robert Frank meets John McPhee—and the real people who come to life on her pages, and their specific and universal dreams and fears, will haunt you long after the book is finished and passed like a secret to a friend. Sure, it's a wrestling book. But that's perfect. Because we are, all of us, imperfect animals on a spinning rock, fighting with the forces all around us, beset even, wrestling off the past and with the future, wishing real life had the simplicity of a 20-by-20 square."

—Wright Thompson, ESPN, author of *The Barn*

"Wrestling exists in a dream state—not just for the fans who come to see good conquer evil, but for the performers who wage constant battles with their flaws and desires. Alison Lyn Miller gets up close to show how the deepest struggles of family and identity can play out even under the dim lights of a dilapidated Georgia gym. You might not know the wrestlers in Miller's book, but when you finish *Rough House*, you'll know their hearts."

—Tommy Tomlinson, author of *Dogland* and *The Elephant in the Room*

"I picture Alison Lyn Miller standing by the backyard training ring, or backstage at the weekend throwdown inside a Georgia strip mall. She's an anthropologist, an interpreter who aims to explain this wildly popular 'chump of sports' to people like me who read books. Neither snide nor worshipful, Miller understands wrestling as violent, cathartic storytelling by 'actors who do their own stunts,' an art form that deserves respect. Read

Rough House to learn about how the 'dulcet thunder of body to mat became a balm' for so many, the bargain between wrestlers and fans, . . . and why it matters to our political moment."

—Ted Conover, author *of Cheap Land Colorado* and *Newjack: Guarding Sing Sing*

"With empathy and grace and insight, driven by respectful and intimate reporting, Alison Lyn Miller pulls the curtain back on a grand American spectacle to show us all that, while suplexes and body slams can be faked, the honest human dramas that draw wrestlers to 'this brutal ballet' are universal and revealing."

—John T. Edge, host of ESPN's *TrueSouth* and author of *House of Smoke: A Southerner Goes Searching for Home*

"In *Rough House*, Alison Lyn Miller proves what fans of professional wrestling have always known: This pseudo-sport is the skeleton key for unlocking the mysteries—and horrors—of the United States. Miller, like the wrestlers she documents, puts in a back-breaking effort to prove that wrestling matters, and the results are as thrilling as any hardcore brawl. Truly, this is a book that belongs on the shelves of not just wrestling fans, but anyone who wants to understand the agonized American soul."

—Josephine Riesman, author of *Ringmaster: Vince McMahon and the Unmaking of America*

"Behind the show and beneath the costumes, *Rough House* reveals some of the best of America. In this soulful and impeccably researched story, Alison Lyn Miller separates the good guys from the bad guys, the babyfaces from the heels, and the myths from the legends. It's a fantastic show."

—Tim Brown, author of *The Tao of the Backup Catcher*

"Pro wrestling may or may not be a sport, but it's without question a magnificent spectacle, the badass American analog of kabuki or pantomime. *Rough House* is a moving and fascinating look behind the scenes of this spectacle at the grassroots level, from the backyard trampolines where boys and girls learn to copy their heroes to the small-town gyms where they try to join them. You'll find yourself rooting for both the babyfaces and the heels, even if you already know who will win and who will lose, because Alison Lyn Miller makes you question what it means to 'win' or 'lose' in this game."

—Ed Southern, author of *Fight Songs: A Story of Love and Sports in a Complicated South*

ROUGH HOUSE

ROUGH HOUSE

A FATHER, A SON, AND THE PURSUIT OF PRO WRESTLING GLORY

ALISON LYN MILLER

W. W. NORTON & COMPANY
Independent Publishers Since 1923

Printed in the United States of America
First Edition

For information about special discounts for bulk purchases, please contact
W. W. Norton Special Sales at specialsales@wwnorton.com or 800-233-4830

Manufacturing by Lakeside Book Company
Book design by Daniel Lagin
Production manager: Julia Druskin

ISBN: 978-1-324-08658-1 (pbk.)

W. W. Norton & Company, Inc., 500 Fifth Avenue, New York, NY 10110
www.wwnorton.com

W. W. Norton & Company Ltd., 15 Carlisle Street, London W1D 3BS

Authorized EU representative:
EAS, Mustamäe tee 50, 10621 Tallinn, Estonia

10 9 8 7 6 5 4 3 2 1

For the workers.

AUTHOR'S NOTE

This is a work of nonfiction informed by five years of reporting, including hundreds of hours of interviews and observation. With rare exception, I use working wrestlers' ring names rather than their legal names.

ROUGH HOUSE

CHAPTER 1

Hunter Noblett parks his Jeep and walks up the leaf-covered dirt driveway.

"Do you mind plugging that in down there?" Jamie Holmes yells to him from behind his ranch-style house in Statham, Georgia. He carries a 1,000-watt halogen work light in one hand. The other uncoils an extension cord as he walks toward the wrestling ring, shielded from the elements by an oversized carport in his backyard.

"Yeah, I gotcha," Hunter, in Deadpool pajama pants and a green Under Armour pullover, says. It's November 19, 2019. In three days, Hunter will turn 17.

Backyards serve as origin story settings for countless professional wrestlers, both established and unheard of. When it comes to training there's no match for a real ring. When none is available, a trampoline suffices. No one wants to practice a back bump on a concrete floor. They're called backyarders at this stage in their careers, where they wobble on the lowest rung of a long ladder to the top. Some start with aspirations of signing with WWE* or AEW,† the industry's most prominent companies. Most settle for the accessible catharsis of wrestling's smallest stages: American Legions, rec center gymnasiums, bars, and churches where, for a few hours, they can be whoever they want to be.

Wrestling was going to be a ticket out for Hunter's father, but it never came. Billy Ray vowed Hunter and his younger brother, Christian, wouldn't waste their lives chasing something so hollow. He steered them toward amateur wrestling, an accredited sport where they'd build strength, stay out of trouble, and most importantly, get college scholarships.

But telling a kid to do as his father says, not as he did, when his father is a professional wrestler, is like taking him to an arcade full of howling flashing games and saying, "Don't waste your time and money on these."

So tonight Hunter drove to Jamie's after amateur wrestling practice at Apalachee High School. He gets all As and has well over 100 career wins on the mat. His parents pay for private training and a college recruiter, anything they can to set him up to attend a four-year college—an experience neither of them had.

In building a life without worry for their children, Billy Ray and Jennifer Noblett instilled a certain privilege, and with it came confidence. In insisting Hunter stay away from the ring until

* World Wrestling Entertainment (WWE): The largest sports entertainment company in the world, headquartered in Stamford, Connecticut, and owned since 2023 by TKO Group Holdings, a subsidiary of the talent and media company Endeavor. It began in 1953 as the Capitol Wrestling Corporation (CWC) under Vince McMahon Sr. The company became the World Wide Wrestling Federation (WWWF), and later the World Wrestling Federation (WWF). McMahon Sr., sold it to his son Vince in 1982. In 2002, it became known as WWE.

† All Elite Wrestling (AEW): Founded in 2019 by Tony Khan, based in Jacksonville, Florida, and named the third most valuable combat sports promotion, behind UFC (Ultimate Fighting Championship) and WWE, by *Forbes* in 2024.

after college, Billy Ray challenged his young son to delay his own gratification, a decidedly mature concept.

Jamie's auburn roots seep into platinum, shoulder-length hair and his midsection fills out a black T-shirt stamped with nWo, the acronym of the late-'90s heel stable New World Order, briefly helmed by Hulk Hogan. At 34, he's wrestled in Georgia rings nearly half his life. For some of those years, he wrestled Billy Ray.

Artists study perspective and chiaroscuro. Wrestlers learn hip tosses and flip bumps. The good ones load up a mental toolbox with moves and pull from it in the ring like Realist painters working with color, layering each action and reaction in a way that appears natural to the people watching.

A few years ago, another local wrestler, Leatherface, unloaded this ring in Jamie's backyard after the City of Winder, Georgia, deemed it an eyesore. Here, he teaches men and women the skills they need to perform. "Big-time big-name wrestlers?" Jamie says. "I can't help them with that. But I can get them started."

The performers' stories are the same. They grew up watching wrestling and come here to fulfill a dream: to be the person being watched rather than the one watching. To embody an outsize character in battle is to feel the thrill of admiration and aversion, to revel in the warmth of attention. It's true for Hunter, and it's true for Jamie's other trainee tonight, 39-year-old high school English teacher Brian Snyder. Hope all you want of being an NFL running back but good luck showing up to the Combine. But if you want to be a wrestler, in this state, you're never far from a ring and a weathered hand to help you up.

Hunter spent his childhood watching wrestlers like Jeff Hardy, CM Punk, and Dolph Ziggler rise to WWE stardom. On weekends he watched his father chase fame on much smaller stages, a bit player in a global show so addictive Billy Ray calls it a drug.

Hunter and Brian warm up by ricocheting between the ropes. Their bodies collide with steel cable sheathed in garden hose, attached by springs to metal posts.

Brian complains he's sore from last week.

"Can I say something?" Jamie asks, watching from the ground. "It only gets worse from here."

Jamie, who delivers home medical equipment by day, performs less frequently these days. Tonight, he still reels from a Halloween-themed casket match in which his opponent Justin Legend assaulted him with thumbtacks and a barbed axe handle. In Hunter, Jamie has a spry stand-in to demonstrate the techniques he wants to teach Brian. Hunter's adept. He's been doing them his whole life.

The tripod utility light—the kind construction workers use to extend the workday—illuminates the canvas, dingy with dirt and sweat. Brian grabs Hunter's wrist and twists his arm downward. Hunter grimaces and lands hard on his knees to amplify the sound. Brian yanks the teenager's arm like a crowbar and flips his 170-pound body into the air. Hunter lands flat on his back. *Thud.* And then bounces up, unfazed.

A ring is a dance floor. You have to be well-versed in the steps to gracefully perform. You have to listen, and you have to feel. A wrestler's opponent has everything to do with how well he's received. The reason a man can hurl someone twice his size across the ring is that the big guy crouches and jumps as the little guy launches him into the air. If your opponent doesn't effectively project pain from your punches, your effort—no matter how skillful—is wasted. It's called selling. The customers are the people in the seats.

The ring's layers—canvas, foam, plywood, and Flexi-Beam—reverberate with every collision between body and mat. The sound echoes off the aluminum roof overhead and across Jamie's backyard, past the bare trees and into the dark distance beyond. To Hunter it's a heartbeat, the soundtrack to his existence.

"Lats are on fire," Brian says, taking a labored breath with his head between his knees.

"I didn't do it," Hunter laughs, gulping water from a 2-liter Diet Dr Pepper bottle.

Jamie steps back from the ring. "It's changed from the generation before me," he says. "This," he points his finger back and forth between himself—a professional wrestler—and me, a journalist, "wouldn't have ever happened."

From its American inception in the second half of the 1800s to the moment in 1989 when Vince McMahon revealed professional wrestling was actually "sports entertainment," as a means of avoiding fees and regulations imposed by state sports commissions, tight-lipped performers were bound by secrecy. No wrestler, not even one on the indie circuit like Jamie, would have let a reporter behind the curtain.

Wrestling is fake. It's the first thing naysayers note about this violent spectacle that straddles theatre and sport. To that, wrestling fans say, "Duh." There's an unspoken truth here, a wink and nod between spectator and performer: The action in the ring is real, but it's not as bad as it looks. Wrestling relies on suspension of disbelief, the same tactic we employ when we sit down with a Marvel movie.

That acknowledgment wasn't always widespread. Though they were often friends off the clock, bad guys (heels) and good guys (babyfaces) were not to be seen together. The ruse is so peculiar it commands its own term: kayfabe. Wrestlers guarded the act like a flame. You want to join the brotherhood? You take the oath. Breaking character was breaking kayfabe, wrestling's original sin.

The best anyone can guess, the word is some butchered, pig Latin version of the word "fake," created to describe a concept specific to professional wrestling: the insistence that characters and events are real. There's no curtain call, no fourth wall. It's Method acting, to the nth degree. This makes sense. Wrestling grew out of carnivals in the mid-to-late 19th century, and performers spoke Carnie in the ring, a mucked-up language unrecognizable to spectators.

So yeah, it's "fake." So are Tarantino movies.

Before he agreed to be interviewed, Jamie asked the person who introduced us—Justin Legend, his opponent in the casket match three weeks earlier—a question only someone in the business would understand. "Is this a shoot-shoot,* a work-shoot, or a complete work†?" Aces in the pro wrestler's vocabulary deck, born of that early 20th-century carnivalspeak. Legend confirmed: The interview was a shoot-shoot. One hundred percent unscripted real-life.

I turned 7 in 1990, the year The Ultimate Warrior took the belt from Hulk Hogan at WrestleMania VI. Wrestling permeated popular culture. I was around it but never in it. I grew up and rested it next to the other relics of my childhood: Micro Machines, Michael Jordan, New Kids on the Block.

Then one February night in 2019 I showed up, out of curiosity, to a wrestling show in Athens, Georgia, where I live. I started asking questions and soon discovered a community bound by a passion for a pervasive but overlooked pastime. Our tendency to imbue characters with meaning and relish in stories—fact, fiction, or somewhere in between—is part of what makes us human.

---

* Shoot: Truth.

† Work: Kayfabe.

Wrestling, I learned, reverberates the chimes of our fundamental existence like no other endeavor.

I guess you could say I came for the suplexes and stayed for the stories. This one unfolds in the shadows of the bright lights and big cities. And like every wrestling story, whether it plays out inside the American Airlines Center or a Georgia backyard, it's bigger than fist and foot.

"Go through tie-ups and chaining—what we did last week," Jamie says, instructing Brian and Hunter to take turns calling the moves, whispering to each other what comes next in the sequence.

They lock arms and the ring rattles again. Hunter, 23 years younger than his bearded opponent, bounces weightlessly. Brian, in knee and elbow braces, bends down to catch his breath again. Jamie folds his arms and leans into the ring.

"Is that the only way you know how to reverse it?" he asks Brian. "The arm wringer?" He climbs the plastic stairs to the canvas to explain the logic and mechanics of the move set. "You don't have to do all that spinning shit," he trails off, demonstrating the move on Brian. "And when you grabbed that headlock, you were on the wrong side. I'll show you a standing switch."

Wrestling showrunners, called bookers, pit heels (bad guys) against babyfaces (good guys). A heel screams "Shut up!" at a heckling fan. A babyface lingers a heel's grip, breaks free only when the crowd gets loud enough to propel him. Every encounter between opponents must project that simple, most enduring conflict: good versus evil.

Timing is crucial. You have to draw out an injury to give the fans time to react, to process. A wrestler's job is to entertain. If you're not there for the fans, and to support your fellow wrestlers, you're "in business for yourself"—another impiety in the unspoken constitution of it all.

Jamie watches as Hunter and Brian lock arms and try again. "Who would've been the heel in that situation?" he asks, raising his voice above the racket.

Hunter answers without hesitation. "Him."

"Would it?" Jamie plies.

"He was grabbing the rope," Hunter says.

"Well you held it," Brian says.

The conversation between them unfolds like it would in a third-grade classroom with Jamie at the chalkboard. Then it starts to sound more like three brothers exchanging verbal jabs.

"Yeah, but the way you carry yourself... I want to smack you," Jamie says to Hunter.

"What is it? The gum chewing?" Hunter asks.

"It's the jock thing," Jamie says. "It's the blond hair, blue-eyed jock."

"Ok, it's your turn to hit the lionsault," Jamie says to Brian. "There's crash pads, but you're a bitch if you use them."

Hunter demonstrates. In one seamless motion, he hops to the second rope, grips the top one, and flips backwards in a spinning catapult, landing on his back. In a real match he'd land belly down onto his opponent, who would be prone in the center of the ring recovering from his last strike.

Jamie feigns annoyance at Hunter's ease, but his tone reveals pride. "Sixteen and no injuries," he says. "Genetic freak."

"Ideally we're still young enough to do it but wise enough to know not to do it," he continues, describing the craft he's devoted his life to, the one he now guides people toward. "But then occasionally crazy enough to still do it anyway."

CHAPTER 2

Hunter James Noblett always knew he'd use his born name as his first name in the ring, but he agonized over James. It felt basic. Forgettable. Not like the names that rolled off the tongue like those inked into his memory: Buzz Sawyer, Kyle O'Reilly, Shawn Michaels.

Wrestlers say their character, or gimmick, is an extension of their true personality. It's easier to amplify what you know than to contrive it. He couldn't think of anything better so he stuck with Hunter James. When it came to his gimmick, he looked in the mirror.

Four months into the COVID-19 pandemic, while most of the world was still adhering to some form of lockdown, Hunter traveled to Glenwood, Arkansas, with brothers Chris and Jerry Nelms—Georgia wrestling lifers working the ring since Billy Ray was in it—and performed in his first show: The Sizzlin' Summer Showdown at the Pike County Fairgrounds. When the promoter asked for his entrance music he replied with the first thing that came to mind. "Look What the Cat Dragged In." His father's song.

He'd been at it for a while: racking up high-school amateur wrestling wins and driving to Jamie Holmes's backyard ring for late-night practice matches. One Saturday a month he ran the music and rang the bell at a show in Athens. He was "paying his dues": showing up and working for nothing as a utility man to one day earn himself a spot on the match card.

He played the part of straight-A athlete when his parents were around but capitalized on their fractured attention. It had been a trying year for the Nobletts. The pandemic put the housing market into overdrive, and Jenn, a loan processor at a local mortgage company, worked 60–70 hours a week. She and Billy Ray grew apart. She moved out in January 2021, starting an official separation in their twentieth year of marriage, Hunter's senior year of high school.

While Jenn was busy at work Billy Ray got busy trying to win her back. Hunter knew if he kept his grades up and performed well on the mat, his parents wouldn't notice he was spending more time at wrestling shows on the weekends. Sometimes after a particularly intense set of conditioning drills at Apalachee he'd look at himself in the mirror and ask, "What the fuck am I doing?" Billy Ray had pushed Hunter toward amateur wrestling. Hunter never loved it. The more time he spent around professional wrestling rings, the more he quietly considered his future.

In March 2021 Billy Ray got a text from Hunter's best friend, Clay Carroll, the cowboy hat–wearing offensive lineman they both affectionately called Billy Bob, after the *Varsity Blues* character. *Have you seen Hunter's Facebook page*? It was a wrestling flyer, covered with blue flames and crowned by the words Anarchy Wrestling: Hardcore Hell 23. Clay knew Hunter was wrestling and thought Billy Ray should know. He was close with the entire family and didn't like being part of the secret. Ensconced between the faces of Georgia wrestlers booked to perform on April 24, a shirtless teenager in wrist tape smiled. Hunter.

I'm going to fucking kill him, Billy Ray thought.

For two and a half years he and Jenn spent $185 a month for a college recruiter and $60 an hour for private amateur wrestling training. They drove him to and from practices. Paid for out-of-state tournaments. All of this to shape Hunter into something an athletic director would offer a scholarship. Billy Ray was ready to set Hunter's Jeep on fire. He refused to see or talk to him. He knew he wouldn't be able to control himself if he did, so he avoided his son. He had a saying around the house. "Don't be gay and don't be a Democrat." *I'd be happier if he was sleeping with a gay Democrat*, he thought.

Billy Ray had spent years laying the path to opportunity for Hunter that no one had laid for him, *for this?* He knew Hunter was destined to get in the ring someday—nothing he could do about it—but they had a deal: Not until he finished college. He wanted Hunter to have the backup plan he never had.

What the hell? Hunter thought a few weeks earlier when the flyer's designer approached him about it. *He's going to find out someday*. And Hunter preferred Billy Ray find out he was wrestling from a flyer. It would be easier than telling him to his face.

Billy Ray preached and preached to Hunter the dangers of

not doing well in school, of not going to college, of chasing a pro wrestling career. But Hunter had seen all he needed to see. He was going to be a star. And a budding star needed to promote himself.

Billy Ray knew once Hunter felt the euphoria of bursting through the curtain and diving into the ring—of living his dream—there'd be no stopping him. That night, for the first time in as long he could remember, Billy Ray did not fall asleep to wrestling on TV. It disgusted him.

Hunter lived with Jenn at the time so avoiding Billy Ray was easy, except that Hunter spent his senior year working part-time with him at WAM, the industrial supplies manufacturer where Billy Ray worked on again, off again, for 25 years and counting. A few days later Hunter gripped a wrench behind his back as his father walked toward him in the warehouse. *Every father and son get into a fistfight at some point*, he thought. *This is it.*

Rather than a punch, Billy Ray delivered a hug.

"I love you, I hate you," he said, putting into words his dissonant emotions. "Fuck you." Billy Ray said he would come to Hunter's next match but made it clear he'd never watch him perform again. Before he walked away he offered an earnest parting sentiment. "I'm proud of you."

Billy Ray and Jenn met to watch Hunter at Landmark Arena in Cornelia, Georgia, a building with peeling paint and a grass parking lot known to those who frequent it as The Church of Southern Wrestling.* The building, with its 70-year-old floors marred by squashed cigarette butts, was sparsely populated. Before the show Billy Ray wandered to the dressing room in the back where Hunter was wrapping his wrists with athletic tape.

* Southern wrestling: relatable characters rather than superheroes and a focus on promos and feuds over physique.

Hunter hugged him and then asked him to leave. "You can't be back here," he said. "You're not a wrestler anymore."

Billy Ray and Jenn sat next to each other watching their oldest son and made plans for his brother Christian's upcoming birthday. They agreed to get together the following Saturday to shop for gifts, an outing that ended at a moonshine distillery in the North Georgia mountains. At Christian's birthday dinner he asked her out again, this time to see a Journey cover band. It felt like a first date.

Hunter walked across the turf at Apalachee High School's football stadium to accept his high school diploma two months later. He finished with a 3.8 GPA and a year's worth of college credits earned in a dual-enrollment program. Coker University, a Division II school in Hartsville, South Carolina, offered him an academic and amateur wrestling scholarship. Billy Ray and Jenn's hard work as parents had paid off.

That August, the family loaded their Jeep Wranglers—Billy Ray's in black, Hunter's in silver—and drove 250 miles east to Coker. The next day Jenn posted a photo on Facebook of Hunter standing next to a mini fridge and microwave in his vinyl-tiled dorm room. She wrote: "Hunter James IS OFFICIALLY A COKER COBRA!"

Billy Ray, Jenn, and Christian, whose baby pudge earned him an enduring nickname, Chunk, said goodbye and continued east to Myrtle Beach for the weekend. "I hope no one has plans this weekend," the wrestling coach said at the team's first meeting that Wednesday. And then he delivered a packed schedule: an all-athlete pep rally Friday, team photos Saturday.

Hunter had plans. He had three matches that weekend: the opening match and main event at Landmark on Friday night and one on Saturday at Southern Fried Championship Wrestling, where he was starting his run for the tag-team title as one half of The Palmetto Express.

"Hey," he said to the coach. "I'm not going to be here this weekend."

The coach asked why.

"Pro wrestling," Hunter said.

He looked dumbfounded. "Pro wrestling," Hunter said again. "You know, WWE? Play fighting in my underwear?"

Coach suggested he could have his photo taken the following weekend. Hunter was booked then too.

"Sounds like you have a lot of thinking to do," the coach said.

Sure, dude. Hunter thought. He was done thinking. He'd run through this scene so many times in his mind, there was no hesitation now, no contemplation, no lying awake at night. *I need one shot,* he thought. *They won't forget me. I'll make sure of that.*

He walked straight to the registrar's office and told an administrator he was dropping out. She handed him a tablet to complete the exit paperwork. He scanned the dropdown menu beneath "reason for unenrollment." He clicked "other" and then typed: To be a professional wrestler.

He'd done the research. He knew college didn't guarantee a higher income. Besides, college-educated people sometimes acted like they were better than him. He didn't want to be around it, didn't want to waste his time, wasn't going to spend one more second doing anything besides the thing he loves.

Jenn's phone rang. "I'm homesick," Hunter said. *Don't fall for that shit,* Billy Ray thought, as he listened to her console her son. He knew what Hunter was up to. "I will graduate from college," he promised. "But right now I'm coming home to do what makes me happy." Jenn hung up and looked at Billy Ray. "Let's go get his Jeep," he said. "Then he'll be stranded there."

It was too late. Coach called. Hunter didn't answer. It was real now. He had to follow through. Hunter sent a text: "Driving. Can't talk. I had fun with wrestling in high school, it kept me in shape, but it's not for me anymore. I appreciate you putting in the effort on me but I'm done." He pulled into the first RaceTrac gas station he came to across the Georgia state line, bought a donut and a Monster energy drink. The coach pleaded with him to return. *We can reenroll you. We can figure this out.*

"That's not what you want to do," Hunter explained. "Because my heart is never going to be in it. My heart was never in it." He'd gotten all he needed from the mat: athleticism and the ability to move safely and skillfully around the ring. He'd be a better professional wrestler for it.

Billy Ray had written his story, now it was time for Hunter to write his. Within hours of dropping out of college, he leapt from the top rope at Landmark. He had never felt so free.

Billy Ray's prediction, the fate he knew would arrive but hoped would come later, was affirmed. Hunter left the certainty of a college career for a gauzy underworld riddled by injury and ruled by an aging cast of washed-up gatekeepers. Billy Ray was disgusted by the talentless, out-of-shape has-beens and never-wills who lurked around the spaces where Hunter trained and performed, people who constantly told Hunter how good he was.

If you're the best in the room, Billy Ray always told him, you're in the wrong room.

Billy Ray knew better than anyone how addictive wrestling is. He knew you could spend 20 years of your life chasing the dream and end right where you started, with nothing to show for it. "People say, 'He's young, he can go back to school.' He's not going to school. He's already started wrestling. Nobody goes back to school after they start wrestling."

In dropping out of college to pursue professional wrestling, Hunter retreated from a father who always pushed him to be better and entered a world where he is almost always the best in the room.

"He doesn't take criticism that well," Billy Ray says. "He loves when people tell him how great he is. If you ask me, that's how come he likes to hang out with the boys in the back."

Despite Billy Ray's intentions, a reel of Hunter's life at 18 mirrors his own at that age, with the days passing in monomaniacal rhythm: work, train, perform, hope someone notices. He lifts, runs, and pounds protein, fortifying himself into a human action figure with one goal: to get signed by a major wrestling promotion.

Success in pro wrestling teeters on confidence and humility, on loyalty and leaving things behind. Hunter's routine reveals his dedication to a bright-lights future. It also reveals an unconscious rooting into blue-collar adulthood, should he fall short. His only backup plan, Billy Ray knows, is to work at the one place Billy Ray told him his whole life he is too good for, the place he's worked for a quarter century.

At 18, Hunter doesn't understand the stakes. He can't feel the ache of inevitability his father feels. He doesn't see the wrestlers all around him who started with the same goal. Men with swollen, broken bodies who continue to show up because the fleeting stardom is a lifeline, a ticket out without having to go anywhere.

"I know what it's like to have nothing, not just in wrestling but in real life," Billy Ray says.

"He better make it," he continues. "Because I'm the type of person that will tell him, 'I told you so.'"

CHAPTER 3

Outside Landmark Arena

Hunter tagged along with his cousin Justin, who wrestles as Chop Top, many times before becoming a Landmark Arena regular on his own. One such night a few months into his senior year of high school, Hunter insisted they linger after the show wrapped. His birthday was the next day. He had a benchmark in mind: he wanted to turn 18 in a wrestling ring. A Landmark trainer, "The Angel of Death" Azrael, texted him the next day with a question: How would he like to start coming to Landmark for ring time?

The building started its life as the Mud Creek School gymnasium in 1949. Five decades later, students of a different sort showed up to this crossroads in the Appalachian foothills of Northeast Georgia to practice and perform. There are no official hours but if you opened the door on any given night between 1998 and 2022 you'd likely find a few professional wrestlers inside.

Wrestlers know the most impactful moments in the ring aren't the moves but rather the pauses between them: the times when a performer writhes on the mat after receiving a debilitating blow or showboats around the ring after giving one. Similarly, the most poignant moments at Landmark aren't the ones captured on camera, they're the in-between times.

A rickety screen door in the back leads to the makeshift locker room where men and women escaping their everyday lives pull on their tights and tie up their boots. Just before 7 o'clock on a Monday evening in August 2021, Azrael sits on a narrow wood bench and sifts through a large suitcase of gear while drawing from the cigarette stationed between his lips.

"My teacher was AJ Styles," he says, name-dropping the WWE Superstar who spent much of his early career in the building. "And Rick Michaels, the person who taught AJ Styles." Landmark's most famous graduate, Styles signed with WWE at 38, after nearly two decades working the indies. He's a symbol of hope, proof that hard work pays off, that dreams come true, and that provenance does not dictate success. To WWE fans across the world, he's The Phenomenal One. To wrestlers and fans in Georgia, he's one of them. The one who got out. The one who didn't forget where he came from.

On September 9, 2017, Styles climbed the ropes inside Landmark and raised WWE's United States Championship belt high. A warrior home with the kill. An AJ chant gave way to something more poignant: Welcome Home.

Styles's speech included parting words redolent with promise: "It's not how you start, it's how you finish." His unannounced appearance "may or may not have been the loudest pop* in the 19-year history of Landmark Arena," Larry Goodman wrote on *Georgia Wrestling History* the next day.

Two weeks before Hardcore Hell 23 Hunter finished his match at Landmark and charged through the curtain, all sweat and adrenaline. Styles, home from WWE tapings, stood watching the action on a video monitor. It was the first time Hunter had been booked for the main event, against two wrestlers from Alabama. He'd employed one of Styles's signature moves: a running corner backflip dropkick. "Don't do it just to get a pop," Styles warned. "Do it and make it mean something."

His words reinforced what Hunter knew but didn't execute. A wrestler's moves are like words in a story. They have to happen in an order that propels the plot. He thought of Billy Ray's big, slow powerslam† and started working on a quicker, more compact version of the move—his own telling of the story.

Like a dirt track on the way to the Daytona 500, no Georgia wrestler, past or present, has missed the opportunity to perform at Landmark. It's an essential step on all paths: paths that lead to the WWE; paths that weave around the South and snuff out quietly.

Azrael and his wife, "The Natural Born Legend" Crystal Rose, run the training program at Landmark and book its Friday night show, National Championship Wrestling (NCW). There's no definitive training rubric or length of commitment, and admis-

* Pop: a big cheer from the crowd.

† Powerslam: a move in which a wrestler, with one arm between his opponent's legs and the other around his back, lifts the guy and slams him down, landing on top of him.

sions are rolling. The real value comes in access to the place, where you never know who might walk in the door. When the pandemic struck, Styles showed up to stay fresh during WWE's production halt. The place is a shithole, but it's a sacred one.

In the ring there are leads, follows, and the occasional whisper in an ear, but most of what happens is an unscripted unfurling of familiar moves, like dancing with a stranger. Trainees who put in the work can expect to perform within a year. But it takes about four years for it to really click, Azrael says. "There's a lot of process to take in," he explains. "Psychology of the crowd, telling a story, being safe with the moves."

Crystal, in jeggings, kneepads, and wrestling sneakers, repeats that last point. "Mainly being safe with the moves."

"Don't worry about getting hurt," Azrael likes to say. "Worry about getting injured. Because it all hurts."

Wrestlers study the art of soft assault. They can heave their opponents overhead with impossible loft and lay down a punch that comes in hot and lands like a feather. They land loud and groan louder, and when it all goes like it should, no one gets hurt—much. They learn how to take a hit and pull themselves up, unbroken. It's a skill for the ring they take to life.

Crystal was shy and small, eternally picked on at White County High School in nearby Cleveland, Georgia. She's not the first in her family to walk these wooden floors. Her great-grandmother was a Mud Creek student. On weekends for as long as she can remember, her family took her to wrestling shows where she discovered a world of brutal promise.

We're taught to control our feelings, to walk away without making a scene. Around the ring we let loose. The quiet acknowledgment that everyone walks away unharmed grants fans license to celebrate violence, and it feels good. Where else can you lob obscenities at your worst enemy without risk of being slugged? It's catharsis, for 10 dollars at the door.

Crystal met Azrael here in 2001. It was a Friday night show, "the same damn show we run now," she says. "He said something, and my dad called him a foulmouthed little bastard." Crystal was 15 and saving the money she made delivering newspapers with her mom to pay for training at the WCW Power Plant, where she planned to go when she turned 18.

That night she approached a merch table and asked the woman there, a wrestler's wife, how her husband learned to do this. The woman went backstage and returned with AJ Styles, then the head trainer at Landmark. Crystal started training with him two days later.

Crystal's entrée into the business aligned with WWE's Attitude Era (1997 to 2002), when women were typically cast as sidepieces rather than contenders. By 2002, WWE "Divas" were competing in Victoria Secret Angel–inspired catwalk showdowns. (Though they represent a significantly smaller percentage of performers, women now have divisions in WWE and AEW.) They often wore short dresses, fawned and fought over male wrestlers, and walked them to the ring, stopping just short of the action in a role known as valet.

"I hated being a valet," Crystal says. "Hated it."

In 2006 she and Azrael married in the ring at Landmark in a Miss Elizabeth and Randy Savage–inspired wedding. When she was pregnant with their son, Leo, Crystal opened presents inside the ropes.

"Without this, I might still be that shy timid little girl," she says. "And I hated the person that I was."

Hunter's laser-focused, young, good-looking, and worry-free, a powerful combination in an industry that rewards the beautiful and self-obsessed. Living with his parents and unburdened by grown-up worries like injuries, bills, and childcare, he exudes a carefree and confident presence notably absent from Crystal, Azrael, and their other trainees. Blake Ridings, a bisexual 18-year-old whose depression had landed him in alternative school, is here with Nathaniel Seabolt, a Taco Bell shift manager who just graduated high school and Ridings's best friend since elementary school when they realized their shared passion for wrestling. Crystal's 27-year-old sister, Candi, mother of four, came with her boyfriend Zackary Blane, a lanky wrestler with a ponytail a decade into his career.

They're country kids who spent their birthday money on WWE action figures and beat each other up in the backyard, who know they can turn the TV on and see heroes who will never let them down. When things got tough at home, they turned the volume up. The dulcet thunder of body to mat became a balm over the years, a security blanket they never put down.

The illusion of violence and triumph hooked them, and they hung on. When they grew up and stared down the impossibility of working-class life in the 21st century they retreated to the one thing that had always offered hope and comfort, an escape from the cruel mundanity of everyday life: the ring.

If they can't command any other stage in their lives, they can be heroes—or heels—in wrestling. Here, they touch something more American than the American Dream itself, a dream they can make come true.

The trainees gather in a circle in the ring and Crystal, who worked all day cleaning houses, directs them in a series of warm-ups. She starts by demonstrating squats and sandbag lifts. Leo gets bored and jumps on her back. She continues.

For years she put in the work, training multiple nights a week, and watched the men around her graduate to bigger, better shows while promoters passed her up.

"I lost my heart," Crystal says, sitting on the bleachers. She quit, and assumed another role—wrestler's wife, and then, mother, until the day in 2016 that Leo, then 4, asked why she no longer wrestled.

"I'm not interested in wrestling anymore," she lied. "Mommy wants to take care of you now."

"I believe in you, Mommy!" Leo said. "You can be WWE Women's Champion someday!"

She kept Leo's words to herself for a week and then returned the ring, where the fire she felt when she was young was there waiting. "I found that first love for it again, that I always had, that I just buried deep down inside my depression."

To earn a living between matches she runs her own cleaning business. "I do that so I can do this," she says.

"Dig deep or get out," she yells. "Hands over head, in through the nose, out through the mouth. You're sweating, you're not dying!"

Hunter watches from ringside in a backward ballcap, gym shorts, and a sleeveless hooded shirt. He's already worked out twice today. As they go through the exercise, he unfurls the contents of a Wendy's bag on the ring apron and tears into a Baconator burger.

He wipes his face and jumps in to demonstrate a clothesline, dropkick, and body slam on Blane. Then he climbs out of the ropes, squats on the ring apron, leaps to the top rope, and dives toward him, taking him to the floor.

"Good," Crystal says from her perch on top of the turnbuckle.

She retires to the bleachers, where her hands work in quick shifts: a tug to loosen the lace of her high-top wrestling sneaker, a pull from an e-cigarette, a slug from a plastic bottle of Diet Dr Pepper.

Tonight she and Azrael have invited Hoax, an aging skateboarder-type in baggy shorts, and Vans to talk about ring psychology, the Method acting that elevates wrestling from bush-league melee to melodrama. In professional wrestling, it's the personalities, not the acrobatics, that unlock our emotions. We want to see jealousy, fear, and rage, because we want to feel them too. Ring psychology is how a wrestler uses his body to dictate the emotions of the crowd. It's what makes a match a character-driven episode of serial storytelling rather than a one-dimensional battle between opponents. Winded and red-faced from the workout, the trainees gather on the risers and fix their eyes on him.

Wrestlers must have physical acumen, but they must also know how to talk. Performers at this level shoot short videos called promos on their iPhones, morphing into character and delivering messages to their opponents, but really, to their fans. The messages move storylines forward and keep fans engaged between shows. Opponents recount the injustice of the last encounter and promise revenge, often drawing on stories from their real lives to prove their grit. They read like Shakespearean monologues for the social media set. "Character builders," Hoax calls them.

"When we're here, we're in kayfabeland," he says.

Sometime around the turn of the 20th century, organizers of

catch* wrestling matches gazed out at rows of yawning spectators and decided they'd better find a way to amp it up. So they played God. They fixed the matches and directed opponents on duration, instructing them to exaggerate blows and follow the audience's cues. Like a comedian bailing on a bad joke, a barrel-chested brawler would change course if the audience lost interest. Bookers became writer-directors who considered stage presence alongside athleticism, the face-offs they designed becoming quick-hitting matches between showboating characters. Back then, carnivals pitted strongmen against cocksure spectators eager to prove themselves under the big top. If the amateur could last 15 minutes in the ring, or take out the big guy before then, he'd win a cash prize. Like human saddle bronc riding, with the horse in cahoots with the boss. To keep the audience interested, the prizefighter pretended to reel with every punch. The real kicker: the amateur worked for the carnival too. The whole thing was a "work," a staged act designed to thrill the audience. This remains the rubric for America's most curious almost-sport. Bad guys cheat, beat up the good guy, the good guy comes back. The encounter ends with a finisher, a splashy, recognizable move to ink the match into fans' memories. The simplistic approach taps into the most rudimentary conflict of our existence. It's no wonder it persists.

"Think about who you are," Hoax continues, his tone somewhere between head coach and college professor. A sense of gravity fills the room. "Think about the reasons that brought you into wrestling in the first place. Don't just jump up there because." He raises a tattooed arm toward the ring.

* Also known as "catch as catch can," a combat sport that incorporates several grappling styles and is known for excruciatingly long face-offs.

They stare back at him like he were a pastor prescribing their salvation. At The Church of Southern Wrestling, he fits the part.

It's about the story, he wants them to understand. He uses Hunter as an example. "His gimmick is the athlete," Hoax says. "He's here for the fame and the glory and the trophy. How do you get there? You gotta fight for it. You gotta earn it."

Seabolt, the Taco Bell employee, who hasn't uttered an audible word all night, takes the floor.

"Friday September 3, right here in the Landmark Arena, NCW's gonna see something they've never seen before," he says, like a television news anchor. "Because you see, I've lived a hard life. I've sweat and I've bled to get where I am today, and not for anyone to take my spot. Because at 3 a.m. when everyone else is asleep, I'm awake, and I'm still thinking. About how I'm gonna mangle, and how I'm gonna strangle, and how I'm gonna beat my way to victory."

Startled by his volume and perfect pacing, the group hoots and claps. Kayfabe.

Hunter uses the lesson as an opportunity to create content. He removes his T-shirt, pulls tightfitting jeans over his wrestling trunks, and slips his bare arms into his Apalachee High School letter jacket. He pulls two high school wrestling trophies from his rollaboard suitcase—the one stamped with a "Future Legend" sticker—and carries them to the ring.

"Hey Hunter!" Azrael yells. "You look fuckboy. Very nice!"

"I know, right?" Hunter calls back, with a knowing smile.

The front pocket of his jeans sticks out of his waistband. Crystal goes for the jab. "Might want to tuck your pocket in," she says.

Hunter deflects. "Why not give 'em something to pick at?" he says, pushing the fabric down. "I'm a heel."

He sets the trophies on a scarred wooden lectern and pulls

three tournament medals over his head. With the brim of a Coker University cap tilted toward his brow, he leans in, grips the trophies, and waits for Hoax to press record on his iPhone.

The room quiets.

Hunter's character—the pompous jock—is too pretty, too perfect, too likely to succeed. It's an irresistible blend: Fans hate him but can't take their eyes off him. Tonight, he looks back at them. "I'm young, I'm athletic," Hunter says and then cocks his head to the side. "My whole life's ahead of me."

Hoax zooms in until Hunter's boyish face takes over the frame. Hunter gives a nod to his accomplices in a heel stable called The Program. "And then there's me," he says. "There's Hunter James."

Skin shining in the big-time glow of stage lights overhead, he tilts his head and smirks. "I'm young, I'm athletic. My whole life's ahead of me. I haven't even hit my peak yet—" he continues, slowing down. "—in the gym, in the ring, or anywhere I want to be."

CHAPTER 4

Billy Ray grew up in Dacula, Georgia, a far northeastern suburb of Atlanta that at the time existed as a rural afterthought dominated by cotton fields not yet converted to subdivisions. It was the '80s, the golden era of professional wrestling. Kids woke on Saturday mornings to *Hulk Hogan's Rock 'n' Wrestling* and carried sandwiches to school in blue plastic WWF lunchboxes. They lined up for autographs at shopping malls, and, if they were lucky, piled into packed arenas in Orlando, Atlanta, and LA to see the spectacular amalgamation of theatre and sport sweeping cable TV.

Instead of family vacations, the Nobletts drove to Atlanta to see stars like Tony Atlas and Terry Funk perform at the Omni Coliseum, home base of Georgia Championship Wrestling (GCW). The live-action show broadcast on TBS every Saturday night at 6:05 later morphed into World Championship Wrestling (WCW), WWE's No. 1 competitor until the company bought it in 2001.

In a Polaroid photo from his childhood, young Billy Ray sits next to Mr. Wrestling II, a GCW star who wore a *luchador*-style mask and built his character around his anonymity. With a page-boy haircut and jeans threadbare at the knees, Billy Ray grips a piece of paper for an autograph and leans into the crook of Two's arm. Like a doughy Mister Rogers in a wrestling mask, Mr. Wrestling II, over 40 at that time, sports an aqua cardigan over a wide-collared white shirt and peers through the mask at the camera without smiling. Billy Ray beams.

By then, pro football teams had fortified fan blocs in the North and Midwest. With only the poorly performing Atlanta Falcons in their midst, the South clung to what it knew best: college football, NASCAR, and professional wrestling. In Georgia, small-town shows have been around for as long as anyone alive can remember, beacons of escape just down the street where magicians of violence perform acts so beguiling that, for a few hours, the outside world slips out of view.

If it hadn't happened already, "The American Dream" Dusty Rhodes calcified wrestling's role as escapist entertainment for the working class in 1985 with his "Hard Times" speech. The real-life son of a Texas plumber would soon take on the very picture of wealth and greed, Ric Flair, in the main event at Starrcade '85. In their previous encounter, Flair had delivered an attack so vicious Rhodes was carried out of the ring.

Rhodes addressed Flair—but really his fans—with the fervor of a television preacher. His aviators sparkled. His tight-curled platinum mullet shone in soft white. He spoke with a lisp.

"Hard times are when the textile workers around this country are out of work, they got four or five kids and can't pay their wages, can't buy their food," he said. "Hard times are when the auto workers are out of work and they tell 'em, 'Go home.' And hard times are when a man has worked at a job thirty years, *thirty years*, and they give him a watch, kick him in the butt, and say, 'Hey, a computer took your place, daddy.' That's hard times! That's hard times!" he screamed, pointing his finger at the camera to shame the proverbial Man.

It was a moment of wrestling transcendence. In what would become widely known as the greatest wrestling promo* of all time, Rhodes admits he doesn't look like a typical athlete. "My belly's just a 'lil big, my heiny's a 'lil big.'" And then he makes a promise to his fans. "I'm gon' take it," he says of the heavyweight title, then slows down, stares into the camera, and extends an open hand. "This time when I take it, daddy, I'm gon' take it for you."

Rhodes confronted the fleeting accessibility of the American Dream in a decade when the kind of manufacturing jobs that could once sustain a family were replaced by machines and low-paying service work. Times were indeed hard, and he offered a resonant promise. The speech was a performance. But to those whose lives were affected by the plight Rhodes described, it was real. As is always the case in professional wrestling, it was about so much more than a belt. Rhodes, the common man, stood high on wrestling's biggest stage and denounced corporate greed. He persevered. They could too.

Billy Ray's mother, Sarah, worked at a casket company, then a chandelier company, and then in the deli of the local grocery store. His father, Robert, drove a forklift for a packaging manufacturer. Money was eternally scarce.

The way Billy Ray remembers it, rec sports in Dacula cost $35 for the season but his parents told him they could only afford one. He chose baseball and played in sneakers, the only pair he had,

* Promo: the plot thickener between matches, often performed as a monologue.

rather than cleats. For Billy Ray the '80s were marked by the deviances of a teenager with a lot of time, little money, a vendetta against his father, and a longing to be the center of attention. Robert and Billy Ray ferociously argued.

"I poured Jack Daniel's in my Froot Loops one day just to fuck with people," he says. "We didn't have any milk but we had Jack Daniel's. Actually, I had Jack Daniel's."

He started smoking pot in eighth grade and stole cassette tapes from Kmart and Roses Discount Store. "People who coughed my way, I was gonna punch them," he says. "I got in a fight in school and while I was in the principal's office I got in another fight waiting for my punishment. I think I had something to prove because I was always the smallest."

If the kids weren't home, Sarah and Robert recorded shows like Georgia All-Star Wrestling and Florida Championship Wrestling (FCW) for Billy Ray and his sister, Penny. One night Billy Ray flipped the channel over to FCW. "This guy walked out that changed me forever," he says. "Lex Luger." It was 1986.

Luger was a 6'3" former football player whose body—sculpted by weight training and anabolic steroids—reflected the industry's increasing preoccupation with oversized performers. A riled-up Percy Pringle plays the role of Luger's manager and ushers him into view, interrupting a deferential Gordon Solie, FCW's announcer, who sits behind a news anchor desk.

"Put the camera on Luger!" Pringle demands. Like an animatronic action figure Luger silently stares at the camera through black sunglasses, responding to Pringle's fawning by flexing his pecs beneath a sleeveless yellow T-shirt.

The screen shifts to a scene of Luger at the gym. The camera zooms in on his melon-wide biceps as he effortlessly curls, pulls, and presses.

A scrawny 14-year-old Billy Ray gazed in awe at Luger's colossal figure, blue eyes, and sandy blond mullet. In a few late-night seconds, his became the body Billy Ray would spend his life trying to build. "I had never seen anything look like that in my life," Billy Ray says at 50. He started lifting weights the next week.

Working out between eighth and ninth grade, he put on 25 pounds and then competed in the amateur wrestling team's 132-pound weight class. At some point a football player friend of his offered him some of the testosterone he kept in his locker. After the kid got busted, he unloaded the stuff on Billy Ray, who tucked the vials and needles in a shaving kit and hid it in an old tire in his backyard. Propelled by the pursuit of professional wrestling stardom with little concern for anything else, he began focusing on creating the perfect body even as he started failing some of his classes.

He knew he'd get booted from the wrestling team, so before his report card came home he quit. He bought a Honda motorcycle at 16 with money he earned selling weed and dropped out of high school the next year. He returned after a year working construction but then quit again, this time for good, and started paying his parents to live in his childhood bedroom.

Professional wrestlers represented a highly visible strata of greater Atlanta's demographic at the time. Drawn to the city by GCW, and later, WCW, icons of the era including Hulk Hogan, Kevin Nash, Abdullah the Butcher, and Diamond Dallas Page bought large houses and often appeared at Main Event Fitness, a powerlifting gym in the suburbs initially owned by Sting and Lex Luger.

One day, Billy Ray and a buddy snuck out of church and drove to the movie theatre. The friend parked the car and offered Billy Ray a sniff of what he had in the back. "Nah, I'm good," Billy Ray said. He'd just smoked a joint. The kid opened a canister of butane and started huffing. Then he leaned back and lit a cigarette.

The Nobletts got a phone call from the local hospital: They were transporting Billy Ray to Grady Memorial in Atlanta. Later the boy's parents asked Billy Ray if he'd take the blame. If it was their son's fault, they said, their car insurance payment would go up.

"I didn't care. I took the blame," Billy Ray says. "I was already a bad guy."

Sarah was used to commuting to Atlanta hospitals with Billy Ray, who was born with a heart defect. Every six months when he was young, she took him to Egleston Children's Hospital for cardiac catheterization. Eventually she brought Billy Ray home with bandages covering his burned face and tended to him the same way she had when he was a toddler. Back then, she'd wait until he was sleeping to administer the liquid medicine he refused to swallow when he was awake. "It destroyed his teeth," she says. Caring for his burns, she gave him a pain pill before peeling away the decomposing skin and replacing the dressing on his face. Billy Ray insisted Sarah cover the mirrors in the house. He couldn't stand to see himself. "The only scar he's got is a little bit around his ear," she says proudly. "I took care of that kid."

Billy Ray can pinpoint with confidence the single most transformative year of his life: 1986. The same year he discovered Lex Luger he heard, for the first time, the glam metal guitar riffs of his all-time favorite band, Poison, on MTV. As soon as "Talk Dirty to Me" ended on screen he begged Sarah for a ride to Roses and stole three cassettes of the band's breakout album. The songs—hype anthems about partying, fighting, and girls—provided a soundtrack for the life he was living, the character he wanted to become.

But it wasn't until 1992 that he met Steve "The Brawler"

Lawler, a Georgia wrestler who borrowed his ring surname from Memphis's Jerry "The King" Lawler and had made it big in a promotion 25 miles south of Atlanta called Deep South Wrestling. On the side, Lawler trained aspiring wrestlers, including Buff Bagwell, Disco Inferno, and Murder-1. "Steve told me what was expected of me, which was $1,000 up front," Billy Ray says. The regimen back then was for the trainer to take their pupils' cash and then work them so hard they don't come back.

He had some money saved from shifts at the chandelier factory where both he and Sarah worked, but not enough. And then a neighbor came to him with a proposition. A friend of hers, who adored Billy Ray, was having a birthday party. She'd pay him to do a surprise striptease.

That night Billy Ray sat down next to the woman celebrating. The song "Wake Me Up Before You Go-Go" by Wham! came on and Billy Ray started dancing. "I've always been a showman," he says. He made $600, enough to cover the rest of the payment.

Billy Ray, 5'6", found out later the amount he paid Lawler was twice what he charged the bigger guys. "You were so little. I was going to break you and take your money," Lawler later admitted, after Billy Ray proved himself and the two became friends.

For Billy Ray wrestling offered deliverance from his past. He stopped drinking, stealing, and doing drugs. The only thing that mattered was "making it" it in wrestling and making it out of Dacula, Georgia.

He wanted to distance himself from his name and any pop country connotations it had in the early '90s, so he devised a character, Jamey Dean, based on America's smoldering native son of teen angst, James Dean. He tucked jeans into cowboy boots painted red, white, and blue, and told ring announcers his hometown was Fairmount, Indiana, where Dean grew up and was buried. When it came to choosing entrance music, there wasn't a question: Poison's "Look What the Cat Dragged In."

"Billy Ray Noblett had a bad reputation," he says. "Jamey Dean didn't have a reputation. I could be anything I wanted."

Soon he dropped the Indiana bit and said his hometown was whatever locale the show was in. It was an easy way to win over the crowd. "Talk about a cheap pop," he says.

Once someone came up to him and said, "We were talking about your match the other day at dinner." People had likely talked about Billy Ray at dinner before, but never in a positive light. It filled him up.

"Everybody's starving for attention," he says. "My job was to steal the show."

He adopted the moniker inside the ring and out. To this day, his mother-in-law calls him Jamey. When his father-in-law died in 2019 the obituary listed Jennifer and Jamey Noblett of Bethlehem, Georgia, among the man's survivors.

Too nervous to eat anything on show days, he'd arrive before bell time, find a seat in the back, and stay there until he heard his music. "Then I'd start bouncing." The adrenaline rush drowned the anxiety as he exploded through the curtain. "That was definitely one of my highs," he says, two decades later, and then stops to corrects himself. "That was the best high."

One day in 1995 he tacked a white sheet to a wall in the family's wood-paneled dining room. He hung an American flag over it and called Sarah in to take a picture. Wrists wrapped in white tape and hair collected in a white headband, the way Poison's Bret Michaels wore it, he flexed his biceps and lats and brought his fists in front of him. He ordered duplicates, autographed them, and sold them at shows. After she photographed him, Sarah cut the stars out of the flag and sewed them on his jean jacket. He was 22.

Billy Ray transformed himself into a man who hit all the marks of wrestling's prescribed masculinity as he saw it—attractive, entertaining, and respectable—and he came to embody them outside the ring too. Bad Guy Billy Ray became Good Guy Jamey Dean.

"Once I started wrestling it was like everything I ever did in the past was gone away," he says. The kid who got into fights just to get into fights. Who faced multiple school suspensions. Who got his first taste of drugs in the eighth grade.

Sometimes he was so broke after paying his bills he paid for a gallon of gas with a handful of change to get to the show. He never revealed his circumstances to anyone in the locker room. He didn't have to.

"If I saw a kid like me, I would think he was trash," Billy Ray says now of his teenaged self. "I was Billy Ray Noblett from Dacula, Georgia. In the wrestling world I was Jamey Dean."

A young Billy Ray had discovered, on his own, the psychological value of self-distancing via an alter ego, a phenomenon called The Batman Effect that's been used by everyone from Beyoncé (Sasha Fierce) to Kobe Bryant (Black Mamba).

"It was my escape," he says. For the first time in his life, he felt the hypnotizing warmth of admiration. "I realized, *holy crap*, these people kind of like me. It changed my life."

Billy Ray wrestled his first match in 1993 at a fundraising event for a camp in Winder, Georgia, for children with disabilities. His opponent, in tribal face paint, was more than twice his size. "I only got a few moves in but I did powerslam a 300-pound guy," he remembers. Billy Ray's trainer, Steve Lawler, watched through the curtain. After the match, he told Billy Ray his was the worst bumping and selling he'd ever seen.

Maybe it was because Billy Ray was just starting out. Maybe it was because his father, at age 42, was recovering from an aneurysm in a hospital 20 miles away. Robert's mother told Billy Ray he shouldn't go. Billy Ray talked to his own mother, Sarah, about it. "Your daddy would want you to go," she said. "You're going."

Lawler's critique deflated Billy Ray and the shame kept him from the ring for the next 18 months. He lifted weights after work and vowed to never again let anything get in the way of wrestling.

"I've never had anyone talk bad about me since," he says. "I busted my ass."

After shows he watched VHS tapes of his matches and beat himself up if he saw a mistake. A Saturday mishap would eat him up until Friday night, and then as soon as he got into the ring again, he'd right the wrong by executing the move perfectly. If an opponent made a mistake, that person would pay.

Once, Billy Ray tore the tendons in his shoulder taking a DDT* from a drunk opponent. The next time they met, Billy Ray started the match by popping him—hard—in the nose, relevelling the playing field in the way only violence can. Blood poured from the guy's face. He looked at Billy Ray and said, "We're even."

"I took a lot more bruises than I should, but I gave a lot more than I should," he says.

For a time, Billy Ray's entrance included a quick blitz through the seats to kiss a different good-looking girl each night. One night at a show in Dalton, Georgia, he peeked through the curtain

* DDT: In the move, a wrestler kicks his opponent in the gut to double him over, locks his head beneath his armpit, and falls backward, slamming that head into the mat.

and didn't like the offerings. "Nah, I ain't doing it tonight," he told his tag partner at the time, the promoter's son, Jerry. Jerry offered up his 14-year-old sister, Jennifer. "I'm still kissing his little sister," Billy Ray says, 28 years later.

Jenn graduated high school in 1999 and moved with Billy Ray into an apartment after a brief stint living with his parents. Instead of going on dates, the couple traveled between wrestling gigs. Late at night after they got home from a show, Billy Ray would pull a tape from his collection of *Nitros*, *Raws*, and ECWs, sink into the pillow, and wait for the singular sound of body to mat to lull him to sleep, just as he had for as long as he could remember.

He fell short of his big break in the mid '90s when Lawler brought him to try out at his friend Jody Hamilton's training center in Jonesboro, Georgia. The place would later be named the WCW Power Plant and become the official talent feeder to Atlanta-based WCW.

After a successful tryout for the cruiserweight tag team class, Billy Ray's physical exam revealed what he already knew: his untreated heart defects—enlargement, a murmur, a hole, and an "artery like a dirt road instead of an expressway," were too high-risk for the wrestling company. It passed on him. But wrestling was too hard to give up. He kept performing, at churches, school gyms, armories, and American Legions—fleeting throwdowns in borrowed spaces across Georgia, where, for a few hours, ordinary people become superheroes.

The wrestling years were a period of selfishness, Billy Ray admits. "Everything I did for the longest time, was, 'I don't care. I'm going to be a pro wrestler.'" His sight line stopped at his next show. He had one goal: to ride a WWE contract out of town.

Even Jenn knew she came in second place. Billy Ray told her as much. "That's how addicted to it I was."

But it was also a time of self-preservation. Without wrestling stardom as a goal, he says, "I'd a went to jail."

When he started training, Steve Lawler asked Billy Ray if he was nervous. "I got one butterfly and it's about this fucking big," Billy Ray replied to his trainer, and spread his hands wide. "When the butterflies go away, stop," Lawler said. They never did.

CHAPTER 5

Hunter and Billy Ray, December 5, 2009

Hunter's most vivid early memory is walking toward the ring with his father at a show in Carl, Georgia. Billy Ray had been a babyface for most of his career, but a few weeks earlier the booker had turned him heel. The crowd didn't buy it. Billy Ray turned to Hunter. "Hey," he said. "I'm turning back good guy tonight. Who do you want me to punch in the face?" "Father John!" Hunter begged. The wrestler wore priest-like gear and teamed with Leatherface in a heel stable called the Unholy Alliance. The spot did its job: Billy Ray went after Father John, and all the babyface wrestlers ran out of the locker room to save him from the wrestler's retaliation. Jamey Dean, babyface, was back.

So many times in his early life, Hunter dressed in a kid-sized version of his father's gear—jeans, a Superman shirt, and a bandana headband—and circled the ring with him, high-fiving fans. Before leaping onto the mat, Billy Ray would lift Hunter over the barricade and into the seats, where he'd watch the match. After, Hunter followed him back to the locker room. On those days he watched his father soften. He felt he was in on a secret, part of a club.

Hunter felt the grip of this violent utopia, witnessed the power it held over people, saw how they looked up to his father. He looked up to him too. In those makeshift locker rooms a bond strengthened between father and son. Billy Ray felt his son's admiration, and it compelled him to keep performing. When Hunter was 8 and Billy Ray had worked the ring for more than two decades, he finally set his dream aside. Billy Ray was becoming the thing he hated: a has-been and hanger-on, wrestling the same aging opponents year after year in front of tiny crowds. The distance between him and the guys on TV had grown too far to travel. He left his final match with a hall of fame plaque and a commitment to fatherhood. "I didn't want to miss a thing," he says, 13 years later.

He doesn't part from the sentiment without acknowledging the what-if. "I could have 'roided up some, and by the time I quit the small guys were out there, but . . . "

When Hunter was born his parents looked to wrestling royalty, Hunter Hearst Helmsley—better known as Triple H—for name inspiration. At the time the wrestler had won the WWE Championship, the company's highest honor, five times and was cast as Stephanie McMahon's husband in the ring. (The couple later married in real life. Now he's WWE's chief content officer.) Hunter's younger brother, Christian Michaels Noblett, is an amalgam of two of Billy Ray's favorites: Christian Cage and Shawn Michaels.

Christian was born in 2008, after years of trying to conceive. "That's the reason he's named Christian," Billy Ray says. "Because he wasn't supposed to happen. Christian became world champion and they said he would never be world champion."

One family photo captures Billy Ray heaving baby Hunter into the air above Hunter's cousins Justin and Austin, who lay on their backs on a trampoline. Hunter, in a diaper, extends his arms forward instinctively, prepared for landing.

These acts reveal how soon parents impose their passions onto their children. The transfer is an act of love, of course. But a name is hard to break away from, and so are the values and customs you grow up with.

The day of Hunter's first amateur wrestling practice, at age 8, he dressed in jeans and a T-shirt and tied a red bandana around his head, just as he did before Billy Ray's shows. He arrived at the gym ready to lay out his opponent with the Shawn Michaels superkick he'd been practicing. When a coach greeted him, rather than a WWE Superstar, he felt duped. He thought there was only one kind of wrestling, the kind he watched on TV with his dad.

Hunter got to know his father and formed an encyclopedic knowledge of professional wrestling by watching it on TV with him. A week before his third birthday in 2005, he crawled onto Billy Ray's lap for the November 14 installment of *WWE Raw*. Eddie Guerrero, the small-framed babyface underdog who'd honed his craft in Japan and Mexico, had just died of heart failure at age 38. The camera spanned the solemn faces of John Cena, Rey Mysterio, Shawn Michaels, and Randy Orton as Vince McMahon teed up a 10-bell salute, pro wrestling's version of a 21-

gun sendoff. A montage of photos and short clips, set to Johnny Cash's rendition of the Nine Inch Nails song "Hurt," followed.

Curled up next to his father, Hunter watched, and then, recognizing Guerrero's face, yelled out, "Viva La Raza!" It was the wrestler's tagline, which translates to "long live the race." Tears welled in Billy Ray's eyes. He ached for Eddie Guerrero, whose death is presumed to be a result of his steroid-aided effort to build a body big enough to fit the WWE script; and he ached with love for his little son, whose early vocabulary was decorated with the language of wrestling. A love language.

Many US households mark the time of year by the start and conclusion of major-league sports seasons. As months came and went, the Noblett TV stayed tuned to wrestling. By the time he was 4, Hunter could mimic, on command, the entrance poses of just about any top-billed WWE Superstar.

Hunter watched his dad chase a pro wrestling career, and then he watched him admonish it. With one young son and another on the way, Billy Ray knew he needed to change course. He didn't want his kids to have to work so hard for everything in their lives as he had. He wanted to set them up for something more.

"The only time I ever missed anything, *anything*, was Hunter's last year of high school because he was wrestling Friday and Saturday at one place and Chunk was wrestling Saturday and Sunday at another," Billy Ray says. "I kept it up and that's still my bragging right."

Noting his strength, Hunter's high school football coach asked him to move from quarterback to middle linebacker. Two weeks after a devastating loss, he wrestled his first varsity wrestling match. Hunter went two and two, looked at the coach and said, "I'll never play football again." "Broke his Mama's heart," Billy Ray says. "But I knew. I kept telling her, 'A quarterback's never going to quit the team. You got all the attention.' But they took him out as quarterback. So it didn't surprise me."

Once during his senior year an opponent suplexed him off the mat onto the gym floor. The ref blew the whistle and Hunter wobbled to his feet, holding his head. Jenn panicked. Billy Ray held his breath and looked closer. Hunter gripped his head in pain but stood strong on his feet. Billy Ray saw his son's toes move through his shoes.

"He's working it!" Billy Ray whispered to Jenn. Hunter was spreading a little pro wrestling stardust in the high school gym: He feigned injury to get the crowd invested. He also tricked his opponent into thinking he was weakened by the blow, and then surged back to defeat him. He smiled. Their little secret.

It wasn't the first time Hunter brought theatricality to the mat. On the team's senior night when he was a freshman, he and his practice partner, a senior, wrestled each other because the opposing team didn't have contenders in their weight classes. "What if we go out there and script our match? Just have fun?" Hunter proposed. The senior would pin him in the end, of course. "We pro-wrestled a wrestling match," Hunter says. The show included a *Dirty Dancing*–style lift.

It's impossible to untangle professional wrestling from the Noblett family web. As a child Jenn swung from the ropes before the shows her father ran. For a stint, her bother Jerry performed as Billy Ray's tag partner. Billy Ray's sister, Penny, married his wrestler roommate, Richard Dutton. Their son, Justin, also a wrestler, first brought Hunter to Landmark.

Hunter and Justin and their respective younger brothers spent countless hours mimicking the moves of wrestlers like AJ Styles, Shawn Michaels, and Chris Benoit on an old mattress at Nanny and Pa Nobletts', where they spent many days as children. Before grappling for the glory of a cardboard belt, they'd run to the kitchen and ask Nanny, who played the role of showrunner, who should win.

Once they acted out a "street fight," a popular hardcore format in which opponents wear regular clothing and use weapons. The boys gathered their usual assortment of munitions: plastic swords, a hammer, a folding chair. Five-year-old Chunk disappeared inside and returned with a days-old loaf of oblong bread. "He beat us until there were welts on our backs," Hunter says. Days earlier a neighbor had picked it up at the food bank and given it to Sarah.

Cross-legged in a beige recliner in October 2021 Justin wears worn-out Zubaz, the brand of blousy zebra-print pants now associated with NFL fan gear but first popularized by the prime-time Road Warrior wrestlers Hawk and Animal. His black T-shirt bears the motto, spelled out in razor-wire script, of wrestler Malakai Black when he performed as Aleister Black in WWE: Fade to Black. He sips from a bottle of Smirnoff Ice and occasionally spits Grizzly smokeless tobacco residue into an empty plastic Gold Peak iced tea bottle. His wife, Leah, reclines in the matching chair next to him, lost in a shapeless floral dress and hidden behind glasses and the screen of a laptop.

After he graduated from West Hall High School in 2014, Justin went to work at Progress Container & Display, where Pa drove a forklift. Since then he's had a host of hourly jobs ranging from installing insulation in commercial chicken houses to manufacturing nuts and bolts. He started wrestling at 14.

The house is small and cheery, free of clutter and with freshly painted walls. Justin and Leah spent the past six months scraping it clean after its previous tenants vacated. When they opened the refrigerator, they found rotting meat. "It was one of those—people who did drugs would hide out in the basement," Justin says. "That's padlocked now."

From the sofa, Hunter rattles off the personas Justin has embodied since starting his wrestling career.

"Luchador, sexy, party guy, backwoods soldier, outlaw, young buck, redneck."

"And then I realized there's too many rednecks out here." Justin smiles. "So I changed it to Chop Top."

The shift happened before a match at Landmark. The death-match wrestler Brad Cash recruited Justin to his grisly Cult of Cash that night but said Justin's character, Hoss Michaels, wasn't creepy enough. Justin borrowed the name Chop Top from the *Texas Chainsaw Massacre* murderer.

"I love being booed," Justin says. "I love when people throw stuff at me. Being out there makes me feel like I'm a star bigger than what I am outside of wrestling. Some people just know me as the guy always outside working on his truck." He pauses. "I don't know. I have this fire that's built in me when I come out there."

That fire burns through the family bloodline.

Billy Ray met Justin's father, Richard, at the chandelier factory. They discovered their mutual love of wrestling and became roommates in a rented singlewide trailer. There, on the living room floor, Billy Ray taught Richard how to wrestle. In duster and cowboy hat, Richard Dutton became Richard Chandler of the Chandler Ranch, a surname borrowed from the 1992 George Strait movie *Pure Country*. Before long he started dating Billy Ray's sister, Penny.

Billy Ray was muscular but knew his height prevented him from playing the role of strongman. "Richard couldn't bench 135 to save his life but he was 6 foot tall, 240 pounds. When we played our match he was the strong one."

Richard's was a body built for character, not speed and acrobatics. Like Justin's, his ring persona changed over the years. He was Dirty Dick Dutton, the American Nightmare, and the American Outlaw, a name Justin borrowed for a time.

When the scene became unevenly populated by heels, he paired a clownlike *luchador* mask he found on eBay with *Family Guy* pajama pants, a Hawaiian shirt, and Converse, and became the lovable Junior. He danced to "I Like to Move It" from the movie *Madagascar* on his way to the ring and tossed candy to the kids. He incorporated an oversized lollipop into his signature move, the Sucker Punch.

Richard married Penny in 1994. Justin arrived in 1995, followed by two more boys: Austin in 1998 and Jesse in 2004. Richard became a regular at Billy Ray's home promotion, Future Wrestling Federation (FWF) in Winder, Georgia, and brought his sons, often in wrestling gear of their own.

One of Richard's closest friends, Cleve Christian, performed as Psycho Man, a psychiatric hospital escapee. Outside it, he coached Justin's little league team. Justin adored him. In matching psych-ward-style teal scrubs, young Justin started his career as Psycho Man's manager. Richard started driving him to Jamie Holmes's backyard when he was 13.

Then in August 2008 Richard took Justin to a show and learned his opponent hadn't showed. Justin, 14, entered the ring for the first time as a wrestler that night, in a match against his father.

Soon they were regularly working shows together, strengthening a relationship that would withstand several traumatic events, including Richard's ugly divorce from Penny and the custody battles that ensued.

Taking bumps* on the weekends and working at a concrete

* Bump: A hard landing in the ring.

block yard during the week wore Richard down. One day he bent down to pick something up and heard a pop. He later underwent a spinal fusion to reconnect his vertebrae. "It looks like a metal spider holding my back together because a lot of my discs are gone," he says. Lifting anything heavier than 10 pounds puts him at risk for further injury. He stopped wrestling in 2018 and started delivering Domino's pizzas.

As it does with many wrestlers, the ring served as the site for several pivotal moments in Richard's life. He met his second wife, Amanda, after she started attending the FWF shows, first as a fan at the behest of a high school friend on the roster, and then as an amateur photographer. Before he proposed, Richard and Billy Ray worked out a plan to surprise her at the show.

Richard, playing the heel, forced Amanda into the ring. "I want you to take pictures of what I'm about to do to him," he roared, side-eyeing Billy Ray. Amanda focused her lens on Billy Ray as Richard reared up. Rather than taking the blow, Billy Ray rolled out of the ring and Richard dropped to one knee. She'd serve up a similar surprise a few months later at a show in Ellijay, Georgia. Amanda had secretly asked one of Richard's best friends, the sardonically named wrestler Tiny, to get ordained. She interrupted the promoter's preshow meeting by revealing the veil tucked into her cowboy hat and married Richard in the ring.

There were times the universe seemed to give him something between a wink and a middle finger, like his first day back to work after being attacked in the ring by a baseball bat wrapped in barbed wire. He rolled open a transport truck door to accept a delivery: a pallet of barbed wire.

It never mattered to Richard that he performed in front of scant crowds in second-rate venues. He knew he'd never make it to the WWE. "It's almost like you're a Superstar when you're out there, even if it's only fifteen people," he says, reflecting on his career inside a Dunkin' three years after leaving the ring for good.

A lot happens at a wrestling show but he can distill the magic to a singular moment that kept him coming back: when his entrance music took over the space and the fans started cheering. Richard lived for that. He never found anything to replace it.

When he hung up his boots he pulled away from wrestling entirely, like a recovering alcoholic dumping bottles of booze down the drain. "I couldn't go and watch it because I wanted to be in the back, part of it, helping create stuff."

The absence led to depression. "I even thought about harming myself, you know, just getting out," he says.

Amanda, a licensed professional counselor, encouraged him to try an antidepressant. Richard demurred at first—he figured if the feeling was inside him he could fix it himself—but came around. It helps, he says, but he still feels the emptiness wrestling once filled.

He worried for his son early on, but watching Justin wrestle, he sees a well-trained performer, unlikely to make foolish mistakes like he did. "He's one hundred times better than I ever was," he says. "I'm super proud of him."

And he remains hopeful that someday Justin will be called up to the Big Time. "He's getting to a point now where life's going to get in the way for him," Richard says. "He's going to have to work so much to support his family. But I still think if he was seen by the right people he could go to Ring of Honor or something like that. I still hope every day for him to do that."

When Justin started performing around Georgia on his own, at 16, Hunter, 7 years younger, rode to shows with him. They'd arrive hours before bell time to run the ropes and bounce around the ring, training. On off nights the boys drove to Walmart, where they lingered over the wrestling figurines and combed through the clothing departments dreaming up their gear. In those late-night, unsupervised hours, they buttressed their dreams.

"I knew Hunter would do it," Justin says of his cousin's wrestling career. "We'd always talk about it. We'd sit there all night and draw up our gear, talking about the moves we'd do."

When they get together now, the conversation weaves through wrestling past and present, from big-name performers they've only seen on TV to small-town guys they wrestled last weekend.

Tonight they revisit one of their favorite matches.

"I made sure I didn't miss you that one night I wrestled your dad," Justin says. He's talking about the night Billy Ray emerged from retirement to join Richard in a best of three falls match. Justin attacked Billy Ray. Hunter ran in to rescue his father, and then turned around to meet his cousin's boot in his face. Hunter stands up to reenact the scene, reeling from the kick and tumbling to the floor in Justin and Leah's living room.

The friendship between Billy Ray and Richard went beyond the ring and endured for years, but tonight their sons struggle to remember the last time the men saw each other.

"Laylin's funeral," Justin says, and the conversation quiets.

"They wouldn't stop talking," Justin says after a moment. "And every time I see your dad he tells me the same story, over and over."

Outside a Checkers drive-thru restaurant, Richard threw Billy Ray over the metal barricade next to the order window and put the boots to him. When the cops arrived Billy Ray popped up, uninjured, and offered a handshake. It was a work.

In a family marred by loss, stories like this one float like buoys between tragedies.

Beneath a decorative sign that says BLESSED, with the quiet

resignation of a man decades older than his 25 years, Justin says, "We lost two children."

Leah was three months pregnant this time last year, but Waylon Cash died on April 5, 2021, fewer than 24 hours after he was born, and just 11 months after his sister, Laylin Louise, perished in utero at 33 weeks.

Leah's placenta had blood clots when she was pregnant with Laylin. Waylon had a bladder obstruction. Despite trips to hospitals in Houston and Atlanta, where Waylon received stents in utero, his lungs collapsed.

While Leah recovered in another room after Waylon's birth, Justin rocked his son in the hospital's neonatal intensive care unit. He found a 10-hour-loop of the song "You've Got a Friend in Me" from *Toy Story* and held Waylon until he took his last breath. Then he called the two people he knew would understand the pain: Billy Ray and Jenn.

Jenn birthed twins five months into her first pregnancy. She was 19. Michael, named after Shawn Michaels, was stillborn. Chyna, named after a barrier-breaking female wrestler, died in Billy Ray's arms.

"Be strong. Know that he's with Michael, Chyna, and Laylin," Billy Ray said. Jenn couldn't speak. She just cried.

Justin didn't recognize himself in the days that followed. He didn't want to work on his truck. He didn't want to leave the house. Two weeks passed before he walked zombielike into the only place he knew would make him feel alive: a wrestling locker room. When he got there the boys pushed one another out of the way to hug him.

Now, when he walks toward the ring he locks eyes with Leah to assure her he's ok. And he imagines their children playing next to her. "And then I have to put my head in the turnbuckle for a little bit," he says.

The cousins move from the living room to the hallway connecting the two bedrooms in Justin and Leah's house, pulling aside a comforter nailed to the doorframe that keeps the cool air in the living room.

After getting home from his job painting utility trailers Justin retreats to this small space, where he stores his collection of wrestling trading cards, posters, and figurines. Someday, he and Leah hope, it will be their child's bedroom.

Hunter scans the wall where Justin has tacked cards and other wrestling ephemera from floor to ceiling. An oversized Danhausen photo, situated above a similarly sized, autographed photo of Arn Anderson, Richard's favorite wrestler, anchors the shrine-like space.

"That's not all my cards," Justin says. "I still got more at my dad's."

"At least you have Perfect up there," Hunter says after spotting a photo of Mr. Perfect. "I'm happy."

"I got Perfect. I got Pillman," Justin says of the wrestler Brian Pillman, who died unexpectedly at 35 from an undetected heart condition.

The way the young men effortlessly spout professional wrestling knowledge reveals their lifelong immersion in it.

"You got the second batch of the Horsemen, when Lex replaced Ole," Hunter notes.

A framed collage of photos from Justin's own wrestling career hangs on the opposite wall, a gift from Leah on their one-month anniversary. Beneath his wrestling names, and the date he started his career, two photos, taken 6 years apart, depict Richard and Justin with the same black eye and blood-spattered face.

Justin's injury came from a cowbell in a Texas deathmatch. He went home, wiped it clean, and superglued it shut.

"Then we went to Waffle House," Hunter says, continuing the story.

Justin looks at the photos and smiles. "I had the same smile my dad did," he says. "He got cut open on the top of his head with a keyboard."

"I still have that keyboard," Hunter says. "It's at Nanny's."

Robert and Sarah cared for the grandchildren—all boys—after school and during the summer, when their parents worked. They'd wrestle for hours on the mattress in the bedroom. Sometimes the brawls would move outside to the ring they made by laying down jump ropes, and neighborhood kids would come watch. Sarah sat on the porch swing and cheered them on.

"I can't tell you how many times she damn near went bankrupt just to buy us a wrestling figure because we did good at school," Hunter says. "She's the reason I still go down the toy aisle." Robert sometimes handed them sledgehammers to smash the broken air conditioners and engines he gathered to sell for scrap. In this way the boys learned to take their aggression out on objects. Just like their play fighting, it kept them from hurting each other or other kids. One day a neighbor kid frustrated Chunk so bad he burst through the door and said, "Pa, you got anything for me to beat on?" He took a sledgehammer to a window unit and it started spraying Freon. "I've never seen that kid run so fast!" Sarah says.

She thinks about those times on days when she's down, and they make her smile.

Sometime during Jenn and Billy Ray's separation, the boys were at Nanny and Pa's, wrestling. "I don't know what Hunter did to Christian," she says. "But he almost hurt him." Hunter, frustrated, huffed and said, "I gotta go lift weights." The whole thing started, she finally discovered, when Hunter got annoyed with Chunk's incessant cartoon voices. "That's the only way he gets to get things out is pretending to be someone else!" Sarah yelled at Hunter. Hunter understood.

Justin asks Hunter to grab some boots out of the closet. "The red, white, and blue ones?" Hunter asks. He picks up a pair of leather boots, their soles burnished by wear.

Billy Ray bought them from his trainer, Steve Lawler. They were blood-spattered, two sizes too big, and painted the colors of the flag of Mexico. Billy Ray made them his own. One time the boots got hung up on the rope as his body flew through the air, out of the boots, and out of the ring. He was out cold for a few minutes. After that he gave them to Richard, who passed them on to Justin.

"I should know these, these are my Dad's," Hunter says and then gets distracted by the bottle of cherry-flavored whiskey on the floor. He takes a swig. "That's dangerous," he says.

"They're worn out but since I'm learning how to sew I might try to fix that," Justin says.

If Hunter's nostalgic about his father's footwear he doesn't show it. "No offense, but you can keep them," he says.

"I'm not a cowboy boot person, I never have been," Hunter continues. "I think it's because of my dad. He was anti-redneck because he saw it all his life. He didn't want anything to do with it. He dreaded the day I started listening to country music."

In the corner of the room an array of acrylic paints sits next to the sewing machine where Justin taught himself to sew after Waylon died.

He lifts a pair of tiny gold leggings from the desk. "I finally finished them," he says. On the back waistband of these never-worn, infant-sized pants he spelled out Laylin's name with tiny block letter patches and sewed on sunflowers. The pants are a miniature version of his own gold wrestling tights.

"I'm working on Waylon's now," he says. He'll keep both of them in his gear bag, a way to keep his babies with him.

In this same small workspace, Justin disfigures WWE and AEW wrestler figurines and reassembles torsos, heads, legs, and arms to mirror the bodies of Georgia wrestlers.

Hunter recognizes one in progress. "Wait," he says, and picks it up. "Are you making a Junior?"

Justin confirms he's working on a figure of his father. It'll be a Christmas present: a 6-inch vestige of a man, who, for a moment, was larger than life.

Hunter examines his cousin's handiwork. "You use The Miz?" he asks and hands it back. Justin nods. "The head is actually Sin Cara's mask and the hair came from Cowboy Bob Orton. I scalped him." He smiles. "See? His Converse," he says, pointing to Junior's shoes.

Hunter and Justin talk about which body parts Justin would use if he were to assemble a plastic Billy Ray. The comparisons come quick. "All you'd need is an Orange Cassidy with a jacked body," Hunter says. "A Hulk Hogan body. Realistically, you'd put a Kazarian body on it. I mean, the head's almost there anyways."

Then they speculate how Billy Ray would react to seeing a figure of himself. He'd keep it but wouldn't display it, Justin guesses. "He'd put it somewhere at work, on his desk." Present, but purposefully out of view.

CHAPTER 6

Brian Blaze, Matt Hankins, and Shane Marx

"I'm Hunter James. I'm eighteen years old and I know I'm in the fight of my life right now when it comes to Hardcore Hell," As the screen flips to footage of him training at Landmark, Hunter sits next to JJ Johnson, a rotund man with a stubble-shaved head, beneath the building's block-lettered sign and international flags.

He starts his story. "I'm a collegiate wrestler. I just signed with Coker University in Hartsville, South Carolina. When my dad showed me this I fell in love," he says of professional wrestling. He credits his start to Billy Ray, his uncle Richard, and his cousin

Justin. "We're all intertwined in this business and it's my turn to step into the ring."

It's four days before the April 2021 iteration of Hardcore Hell—the bloody who's who of Georgia wrestling that premiered in 1998—and Hunter's the subject of a rudimentary behind-the-scenes hype video. It begins with a montage of his recent matches, an episode recap of sorts that culminates with footage from Hunter's first appearance on the show a month earlier. He comes at Brian Blaze with a metal chair after Blaze attacks Adrian Hawkins, one of Hunter's mentors, from behind. "I'm not sure who this young man is," the clip's commentator says. A character introduction.

Matt Hankins, in tie-dye denim jacket and newsboy hat, takes the mic. "You want to walk your punk ass out here and make challenges?" he thunders. "Well we accept your challenge, but it's going to be on our terms." The page-turner.

Every seat was filled on April 24, 2021, which was to be expected for Anarchy Wrestling's premier event, a show known for its shock value. In standard pro-wrestling matches, opponents quickly volley exaggerated attacks. In a hardcore match, they draw out the ghastly action. Wrestlers bang cookie sheets on skulls, press crutches to throats, and smack each other with shovels. There's blood, and it's real. It's the snuff film of professional wrestling, a discipline of the art that eliminates disqualifications and invites thumbtacks, light tubes, and barbed wire into the ring. It attracts a certain subset of fans who relish the thrill of knowing anything can happen. Many prefer the comparatively more PG style of traditional professional wrestling. But for fans of hardcore wrestling, witnessing opponents bloody each other in the ring satisfies a desire for violent performance that literally cuts deeper.

In the eighth match of the night, Hunter, in baby blue tights, white boots, and a black satin bomber with the words "Future Legend" stitched across the back, jogs around the ring slapping hands as his opponent, Brain Blaze, sits unbothered on the bottom turnbuckle. Hunter climbs to the top of the opposite corner to hype the crowd. And then in one swift move Brian rises and lunges toward him. He meets the fistful of baby powder Hunter's been hiding, and Hunter sunset flips him for the pin. The battle lasts the length of bull ride. Hunter jumps to each turnbuckle and revels in victory. The audience approves. And then the swerve. Brian comes from behind, yanks Hunter to the ground, pummels him in the face. The referee tries to break it up, but the bell rings again, and the match—deemed no rules, no disqualifications, per Hardcore Hell's rubric—continues.

Brian's in charge now, and like a horror movie villain, he takes his time. He pulls a metal folding chair from beneath the ring, slams it on Hunter's back and then uses the chair to pin Hunter's neck to the ground. Hunter flails. Brian moves to a folding table on the floor, drags Hunter toward the edge of the ring, lifts him onto his shoulders and slams him onto it, breaking the table in half. The crowd grimaces.

Brian walks slowly around the ring with a knowing smile. He reaches under the apron for a final tool of torture. Four referees tend to Hunter, panting on top of the smashed table. When they see what's in Brian's hands, they jump to their feet and plead with him to stop. Brian pushes past them. He bends down, and in one swift motion, pulls the rope around Hunter's neck.

It's been 13 months since COVID-19 pressed pause on the world. Fourteen months since three white men chased and shot to death Ahmaud Arbery in coastal Georgia. Eleven months since

Minneapolis police officer Derek Chauvin pressed his knee into George Floyd's neck.

The mob of white spectators watching Brian and Hunter in the ring conjured up Jim Crow lynching albeit with one important historical edit: the aggressor was Black and the victim was white. On the blank page of the wrestling ring, Brian Blaze rewrote history. The mostly white audience waits as Hunter lays lifeless on the floor.

Brian yanks him toward the ring. Hunter's head rests on the edge of the mat. Brian holds the rope in his hand like a dog leash as he climbs. Somewhere in the seats, a baby cries. Brian jerks the rope, pulling Hunter off the floor like a marionette. Hunter grips the noose and kicks his legs. His face becomes flushed.

The jab at mortality plucks an existential string inside every spectator. Breaths linger in barreled chests. Eyes squint in horror and wonder at the ring. We all have these eyes. Eyes that can't bear to look but can't look away.

The bell rings. Brian holds the rope taut. He sits motionless, menacing, admires his handiwork for a few long seconds before tossing the rope—and Hunter—to the floor.

"That was racist!" someone yells, prompting a staccato clap. A chant begins.

Brian's music—the Beastie Boys song "Sabotage"—interrupts and he walks toward the locker room, leaving Hunter in a heap, gasping for breath.

Backstage before the event, bookers Rick Michaels and Matt Hankins, who also plays the role of Brian's manager, talked through the match. Brian had been an Anarchy regular for years. He was a heel, but the crowd had warmed up to him. They needed something to affirm his role as the bad guy. He was in the middle of a feud with Adrian, but Adrian couldn't make it to the show. Hunter's new role as Adrian's trainee could help take care of business in his absence. Rick proposed Hunter throw powder in Brian's face then quickly roll him up for the win. But how to get the heat* back on Brian?

"Brian, you got your noose?" Matt, the son of a white mother and Black father from Muscle Shoals, Alabama, called out in the locker room.

"In my bag," Brian said. Brian had purchased the thick rope at Home Depot a few months before, for a Hangman Match with Butch Her at Platinum Championship Wrestling (PCW). He'd been a Boy Scout. He knew how to tie the knot.

"We're gonna hang him," Matt said.

As a booker, Matt's job is to get fans to forget everything they think they know about wrestling. Everything that happened to them this week. Everything that's going to happen tomorrow. "That means that at some point in the show, I have to do something heinous, something extreme. I've got to walk you up to the point where we crescendo," he says. Because then, they'll come back for more.

"You need really in-depth, layered storytelling," Matt continues. But not every match can have a resolution. You have to draw it out, let it ebb and flow. "But in times when you're not telling a great story the whole goddamn thing needs to feel on the razor's edge."

I know exactly what's going to happen, Brian remembers thinking at the time. The fans would boo, and they did. "That was the point." In wrestling a move fails if it doesn't get the intended reac-

* Heat: vocal fan disapproval (a good thing).

tion from the crowd. "For them to start chanting, 'This is racist' was exactly what we wanted."

An edgy cleverness undergirded the match card the night Matt attended his first Georgia wrestling show in 2010. Dwight Power, Rachael Tension, and Simon Sermon were set to appear. *That's a place I have to go,* he thought.

Matt's father Larry worked third shift at the tire plant, but Friday and Saturday nights, father and son stayed up late watching TV. One night in the late '80s a new show, *Glow: Gorgeous Ladies of Wrestling*, appeared on Fox, one of the few channels they could view on their TV without cable. A low-budget production filmed weekly at Las Vegas's Riviera Hotel, *Glow* featured a cast of strongwomen who wrestled, spouted G-rated jokes, and rapped both the show's theme song and their own introductions while grooving to a synthesized beat in the ring.

"That is one of my earliest wrestling memories," Matt says over breakfast, nearly four decades later. "And it shaped me—and what I think wrestling is."

The Gorgeous Ladies of Wrestling weren't just eye candy, they were entertainers. Louisiana voodoo queen Big Bad Mama put curses on opponents, Godiva rode a horse to the ring, and fans chanted the name of Matilda the Hun's theme song "Raw Meat." There was the farmer's daughter, Babe; the Russian colonel Ninotchka, head of the KGB; and the hair metal dames of horror, Chainsaw and Spike. They would later inspire the 2017 Netflix series. *WWF Superstars of Wrestling* had a Saturday nighttime slot too, joining *Saturday Night's Main Event* and other shows in a professional wrestling viewing schedule that stretched from morning to night. Matt was hooked.

When Earthquake crushed Hulk Hogan at 1990's SummerSlam, 9-year-old Matt thought the wrestler's career was over. In a promo for their rematch, Hogan groused from a hospital bed, "For sixty-five days, and sixty-five nights, my back was glued to the stretcher." Announcers encouraged fans to write to Hogan to cheer on his return. "It isn't worth it," Matt scribbled on a postcard, begging the Hulkster not to get back in the ring with Earthquake. A few weeks later, Matt (and presumably many thousands of other kids who acted on the company's targeted messaging) received a signed thank-you card. On another formative day in his childhood, he watched in awe as Black wrestler Koko B. Ware, in a white tuxedo jacket with his pet macaw on his arm, came down the ramp. It signaled to him that the ring wasn't just for white people.

Historically, WWE has pushed white wrestlers to the top faster and with more frequency than Black wrestlers. In 2021, Bobby Lashley, at age 44, became the fifth Black man in the company's 68-year history to hold its highest title.

Pro wrestling has only recently seen noticeable inclusion at its highest levels. Those changes, though, first appeared at the bottom, at small wrestling shows like PCW, the first show Matt attended after moving to Georgia. He could see the prickly complexity that simmered inside the heel faction Violent Majority and its attacks on the gay wrestler Simon Sermon, who fans adored. They were characters who jabbed at our country's past and present, forced an audience in an evolving American South to adjust themselves in their seats.

"If it's too on the nose I ain't gonna like it," Matt says. "There's got to be a slant. It can't be straight-up wrestling. That's boring." It's about the story. The subtext.

Wrestling's grip is stronger on a small stage than it is on TV or from the seats of your nearest pro sports stadium because the hero isn't out of reach, he slaps your hand on his way to the ring.

"When the quarterback is hurt, he doesn't reach up to the crowd for help," Matt says. "I can't go yell to Hamlet, 'No, don't do that!' I can't tell Romeo, 'Yo! Juliet's not dead, dude! Don't drink that!' They won't listen. But a wrestler will."

Fans have agency over the action in a wrestling ring. That's powerful in places like Covington, Georgia, PCW's home from 2019 to 2024, when the median household income there hovered just below $50,000.

"For the people that make up my audience, that might be the only time they felt heard all week," Matt says.

It didn't take long for him to part the ropes and play the role of manager, escorting wrestlers to the ring and heckling fans along the way. Call him the BlacKkKlansman of Georgia wrestling: Matt didn't look like most of the fans in the seats, but he had the same countrified drawl. In that dichotomy he saw opportunity.

"They see me and think, I know how to react to this dude," he says. And then he talks. A manager plays a huge role in bringing heat to a heel. Matt ribs them for living in trailers, for having relatives on perpetual disability. It comes from recognizing a shared experience. There's a pathos there. "I can burn you because it will be real," he says. "Because I know that life."

Matt took over PCW in 2014. Even before the shift though, most of the roster was Black, he says. "When those guys would come down here to PCW," he says of Black wrestlers who traveled in from other Southern states, "they felt like they'd gone to Wakanda."

Historically, professional wrestling scripts, like most in American popular culture, have been written by white people. Promoters cast clean-cut white men, often former college football players or amateur wrestling stars, as babyfaces, while those born outside the US—or whose nationality was perhaps less apparent—were written as heels. In the mid-to-late twentieth century, promoters employed the American fear du jour to bring the heat. No one could rile up a Cold War crowd like Nikolai Volkoff singing the Soviet National Anthem . . . except maybe the keffiyeh-wearing Iron Sheik, who would yell, "Russia number one, Iran number one, USA?" and then spit on the ring.

"In the South," Matt says, "you can take the most ardent, hardcore, right-wing racist. You look in that person's life. There's a Black dude named Charles that they love at work."

In this way Georgia wrestling glimpses a granular South rendered invisible in the blinding light of assumption.

"I have to play on that," he says. "I have to present all sorts of different people in different ways so that they can come to love them. And if I have a Black guy who identifies as a street dude and that's the character he wants to play, I have to let him play it. And I have to let him be the heel in the beginning because the natural inclination of the audience is to see that guy as the heel. But then I have an opportunity to tell a story that redeems him and that makes him relatable to those people."

"I call it hiding the vegetables," he continues. "I can't come out and say, 'Here at PCW, we respect this or that.' Because then I'm preaching." In seeing that any person can play any role in the ring, fans come to believe they can be any person outside it. A Black Lives Matter sticker doesn't evoke empathy. An affecting character does.

"Nothing has ever made the world make sense to me like wrestling does," Matt says, between bites of a biscuit sandwich. He grew up Christian and compares it to religion. Wrestling—religion—has a lot to do with believing.

"I'm fully willing to admit it might just be a story," he says of his faith, and wrestling. "But it's a story I like. It's a story that gets me through. And in the end if it was all a work, guess what, I got worked."*

Under his direction, PCW's inclusive, experimental ethos persists and Black fans fill more seats at shows than ever. Talent comes in, stays awhile, graduates to bigger shows, but often returns, where Matt awaits. "We are the launching pad, we are not the establishment," he says. "My goal is not to make money at PCW, my goal is to train the next generation."

Hunter James is among that talent. Matt refers to young performers as his wrestling kids. He gets just as many texts from them about their relationships as he does about their matches. He's the guy they call if they get a flat tire. The guy they ask to officiate their weddings.

A network of unofficial leaders governs the scene at this level. They'll help you tighten your dropkick and get you on a show in the next town over, but most importantly they offer eyes and ears interested in seeing your moves and hearing your story. "This is the power of belief," Matt says. "Knowing somebody believes in you can often be the difference in how you get better, how you get confidence."

Young wrestlers venerate Matt, and he's grateful. "But there's a sadness to it, too," he says. When he sees some wrestlers react to praise and encouragement, it's clear they have never experienced it before. "That means that everyone that was in their path up until they got to me didn't give them the sense of belief in them. That's terrible. Because that's free."

---

* A work is a put-on; a wrestler's actions when he's in character. When something is a "work" it's untrue, by reality's standards. If someone gets worked, it means they bought into the deception.

On November 12, 1966, 18-year-old Robert Smith, the plain-named perpetrator of the Rose-Mar College of Beauty shooting, walked into the Mesa, Arizona, building holding a .22-caliber revolver for all to see. If the entrance fazed any of the cosmetology students or their clients, they didn't show it. Smith fired at a mirror to get their attention, then ordered them to lay like wheel spokes on the floor. His shots, fired at close range, killed four women and a toddler. "I wanted to get known, just wanted to get myself a name," he told police.

In 2023, a team of NYU researchers analyzed 189 mass shootings and found the attackers in eight of the ten most widely known events between 1966 and 2021 were motivated by their hunger for fame.

"Mass shootings perpetrated by shooters seeking fame are the most lethal and, likely, the least understood," their article, published in the *Proceedings of the National Academy of Sciences*, declared. It's human to want to be seen, to be remembered. Self-mythologizing is an act of self-preservation. We want people to see us when we're at our best—or worst.

"Directors will be fighting over this story," Columbine shooter Dylan Klebold said in a home video filmed in the weeks before he and Eric Harris killed 12 students and a teacher, and then themselves, at their high school in Littleton, Colorado, in 1999.

Wrestling solves problems through violence, and that attracts a certain kind of person, Matt says. It's a balm. When done safely, wrestling's incomparably cathartic, a way to experience the thrill of combat without harm. It begs the question: What happens when you dance with brutality but don't bring it home? Wrestlers know the answer: You dance again.

From the outside, wrestling's grotesque. Chairs slammed over backs, foreheads oozing blood, bodies hurled into the air. But behind the brutality, quiet control and prevailing trust nurture wrestlers and fans escaping real-life despair. Violence, depression, addiction—they hide like rattlesnakes beneath the rocks. To avoid the bite, some wrestlers know the best thing is to keep moving. Keep wrestling.

Jamie Holmes, whose ring Hunter practiced in during high school, can trace his depression back to elementary school when he sometimes rubbed his arm along an exposed spring in the recliner until it bled. It was a pain he could control, a pain that somehow made him feel better.

"The psycho gimmick I did? I got it from when I was hospitalized," he said, sitting on the couch in his living room after Hunter and Brian Snyder left that November night in 2019. Across the room rows of wrestling figurines, entombed in their packaging, hung on the wall like art.

Jamie was "good" for a while after a stint at a behavioral hospital his junior year of high school. He married his high school sweetheart, had kids. But soon they grew apart. "I was cutting myself again," he says. "And hiding it." One night while driving he pulled over on the side of the road. "I carried a gun right there in the center console and I just pulled it out, put one in the chamber, and . . ."

One thing stopped him from taking his own life. He wouldn't abandon his kids the way his father had abandoned him. Jamie's dad left when he was 2. "My mom was there, she just wasn't the best," he recalls. "She would drink, and her boyfriends would drink, and that was my escape. I could go in my room and turn on the TV and there was wrestling."

Why are more aspiring wrestlers parting the ropes now than ever? The same reason LARP and cosplay and immersive theatre are familiar terms and Airbnb recreated Marvel Animation's X-Mansion in Westchester, New York. To escape. And to find community.

In 2023, Surgeon General Dr. Vivek Murthy granted epidemic status to loneliness and isolation in the United States. The research cited in his report shows that even before the pandemic, about half of American adults experienced "measurable" levels of loneliness and warned that social disconnection's reach is wider than diabetes or obesity, and is linked to heightened risk of cardiovascular disease, dementia, stroke, depression, and anxiety. The American Psychiatric Association followed up to say 25 percent of us are lonelier now than before COVID-19. Most modern lives lack meaningful social connection. The absence is especially vast in people aged 18–34.

Passion's an unrivaled elixir, Matt says. "It is the thing that can open your eyes to other people's experiences without beating you over the head with it. It's a place we can stand together, and these days we have so few places we can stand together if we're from disparate backgrounds."

Nothing is more primal than wrestling's playful violence. Watch toddlers roughhouse each other without injury, or dogs taunt and tackle one another, then walk home, leashed, satisfied, and better for it.

Play fighting into adulthood is adrenaline-fueled social play that reinforces boundaries and releases dopamine. The act of violent role-playing night after night buffs out the hurt and hate and breeds community.

Friendships form between teammates, opponents, managers, and bookers across race, gender, sexual orientation, and politics. For those whose lives exist in the margins, the benefits of the ring far outweigh its risks.

CHAPTER 7

Hunter pulls a Coker University shirt over his head and climbs out of athletic shorts, revealing his show attire: red Lycra trunks, trimmed in gold and stamped with his initials. The December air spills through the propped-open back door of this makeshift pro wrestling arena: a former grocery store in a low-rent strip mall 40 miles north of Atlanta.

This borrowed space, next to a Family Dollar and a Salvation Army store, reflects the industry's transience at this level. The windowless venue hosts concerts and comedy shows. On Sunday, congregants of Canton, Georgia's, Action Church will gather beneath its drop ceiling to praise. But tonight it's Southern Honor Wrestling. If McMahon's WWE is the MLB, then smaller companies like Total Nonstop Action Wrestling (TNA), National Wrestling Alliance (NWA), and Major League Wrestling (MLW) are the minor leagues. Small shows like this one amount to a Saturday afternoon softball game. Which doesn't make it any less thrilling—or satisfying.

Nearly naked, Hunter, 19, runs in place in the raw drywall threshold between backstage and the ring. Out there, stage lights, loud music, and highlight reels on projector screens add an air of prestige.

With fewer than 10 minutes until their match, he and Joe Black, a cannonball of a man who's worked the ring for more than a decade, rehearse the moves of their fight. In the quiet hallway, marred by Sharpie signatures (including Lynyrd Skynyrd drummer Artimus Pyle's), they step out a dance and speak a language only an insider would understand.

"Catch, go to kick, face bump, throw me back in, angle's to the buckle, one line, two line, send me off inside out," Hunter says, miming punches as Joe watches like a sensei, nodding his head.

"Don't forget the enzi after the jump," Joe says, leaning into the black cane that complements his *Blade*-inspired sleeveless overcoat.

"Shit," Hunter says. "Enzi, enzi, enzi. I keep forgetting that," he mutters under his breath, eyes fixed on the floor as he paces, his mind running through the mechanics of the moves but also their potential. Every Friday and Saturday night, independent wrestlers—almost all working-class men like Hunter—finish their shifts and drive dark two-lane Georgia roads to shows like this, embodying characters and colliding with each other in hopes that someone important will notice. Wrestling shows replace community theatre in small towns across the state, where pro wrestling's roots run deep. Where front yard trampolines with frayed edges become practice rings for second-generation ring workers. Where kids like Hunter don't dream of college, they dream of the day the crowd chants their name.

Atlanta was once the nation's capital of professional wrestling; its marble-clad Municipal Auditorium was its White House. For those whose paychecks didn't wield tickets to Judy Garland or the Jackson Five, it was known for something else: its Friday night wrestling shows, which had drawn at- or near-capacity crowds since GCW premiered there in 1944.

This is the Georgia of Ted Turner, who, in 1972, convinced GCW—then the highest-rated TV program in Atlanta—to move from the local ABC affiliate to his burgeoning independent station. Later, when Turner's Techwood Drive studio doubled as headquarters for his next venture, CNN, news producers working the weekend shift shook from the rattle of wrestlers like Abdullah the Butcher and Dusty Rhodes crashing onto the mat upstairs.

And this is the Georgia of Jimmy Carter, who invited Mr. Wrestling II to his 1977 inauguration and nominated GCW co-owner Jim Barnett to the National Council for the Arts. (Two declined after the Secret Service insisted he leave his mask at home.) Carter shared his fandom with his mother, Lillian, who told a *National Enquirer* reporter, "The more brutal it is, the better I like it."

Here, the Big Time has always trickled down to the backwater and the backwater has always fed the Big Time. Arn Anderson, Ron Simmons, Jake "The Snake" Roberts, Road Dogg, AJ Styles, Xavier Woods, Austin Theory—all celebrity wrestlers who got their start performing in Georgia venues like the one Hunter performs in tonight. The list goes on and lengthens with new contract signed with the industry's powerhouses, AEW and WWE, today. In their wake, countless uncelebrated wrestlers bob like plastic ducks in a carnival pond.

The reality, behind the bravado, is that it's nearly impossible to make a living as a professional wrestler. It's dangerous work with limited opportunity. Many wrestlers call themselves "the best in Georgia." Without that confidence, the crowds wouldn't believe the act. But it's a long road to the majors. The average age of male WWE and AEW wrestlers hovers around 35.

There's no singular path to success. AJ Styles toiled away in the minor leagues until he was nearly 40. Cody Rhodes and Xavier Woods competed as rival high school amateur wrestlers in the suburbs of Atlanta. Woods went to college. Rhodes, to LA to study acting, and then to the ring.

After clinching his final high school match, the announcer declared the victor of the Georgia State Championship, Cody Rhodes, using his father's pro wrestling moniker rather than the family name, Runnells. Cody had asked him to do it. It was a nod to his father and a signal of his plans.

Dusty helped 20-year-old Cody get in at Ohio Valley Wrestling, a well-regarded WWE developmental program. He had wrestled fewer than 50 matches when he debuted on *Raw* against Randy Orton, in his father's yellow boots, in 2006. He played a series of generic cocky athlete bits, then toiled as the maniacal goofball Stardust—a character part WWE assigned him. After a decade, he threw up his hands. He wanted to be great, not goofy.

Swept straight to the top by the mighty hand of his father, Cody bypassed the slow-churning backwater at the bottom of the business. After he left WWE, he went looking for it. Performing in school gyms and community centers, he learned to channel his emotions into a believable character and connect with the crowd. He bet on himself and won their hearts, through authenticity.

Dusty died from septic shock in 2015. In an emotional promo after a match at Crosby High School in Waterbury, Connecticut, Cody held back tears. "What happens on the morning when you wake up and there is no shadow anymore? What do you do? You kick, punch, bite, scratch, and tell every son of a bitch who said you couldn't do it that you can do it!" The fire and fervor of the "American Dream" Dusty Rhodes.

He joined AEW as executive vice president shortly after its inception in 2019, and in 2022, returned to WWE as the "American Nightmare" Cody Rhodes. He was 36.

Hunter's face-off tonight is a squash match. It's a quick-hitting, 2-minute brawl early in the show that Hunter will lose. Before he does, he will recoil from Joe's chops and kicks so much that the crowd leans in and thinks, *wow, he's getting killed out there*. Wrestling's about manipulating emotions. It's more about selling the action than who wins or loses.

Joe was the smallest guy in the ring when he started training in 2008. He remembers his trainers discouraging him from trying difficult moves because of his size, 5'9", and, at the time, 130 pounds. He reclined into the ropes, watching, the word "no" ringing in his ear.

Some nights he snuck into the building and practiced alone in the dark. One night an older, more seasoned wrestler, William Huckaby, pulled him aside and offered feedback: If you want to be taken seriously you need to gain 50 pounds. If he did, Huckaby promised, he would be undeniable.

Joe stopped blaming the trainers, the gatekeepers, and the industry and started focusing on himself, powerlifting between night shifts at Walmart. One night at the gym he dropped a 465-pound weight on his leg. He wiggled his toes but when he stood up, the leg felt like jelly: a ruptured quad. On March 22, 2019, doctors told him he'd be away from the ring for six to eight months. Three months later he tossed his crutches aside and climbed in.

To earn entrée into a promotion—a company that runs wrestling shows—a wrestler must feign a good beating. The narrative works because it speaks to our instinct to protect "our" people. *Don't come in here and threaten our guy.* Night after night in arenas big and small, the act is the same: Cocky new guy shows up, challenges the champion, gets tossed around the ring, hobbles away, comes back for more. The booker—the person casting the roles and determining the victors—draws out the conflict just long enough, and then *boom.* A win. The new guy's on the roster and fans are hooked on the story.

The phrase "you win some, you lose some" may as well be woven into the mat Hunter peels his face from tonight. Fans get bored watching the same person win, week after week, month after month. They need to see him get pummeled and rise up. Fans live for what promoters call swerves: plot twists that make them squirm.

Swerves boost ticket sales because when fans are mad, they show up to see what happens next. A booker engineers an ascension and then wallops the crowd with a fall from grace. Attack, revenge. The volley keeps us watching.

Wrestling's about strength and speed and style—but also how well you can act and how long you stick around. Any match—even a one-sided match—increases Hunter's exposure. Tonight, he's made it to one of Georgia's top shows. He knows it's only a matter of time before he catches the attention of someone in the locker room or in the seats, someone who will take him to that place where doing what he loves earns him a paycheck.

Brandon Thurston of the industry analysis site *Wrestlenomics* backyard-wrestled as a teenager in a Buffalo suburb in the early aughts. He started training in 2003, at 18, and wrestled in independent promotions until 2021, the year he turned 36. In the latter part of his career he trained others hungry for the thrill of the ring. At the onset, he listed four factors that determine the likelihood of getting booked on a show, in order of importance. Number one, who you know. Specifically, who will recommend you. Two, how you look. Three: Your gimmick. Lastly: How you wrestle. "It's a reluctant admission but that's the thing that matters fourth most," he says, calling from his office in western New York.

By Thurston's calculation, Hunter's instinct to lean into his network, no matter the uncertainty of its influence, is a good one.

Hunter keeps his head down and puts his faith in Georgia wrestlers and promoters whose influence is unquantifiable. He controls his training and physique; they control the rest. "You have to know people," he says, because that's what he's been told. "If you don't know people and they don't know you, it's the same question as 'Does a tree make noise if it falls in the woods and no one is there to hear it?' "

"Why are you ok with them doing your bidding for you?" Hunter's boss at work asked him one day. "They know what they're doing," he said. "I don't."

Tonight a lifetime of training can't quell his nerves, which propel Hunter into last-minute wiggles and adjustments familiar to any athlete approaching the starting line. He squats, kicks out his legs and sinks into a set of pushups. Stands. Slaps his biceps. Unties and ties his boots. Lifts his right leg, ballerina-style, onto the railing, and leans into it.

Beyond the wall a body hits the mat, igniting a swell from the crowd. Joe hovers near the curtain, parting it just enough to peer out. Jeremie Prater, a landscaper in referee stripes, sneaks a look. "They're about to go home," he says, issuing a warning. Hunter adjusts his knee pads, retreats down the hallway, returns, runs in place again.

Lupe Fiasco's "Put You on Game" cues Joe's entrance to the stage. As the music plays, a professional-looking highlight reel, inspired by the ones WWE plays on its jumbotron, appears on screens flanking the catwalk that leads to the ring. The footage shows stills of Joe, with six-pack and bulging biceps. In some he kneels above a downed opponent. In others he glares at the camera with crossed arms.

And then the synthesized bass line of Poison's "Unskinny Bop" explodes from the PA. A teenager with shaggy, sandy blond hair smiles on screen as commentator Diana Michel yells into the mic, "Weighing in at 207 pounds from Myrtle Beach, South Carolina, the Varsity One, Hunter James!"

Hunter has a role: to swiftly identify himself as the good guy and take Joe's beatings. He will reinforce Joe's role as a heel. But the fans know Joe. He's earned their respect by being a consistent presence at the show, and he's just back from a devastating injury. Hunter raises his arms and bops toward the ring, trying to get the crowd behind him, but the reaction is muted. The plan doesn't work.

Todd Sexton, one of Hunter's trainers at Landmark and the booker of Southern Fried Championship Wrestling, where

Hunter's a rising star, watches from the wings. After the match Todd, one of the people Hunter trusts to guide him through the industry, approaches him.

"Dropkick. Your timing was off," he says.

Todd knew he wanted to be a wrestler in fourth grade. His parents shrugged it off. It was 1990. What 10-year-old boy didn't? He never grew out of it. In high school when most kids fought to sleep in, Todd got up at 5 and lifted weights before the morning bell.

By 20, his life had become a cadence of parties, concerts, and odd jobs around Atlanta. He knew if he were going to give this a shot he'd have more success training away from his hometown. He heard his favorite wrestler, Shawn Michaels, had opened a wrestling school in San Antonio. He saved up $5,000 and on a July day in 2000, drove the thousand miles to start training at the Shawn Michaels Wrestling Academy.

Known for his match-ending superkick and his role as de facto caption of the D-Generation-X stable in the late '90s/early aughts, the Heartbreak Kid is one of the most revered and recognizable wrestlers of all time. Billy Ray's favorite. Hunter's too. At 6'1", 225—smaller than most people in the ring at that time, his charisma and technical aptitude propelled his fame. He often played the underdog.

Sexton trained with Michaels and Rudy Boy Gonzalez in an unairconditioned space on the second floor of a Mexican restaurant. On weekends, he traveled to border towns to perform in shows under Michaels's Texas Wrestling Alliance promotion. Michaels shuttered the school soon after. "We taught our students well and had no problem filling slots," he wrote in his 2005 memoir, *Heartbreak & Triumph*. "The Shawn Michaels Wrestling Academy was profitable. I just couldn't look a young man in the eye and take his money, knowing full well that he didn't have it in him to make it in this business."

Todd had prepared. Working out, running, strengthening his wiry 5'11" frame. But after the first round of calisthenics and drills on day one he ran to the bathroom confident he was going to throw up. Sweating and panting, he let his head hang limp and stared into the sink. Somewhere in there, he found what he needed to keep going.

At one point while he was training, his tag partner, who lived with him in an apartment near the school, asked Todd what he was going to do if he didn't "make it."

"I'll keep doing it," Todd said. "Because I've waited my whole life to do it."

His roommate dissented. "If I don't make it, I'm going to quit," he said. For him, it was the golden ring: WWE, or nothing.

The difference between wrestlers hell-bent on making a living from it, and wrestlers who relish the joy of performing, despite the injuries, low pay, and slim crowds, is something Todd has come to understand more deeply in the decades since. Having observed, thousands of times, the adoration fans give to local wrestlers, Larry Goodman, lead writer on the show-review site *Georgia Wrestling History*, gets it, too. "There's a love there that's so incredible," he says. "For a lot of these guys, that's enough."

"It can be a release," Todd says. "That's why so many guys want to do it, even though it may not be in their best interest financially. They need that release to get out there and enjoy the moment, to feel like they're somebody."

And then there's wrestler's depression: the emptiness that takes over the days that follow a match. "Performers need something immediately to focus on next," he says. "In that way it's a drug."

Less than a year after arriving in San Antonio Todd returned to Atlanta and entered the independent wrestling circuit with a mighty accolade: He'd been trained by the Heartbreak Kid himself, Shawn Michaels. In Georgia he found the wrestling world abuzz about NWA Wildside, a developmental show for Atlanta-based WCW. It was filmed at Landmark Arena in Cornelia. Soon he became a regular there.

"CBGB," he says, equating Landmark's role in Georgia wrestling to the New York City venue's role in music. "It may not draw the biggest crowd at times, but if you played there it was a big deal." Wrestlers vie for a spot on the card at Landmark because they know it's holy ground, marked by the footprints of gods: AJ Styles, Xavier Woods, the Briscoe Brothers, Christopher Daniels, Kenny Omega, and New Jack.

On June 14, 2015, Todd's brother, Brent, died in a car accident. "I'd never experienced that kind of grief before," Todd says. The only thing he could think of that could free him from the pain was the ring. He wanted a match with Sal Rinauro, a close friend to both him and Brent.

Safe inside the ropes, he could rip himself open and pour his anger and sadness into his moves. "When the bell rings it comes over you like a tide," he says, 6 years after Brent's death. It didn't wash him clean but it cleared enough debris that he could see a path forward.

As much as wrestling hurts, it heals. In the ring, you reel from punches but walk away unscathed. Outside those ropes, that's the scary place. The place where punches land hard; where they kill.

Todd had a knack for ring psychology. He understood early on that successful wrestlers didn't perform moves just for the sake of performing moves, they did it to tell a story. He knew each action needed to signal his motivations, reflect his personality, identify feuds, or introduce allies.

He equates the difference in wrestling for moves and wrestling for story to the layering of sounds in a hit song. "Welcome to the Jungle," he says. "If you take out the rhythm guitar, you know something's missing."

He wrestled around Georgia until 2006, even scored some bookings in bigger indie shows in other parts of the country, like Ring of Honor, Combat Zone Wrestling, and International Wrestling Association. He wanted to be famous, he says. "But goals change." When his son, Xander, was born in 2006 he stopped wrestling and started booking shows at Landmark, and later at Southern Fried, where Hunter debuted in July of 2021, two months after graduating high school.

As a booker, he's the master of fates for every character in the cast, the chief puppeteer of a rotating roster of itinerant showmen and women. As the person hiring the talent and writing the script, Todd looks for the "it" factor. It's more of a feeling than a rubric, but it involves some concrete parameters: in-ring technique, the ability to connect with the crowd, camera work outside of the ring, work ethic, attitude.

He watches early-career performers, offers feedback, and then waits for the light to go on, for them to put it all together.

Hunter has an edge, Todd says, because he grew up in it. "It's second nature."

Does he think Hunter can make a living as a professional wrestler? "It's too soon to tell," he says. "I've seen people who I thought for sure were gonna get signed within a couple of years and then they flaked out. I've seen people that should've got signed that are still plying their trade."

The path to stardom isn't one you can map out on LinkedIn. It starts in the bog of indie wrestling, and it's governed by a cast of gatekeepers with varying connections to the industry, many of them worn thin by time. They're in it for the same reason the wrestlers are: to feel like they're somebody. Many perform the simultaneous duties of showrunner, father, coach, and friend.

They write the stories. You learn by jumping in, sticking around, listening, and kissing ass. Hunter embodies the confidence and humility Billy Ray never had. He knows how to work a room. He understands the transactional nature of the business: he has to put in the unpaid work to earn the big payout. Billy Ray refused. He was too good for that.

In Georgia, two decades after he started his own wrestling career, Todd himself now plays the role of dream maker.

By day, he works at an adult day center in Gainesville. "It's like the Avengers or Justice League," he says. "Everybody's got a superpower. They're all different. You just gotta figure out what works best from working with them to unlock them."

He's speaking about his job working with adults with developmental disabilities but the same could be said for his role as a Georgia wrestler elder. His phone constantly chimes with texts and calls from wrestlers trying to find their way. "For something that's not a full-time job, it becomes a full-time job," he says.

Some nights he gets home from work and has to summon the muster to drive to Landmark on training nights. On the way home, after several hours of ring work, he's high.

"We're in the mud and blood, there's no politics, no people pushing for themselves, nobody bullshitting," he says of those nights. He leaves feeling renewed.

Todd's boots had been hung up for a while by 2020, when AJ Styles was home from the WWE during the pandemic and called him to run drills. The training bug bit again. He devised a heel stable, the Sexton Alliance, with his wife, Kelly, and his best friends Judais, Adrian Hawkins, Bobby Moore, Billy Buck, and Nick Halen, and played the pro wrestling equivalent of actor-director. Like most things that work well in wrestling, it's art imitating life. "The best things click when what the fans see is real. The relationship we have is real. It resonates."

CHAPTER 8

A photo of wrestler Jimmy Rave at his memorial service

A few paces past the metal doors that lead to an indoor sports court in Cartersville, Georgia, on a February Sunday in 2022, Todd Sexton leans over to sign his name in a guest book, splayed open on a table draped in black fabric. Failing to come up with something poetic for the "thoughts and memories" column next to his name, he settles on two words and a form of punctuation that suggests perpetuity rather than an end:

"A lot . . ."

Next to the book, an arrangement of white lilies and cascading green leaves splits the distance between a box of Kleenex and an oversized photo resting on an easel. In it, Georgia wrestler Jimmy Rave stands shirtless in baby blue compression tights, wrists wrapped in white tape, hair slicked back, scowling at the camera. The photo dates from the early 2000s, early in his career.

Drugs are drugs and wrestling is a drug, and when one is beyond the reach of a wrestler, he will sometimes reach for the other. It's difficult to tell which is more dangerous and addictive.

Here, on a shimmering basketball court in a massive youth sports complex, fewer than 100 people sit in folding chairs, staring at an empty podium and an image projected onto the painted-cinderblock wall above it: Jimmy Rave 1982–2021.

Wrestler Sal Rinauro claims a spot in the front row, away from the others. He twists sideways in his chair, crosses ankle over knee, and rests an elbow on the chairback. Every few minutes for the next two hours he rests his forehead into his arm as people speak into a microphone about his best friend James Guffey, known to wrestlers and fans as Jimmy Rave.

Caprice Coleman steps up first. He scans the rows of men, their thick thighs and biceps stuffed into standard-issue black slacks and button-down shirts, men known for riotous, violent behavior who today sit silent and motionless except for the occasional wiping away of tears. Caprice begins. "A lot of you I look at as family, because we grew up together chasing this dream."

"Some of us made it, and some of us didn't," he continues, his tone calm and confident from years as a pastor. "That wasn't the point. The point was a teenager named James Guffey set out to grab his dream and he grabbed it. And he never forgot where he came from."

Jimmy Rave made it. The troubled kid from Georgia performed in the United Kingdom and Japan and India and feuded with WWE Superstars before they got big. When he died on December 12, 2021, the *New York Post* published a story about him with a photo from his Twitter account.

Instead of the athletic young man with button nose and pouty lips sending his famous two-finger salute toward the sky, a bloated Jimmy lay on a hospital bed, both legs and one arm amputated, giving a hardened thumbs down.

"I love this sport that we grew up in," Caprice says. "But it's a hate thing too."

"Because it's the type of sport that . . . " he pauses, as if considering whether or not to deliver the blow.

"It'll bring you in, put you up high, and it'll slam you and kick you out when it's done with you."

He reads from First Peter, Chapter Five: Be alert and of sober mind. Your enemy the devil prowls around like a roaring lion looking for someone to devour. Resist him.

You spend years trying to get back to the glory days, Caprice warns. The days of being on top, of the crowd chanting your name. When those days wane, some wrestlers still show up to breathe in the recognition that comes with being a legacy. Some of them go out quietly. And some of them go out with a bang.

It was a warning to a room full of men who wake every day fiending for the adoration they feel on Saturday night.

Like Hunter, like AJ Styles, like Todd Sexton, and so many others, Jimmy got his start as "one of the boys" at Landmark Arena. But he found drugs before he found wrestling, and before that, trauma found him. In 2013 Jimmy told a reporter from Atlanta's public radio station, WABE, he had been molested by a relative. "My mother was an alcoholic, and she died at the age of thirty-four, so I really felt like I was on my own since I was fifteen," he added.

For a time, wrestling replaced his addiction to drugs. He even worked for the Georgia Mental Health Consumer Network under his born name, James Guffey. But he broke his jaw in 2008 and got hooked on the prescribed painkillers. He attempted suicide in 2009.

A slideshow in front of the crowd displays the duality of Jimmy's life. In one series of photos, a sinewy man with piercing blue eyes poses in wrestling gear. A few shots later the same man nuzzles a newborn baby, then stands with his family in matching white shirts. In another, he poses soldierlike behind the governor celebrating the state mental health day at Atlanta's Capitol. Then next to his daughter, Kailah, dressed up for a high school dance. With his son, Little Jimmy, tugging on his neck. The roaring lion of his addiction hides just outside every frame. Toward the end of the service Jimmy's ex-wife, Felicia, stands at the podium.

"I've always had a love-hate relationship with wrestling," she says, after taking a breath. "I wanted to love it because he loved it, but I hated it, because like Caprice said, it would pull you in, put you up top, and then chew you up and spit you out and stomp on you. While all of this has been very difficult, I have a little more love for it because you guys have been absolutely amazing."

Hunter wasn't there that day. He didn't feel he'd earned the right to be present at such an intimate gathering. But maybe he wasn't ready to hear Caprice Coleman's truth. Hunter started young, too, and committed his life to the goal Jimmy Rave died trying to achieve. Trauma and grief hover at arm's reach all around Hunter. For now, he deflects, stays focused on his goal. Maybe wrestling will serve him when he encounters his own hard times. But what will he reach for when injury inevitably takes it away?

Jimmy spoke slowly in his interview with the hosts of *Georgia Wrestling History*'s podcast *Tipping Point* on November 2, 2021. A year earlier he contracted MRSA after having his left arm amputated due to infection. In June 2021 surgeons removed both of his legs after finding the antibiotic-resistant staph infection.

"You've been through a whole lot," Larry Goodman says. "I gotta ask, where are you at mentally?"

Jimmy responds with a line about opportunities but then trails off. "Day to day it's difficult, for sure. Day to day."

Then silence.

His resigned tone stalls Goodman and his cohost Stephen Platinum, the founder, in the early aughts, of PCW, who have known Jimmy since he began his career.

Jimmy talks about watching wrestling in the hospital, about his desire to continue working in the industry. "I would love to land a job in pro wrestling somewhere, just helping out," he says meekly.

"I imagine you will work in wrestling as long as you care to," Platinum says.

He died less than two months later.

CHAPTER 9

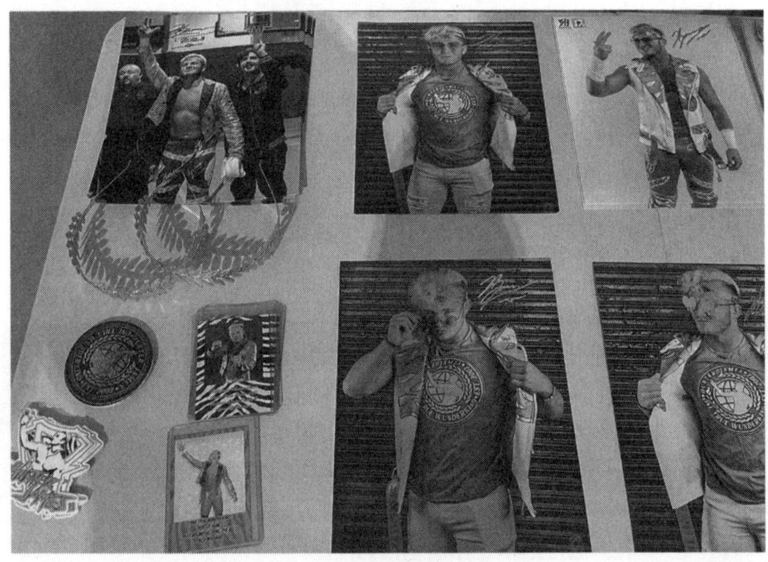

Hunter's merch table

The pre-show gathering—more whiling away the hours than running drills—is part of wrestling's appeal: Under the guise of a performance call time, you hang with your friends. Like groomsmen before a wedding, they arrive to the Walton County Boys & Girls Club in Monroe, Georgia, for Southern Fried Championship Wrestling's show, Grapple Mania, on April 2, 2022.

Dragging a wheeled rollaboard or a duffel, or with a garment bag slung over a shoulder, some stop to read the rundown taped next to the door, a one-page document that lists the matches, in order, and their victors. One wrestler covers himself in a bath towel, removes his shorts, and pulls on a pair of trunks. Another sits on a dining table bench, tightening laces through the grommets of calf-height boots.

Hunter arrived early and flopped onto the L-shaped couch in the gymnasium annex. Laminate wood flooring, exposed wood ceiling, and cinderblock walls painted white, orange, and blue-gray lend a clean and well-funded vibe to the space, home base for a burgeoning youth lacrosse team made up of Walton County Boys & Girls Club kids.

Hunter is bigger, tanner, and more confident than he was 10 months ago when he graduated high school. Young in life and young in his career, he does what he's told. Each match, no matter who wins, is one more bang on the drum he hopes someone will hear.

The people around him keep a steady flow of oxygen to his ego, like they're fanning a fire. A whisper in the ear as he sits on Landmark's bleachers gulping water between practice matches. "You're the youngest person to ever be a regular here." Another whisper: "Fastest win in Hardcore Hell history."

In gym shorts and a T-shirt depicting the early-'90s WWE star Mr. Perfect, Hunter props his Nike Blazers on a throw pillow and pulls up WrestleMania 16 on NBC Universal's streaming platform, Peacock, which purchased five years of exclusive streaming rights to WWE content in a multibillion-dollar deal in 2021. The event was filmed before he was born, but it reminds him of being a kid, of watching wrestling with his dad.

Sal Rinauro, in athletic pants and a "Jimmy Rave Approved" T-shirt with its sleeves cut off, sports something between a five o'clock shadow and full beard and sits on the other end of the couch, at ease. It's been two months since he donned dress shoes and a tie and spoke at Jimmy's memorial. He and Hunter, 20 years his junior, talk about working out. Hunter started bulking up after graduating high school at 170 pounds. He plateaued at 198 and couldn't move the needle. But just the other day he stepped on the scale: 200.8. An important threshold to cross in his quest to shape himself into a WWE Superstar.

Bill Behrens walks in, hands tucked into the pockets of a black leather jacket. A slight, elder statesman sporting black slacks and a comb-over, Behrens is to Georgia wrestling what Rick Rubin is to music.

Behrens got started in the business in the early '90s, when he used his career as a television program syndicator to sell Memphis-based United States Wrestling Association (USWA) programming to TV stations across the country. As an agent he launched the career of hometown hero AJ Styles and worked with everyone from Diamond Dallas Page and Rick Steiner to Slim J and Sal Rinauro. Tonight, he shows off two of his latest successes, Griff Garrison, a 6'3" babyface with long blond curls, who signed with AEW in 2020, and Marcus Kross, his partner in the tag team Master & Machine, which Behrens helped design. Tonight, they'll battle Southern Fried's home team, The Approved, a nod to Jimmy Rave's heel stable, in the main event.

On the TV, Hardcore Holly bashes a box fan over his cousin, Crash. Behrens squints through metal-framed glasses. "This is older wrestling," he announces, in newscaster brogue. "There are Hollys." He pauses. "If there are Hollys it is really old."

"What year is this, 2000?" he asks. From the sofa, Hunter affirms.

Behrens's role is part businessman, part coach, and all sage. He has a BA in psychology from Emory and talks about wrestling in terms of "economics of movement" and refers to it as a "unique art form of improvisation." He has an eye for talent. If Behrens huddles with you after your match, he sees potential. And he always has notes for improvement.

An effective wrestling match, he says, establishes somebody the crowd wants to win and somebody the crowd wants to lose, creates a story involving them, and keeps the audience engaged. "You can also entertain an audience with fireworks," he said, a few days earlier, calling from his home in Eatonton, Georgia, just back from 5 days of TV tapings with NWA. "The problem with fireworks is they're immediately forgettable."

Anyone can learn to wrestle, Behrens says. There's a limited number of wannabes who can wrestle and tell a story. And even fewer who can wrestle, tell a story, have the look, and be a star. In Hunter, he sees the potential of it all. "He's got all the tools," he says.

Hunter has natural instincts that can't be taught, Behrens says, and he can play babyface or heel. Or, as Behrens puts it, "He's got the looks, but he also has a wonderful eat-shit-and-die face."

"Hopefully he doesn't get hurt," Behrens says. "Hopefully he doesn't get lazy. And hopefully he realizes that no matter how good-looking he thinks he is now, how in shape he thinks he is now, he can be better."

"To make it, better is going to be important," he continues.

Matt Hankins enters. He turns to Sal, one of his opponents in a funhouse match in two weeks. Tonight, they'll tease it with some ringside hijinks.

"Sal, what are we doing in this fucking funhouse?" Matt pauses. "Actually, what are we not doing? Let's just start there."

"Hurting each other?" Sal asks.

The setting for a funhouse match is often nowhere near a ring. It's more skit than brawl, and—with a WWE budget—involves multiple camera angles and previously recorded footage. In a moment of desperation-wrapped genius at WrestleMania 36, in 2020, filmed in the fan-less WWE Performance Center in Orlando when COVID-19 lockdown orders were in effect, WWE pitted Bray Wyatt against John Cena in the symbolic, psychologically horrifying Firefly Fun House Match. Cena wrestled phantom opponents, creepy puppets provided commentary, and fans glimpsed scenes from Cena's career, in black and white, as the menacing Wyatt, first in grandfatherly sweater and later in toothy Fiend mask, narrated and taunted. The match finishes with Cena beating Wyatt's Huskus the Pig Boy puppet in the center of the ring.

Fans who knew the wrestlers' careers understood the symbolism. Cena's entrance into the arena is really Cena entering his own consciousness. Alone in the ring, he maneuvers through high and low points of his career, known for its rapid early success and recent sputtering. The tortured loner Wyatt, and his puppets, act as Cena's tormenters, commentating the action.

Sachin Hingoo of *The Cultural Gutter* (tagline: thoughtful writing about disreputable art) called it "one of the most avant-garde, genuinely scary, and high-concept 'matches' the WWE, and I daresay any wrestling promotion, has ever produced."*

Sal talks through an idea he formed at the concession stand. "I was looking at stuff and I was like, 'I could definitely open a bag of these Airhead Xtremes and choke somebody.'"

"I'll fucking take that spot," Matt says, and laughs. Then he spitballs ideas with Sal about force-feeding him the sour candy

* Sachin Hingoo, "The Firefly Funhouse," *The Cultural Gutter*, September 21, 2023.

and feigning a diabetic emergency. It's a start—one Matt knows will resonate with the crowd.

On screen, Test and Albert battle Al Snow and Steve Blackman, who form a tag team called Head Cheese. A man wearing a costume shaped like a triangular hunk of cheese parades around the ring, slapping his ass through two strategically placed "cheese holes." "Jesus Christ," Matt, delighted, yells to Brian Blaze. "Wrestling used to be so good, Brian!"

Hunter doesn't have to watch WrestleMania 16 to know what happens. Like so many other wrestling events, it's inked in his mind.

The names of WWE Superstars past and present form a significant part of a wrestler's lexicon. Famous performers whose names, like artists, evoke a style or era or technique. "Give him an Angle Lock." "Jeff Hardy it." "I want some Dusty color tonight."

Wrestlers use these eponymous terms to impart to their teammates and opponents specific moves and move sets or describe the look and feel of a match. The names come to embody entire spans of wrestling history. There's no Attitude Era without Stone Cold Steve Austin, no Era of Ruthless Aggression without Shawn Michaels, Triple H, John Cena, and Batista. Wrestlers align themselves with specific performers, who serve as character archetypes. Hunter's a self-described Shawn Michaels guy. It's a way for him to see himself and for his opponents to know what they're up against.

"Are there any women here?" someone asks above the din.

On the TV, female wrestlers The Kat and Terri Runnels, in catsuits and high-heeled boots, shriek and yank each other's platinum hair. The Kat sneaks up on Terri and then rips through the back of her opaque black getup, revealing a flesh-toned G-string. The camera zooms in before Terri, humiliated and disheveled, stumbles away. The sexed-up competition, filmed 22 years ago, hasn't aged well. An audible cringe erupts from the living room–like space full of men.

WWE pegs its female viewership at nearly 40 percent. The seats around small-town rings are similarly proportioned. Wrestling's catharsis smashes through gender and race lines. Men outnumber women in Georgia rings but the absence has more to do with women's roles as working mothers than with discriminatory gatekeeping. In Georgia, the consensus around why fewer women perform in small shows than men is twofold. One, promoters can't afford them. It's supply and demand: Because they're not abundant, women can charge a premium. They're also quicker to climb the ladder to larger promotions.

Los Angeles Lakers owner Jeanie Buss has invested millions of dollars in Women of Wrestling (WOW), syndicated via Paramount. In 2019, Ronda Rousey, Becky Lynch, and Charlotte Flair headlined WrestleMania, the first time in the event's 35-year history that women competed in the main event. (Becky "The Man" Lynch triumphed—in long sleeves.) Two years later, Bianca Belair defeated Sasha Banks on night one of WrestleMania 37, the first time two Black women headlined.

When women graduated from arm candy to in-ring WWE competitors in the aughts they performed as "WWE Divas" and went at each other in schoolgirl skirts and lingerie. Match themes included pillow fight and wet T-shirt contest and there always seemed to be a liquid-filled tub nearby for them to flail in. In 2015 wrestling fans reacted with #GiveDivasAChance, a call to WWE to take women seriously. A year later WWE ditched the Divas moniker and replaced the WWE Divas Championship with the

WWE Women's Championship. Since then, female WWE performers are called Superstars, just like their male counterparts.

Southern Fried has run its shows in a bar, two municipal rec centers, inside one church, and in the parking lot of two others. Since August 2018, the Walton County Boys & Girls Club has provided a consistent home. Monroe is a former textile town navigating an evolving identity as an exurb between Atlanta and Athens.

Most of the fans who walk through the doors on Saturday night come to every biweekly show. Many arrive hours before it starts. The scene resembles something between church basement fellowship and youth sports league, down to the hot dogs, popcorn, and soda for sale at the concession stand and the lady selling 50–50 raffle tickets. The Southern Fried Fan Club group on Facebook often reads like a prayer request ledger.

The show's owner, David Manders, knows no one's making a living by performing at Southern Fried. "I'm giving them a stage to live their dreams on," he continues. "Hunter James," he says. "He's going to get signed with WWE. I gave that stage to Hunter. He's going to make it."

An hour before the start of the show Hunter and his tag partner, Luka Daniels, along with their opponents Alex Kytel and Caleb Crocker, gather in the lacrosse team's locker room. Hunter's white rollaboard suitcase with a championship belt fastened around its extension handle is parked in front of a gear locker. Inside it, a pair of white wrestling boots sit below a lacrosse helmet.

"You want to do that double atomic double neck we were talking about?" Hunter asks Luka.

Luka responds by miming the moves but his motions lack confidence.

Hunter's not convinced he understands. "Look," he says. "Say you have him," Hunter points to Kytel. "I have Crock. We do the atomic," Hunter kicks his foot up, "then we switch. I'll run to him, neckbreaker."

In gold kneepads, white boots, black trunks, and his Mr. Perfect shirt, Hunter never stops moving and talking as he plays out their match in his mind and relays the action to his partner and opponents. It's clear he, at 19, is in charge.

"After that we're fucking hyped. Y'all two are not legal," he points to Caleb. "I'll get in the corner, I'm fucking excited," he walks in a circle as he talks, his arms and feet gesturing wildly as he goes. "Kickflip," he says, demonstrating the move with Kytel. "I'm great, I'm athletic, up-and-over me, woo!" he jumps in the air. "Oh shit, you son of . . . ," he feigns a kick to Kytel's face and Kytel stumbles back. They meet again and Kytel discus-elbows him. "And then I'm limp, and y'all start. We got, like, six," he says, referring to the number of minutes for which the match is scheduled.

Tonight's show, Grapple Mania, will open with Hunter and Luka's team, the Palmetto Express, issuing a promo to fans to hype their first defense of Southern Fried's tag team title. Bill Behrens enters to offer some guidance.

"Address how you won the titles," he advises, as Hunter wraps his wrists. Hunter and Luka triumphed in a triple-threat ladder match the month before that nearly went awry with Luka's dive from the top of the 10-foot ladder. He didn't communicate the move—a crossbody—to anyone in the ring, so no one stabilized the ladder. As he jumped from the top, it gave out from beneath his feet and he landed on the ropes rather than on top of Palmetto Express's opponents. (Hunter followed up with a flawless moonsault from the other ladder.) The match ended with their opponents so distracted by their own bickering that Hunter and Luka handily scaled the ladders to nab the belts, which dangled from a cable overhead.

"This is your first defense so this is primarily going to be Bumpy McBump Bump for you guys," Behrens continues. "So just pick a dance partner, tag in, get over,* protect."

The more seasoned among Southern Fried's roster assemble in the teen room of the Boys & Girls Club, where David Weakley, in referee stripes, and his son, sit on the pool table next to an open suitcase filled with wrestling gear. The large window looking out to the sport court has been covered with black paper. Later a corner of it will suddenly fall. "Kayfabe!" someone will yell, and everyone will hit the floor.

Across a small corridor, Alex Kytel sits in a black rocking chair next to a bookshelf of kids' books and DVDs. Hunter, in SFCW Tag Team Champion belt, paces. Motivational phrases mounted on construction paper decorate the walls. YOU DON'T GROW WHEN YOU'RE COMFORTABLE. DOUBT KILLS MORE DREAMS THAN FAILURE EVER WILL. They're meant for kids but feel apropos in the moments leading up to each match.

Kytel comes toward Hunter for a hug. "Love ya, we'll talk," he says. Luka, looking exhausted, walks toward the door. Hunter stops him. "Calm down," he says. It's not time to go yet. Luka returns to his chair, sips from a bottle of water, and then lowers himself to the floor for push-ups to pump up his arms and pass the time.

---

* Getting over: getting a reaction from fans. For heels, this translates to boos and pejoratives. For babyfaces, it's cheers.

Ring announcer Rick Richards, in suit and tie, introduces the show. "Y'all ready for a Southern Fried Saturday night?!"

He thanks the sponsors—Jimmy James Towing, C&K Delivery, Absolute Tree & Stump Removal, Just For Fun Radio, and Monroe Small Engine—and introduces the new "Southern Fried Tag Team Champions, The Palmetto Express!"

A few bars into the Poison song "Unskinny Bop," Hunter and Luka tear through the curtain, belts held high.

After their match a little girl in pigtails stands waiting on a folding chair next to the barricade nearest the curtain. When Hunter passes she hands him a letter. Written in pencil in mangled spelling above a barrage of hearts, it reads: I want you to be my boyfriend.

Behrens meets them backstage with a critique. "Let the heel throw the first punch," he says. "And don't rush at the beginning. Wrestle. Arm drag. Get up. Body slam. Simple, simple. Then escalate."

"The reaction for the newly crowned tag team champions was off the charts," *Georgia Wrestling History*'s Larry Goodman writes on the site the next day. "They love Palmetto Express in Monroe. Pure babyface rah-rah and the crowd ate it up."

During intermission, wrestlers in search of an ego boost and some extra cash spread T-shirts, stickers, and autographed photos across plastic folding tables. Behrens, carrying a portfolio briefcase, escorts Garrison and Kross to one and a line quickly forms. Ten yards over, Hunter stands alone behind his array of Hunter James stickers, photos, and shirts. The crowd mills, but for a few minutes, no one stops. Finally a kid in khakis and a "homework ninja" shirt stands next to him and poses for a picture. Before the cell phone camera clicks, Hunter drapes Southern Fried's tag-team champion belt across the boy's shoulder and shapes his lips into a sideways pout. The eat-shit-and-die grin.

"Bill, your boys stole my thunder out there at the merch table," he tells Behrens in the locker room after. And then he embellishes, shaking it off. "Hey, they came to me after y'all, alright?"

There's danger in exaggerating the truth to manipulate people's emotions. But consider its possibility for good. If, every Friday and Saturday night a small crowd deems you the greatest of all time, do you eventually become it? Or at least believe you have? When it comes to self-fulfillment, isn't it the belief that matters?

The bell time of tonight's show coincides with the start of WrestleMania 38, so before they batter each other in front of a crowd of 250, Southern Fried's wrestlers watch WWE Superstars like Brock Lesnar and Roman Reigns perform in what WWE will later call the most-attended and highest-grossing event in WWE history.* The sculpted bodies and cinematic vignettes on AT&T Stadium's 160-foot jumbotron: It's the dream. The ring in the middle of the Boys & Girls Club basketball court, the muffled PA, the guy turning hot dogs on a propane grill: It's the reality.

Around 10 p.m. the wrestlers all convene in front of the TV for WrestleMania 38's night one main event. Dallas's AT&T Stadium goes dark and then lights up blue as American flags, emblazoned with the wrestler Cody Rhodes's skull logo, unfurl and the wrestlers' song, "Kingdom," plays.

"No fucking way!" someone yells.

Cody Rhodes, son of Dusty, rises through a cloud of fog from

* Before WrestleMania 36 in 2020, which spanned two days, WWE's annual tentpole event took place on a single day. WWE's WrestleMania 38 calculations account for attendance and ticket sales ($15.6 million) for two days. But ticket sales from WrestleMania 32 in 2016, a single-day event, totaled $17.3 million, more than WrestleMania 38 without even adjusting for inflation. WrestleMania 40 in 2024 shattered both numbers: ticket sales for the two-day event totaled $38.5 million.

beneath the catwalk, wearing a long, military-inspired red, white, and blue coat: a dignified return to the company he left in 2016.

"From Atlanta, Georgia, weighing in at 222 pounds, the American Nightmare Cody Rhodes!"

Dusty was sweaty and bloated, red in the face and riled up when he spoke to fans. Cody has carved a different character for himself: calm, calculating, chiseled. The fans followed the story he told in the ring: a goofy cartwheel—a fuck you farewell to Stardust. The bionic elbow. A nod to his father. He pounded his chest. He was here to win a championship, the thing his father never did. He'd found himself inside the ropes. "We tell stories in the ring," he said in the 2023 Peacock documentary about his career. "And I needed that story to be told in the ring." He finished with a Cross Rhodes—his finisher—pinning Seth Rollins at the 21-minute mark. Afterwards, he leaned into the turnbuckle and looked skyward.

The announcer's voice breaks up the action. "Right now, high above the clouds, a certain son of a plumber is grinning ear to ear." A story, two generations in the making, continues.

The next day, Hunter drove to Gulf Shores, Alabama, to meet his family for a beach vacation, his first in three years. As he cruised south on I-85 he listened to the WWE Hall of Fame event from two nights before. He had saved it for the drive.

Inductees included Vader, Queen Sharmell, the late Shad Gaspard, the Steiner Brothers, and, as the voice in the show's introduction put it, "the most prolific performer in Wrestle-Mania history, by many considered the greatest of all time," The Undertaker. Fans held posterboard signs cut into the shape of headstones that read Thank You Taker.

"For thirty long arduous years this man has performed for you," Vince McMahon said, "traveling thousands and thousands of miles, night after night, enduring countless injuries and surgeries, learning to live with the pain. Learning to live with the toll that it takes on the human body."

Before the arena went dark and The Undertaker's trademark bells tolled, Vince delivered the punchline. "Safe to say, he's been to hell and back."

"For the last thirty years, my identity has been Undertaker," Mark Calaway said. A crowdswell swept over Dallas's American Airlines Center. When it quieted, The Undertaker named the personas he embodied. The Phenom. The Deadman. The American Badass. The Taker of Souls.

And then he addressed his fans as the man beneath the black hat. It would've been easy to keep that person hidden, he said, but that wouldn't be fair. The address acknowledged another unspoken agreement between fans and performers. It was an act of respect, given to the fans in return for the respect they had showed him.

"You are loyal, you are passionate, and you guys were the motivation I needed on many nights, to get up off of the training room table, work my way down here to the ring, push through the pain, and perform."

Then he told a story. He's sitting in his brother's living room, a semester away from college graduation, in 1986. He'd spent the previous decade playing basketball and had been offered a contract by a European scout. "I don't know what to do," he tells his brother. "Do I graduate? Do I go overseas and play pro basketball?" Despite being inside the home arena for the Dallas Mavericks, the fans respond with a chorus of *boooo*. "Basketball isn't what I want to do. My heart is already into wrestling."

Calaway had only recently started training but knew already there was nothing else he'd rather do. But he worried about disappointing his teammates and parents. "Mark," his brother said. "You can't live your life for what mom and dad want you to do. You can't live your life for what your teammates want you to do. You can't live your life for anyone other than you."

Undertaker's words didn't stick with Hunter in the moment, but later, they would. He would understand then that both he and Mark Calaway reached a turning point in their lives, a choice to do what they were supposed to, or do what they love. Taker's words reminded him of something Nanny had said to him when he told her he wanted to train rather than go to college. "This is your life. You have to do what you want to do."

When Calaway told his parents he was dropping out of college to pursue professional wrestling, they were disappointed. Like Hunter, he was on track to be the first in the family to earn a college degree. In The Undertaker's episode of *Biography: WWE Legends*, Calaway sits in his mother Catherine's kitchen.

"I don't think y'all approved too much of that decision initially," The Undertaker says.

"No, when you told me that, I said, 'You're on your own. Don't call me for money.'" She says it with a smile now.

Calaway didn't have any industry connections. He hadn't been properly trained. But he had his body: 6'8", 315 pounds. He chased his dream, sometimes sleeping in his car and skipping meals because he couldn't afford them. For eight months, he drove once a week to the Dallas Sportatorium. Finally, Fritz Von Erich noticed him and booked him for a show. He made it in wrestling by showing up.

CHAPTER 10

Hunter woke up early on the morning of Friday, August 5, 2022. He went to the bathroom, looked in the mirror, and thought, *Am I tan enough?* Downstairs in the kitchen, he cracked eight eggs, dumped three of the yolks in the sink, and scrambled the mixture in a pan with two sliced-up turkey hot dogs. He drank water instead of coffee. He needed his heart rate to stay low.

At 9 a.m. he climbed into his Jeep and started heading north. After an hour he pulled off and picked up another wrestler, Hunter Knott. They were invited to be extras in the live-audience taping of one of WWE's flagship programs, *SmackDown*, at the 15,000-seat Bon Secours Wellness Arena in Greenville, South Carolina. They may as well carpool to save on gas, they agreed.

A few months earlier, Hunter completed WWE's application for enhancement talent. This would be his second booking, just seven days after he extra'd on *SmackDown* in Atlanta. In official-looking black polo shirt and pants, he entered the frame as a security guard and pleaded with wrestler Happy Corbin to stop assaulting color commentator Pat McAfee with popcorn. Fifteen seconds of fame, just off center from the focus of the shot.

On the road, the two Hunters tried to guess how WWE's producers would cast them. Would they play security guards and get beaten up by Brock Lesnar or Ronda Rousey? Would they pile onto a pull-apart between Lesnar and Roman Reigns? Hunter pulled off at a QuikTrip gas station a few miles from the arena. They grabbed their garment bags from the back seat and went inside to change into suits, as directed.

Inside the arena producer and former wrestler Shawn Daivari spotted them looking lost, luggage in tow. "You looking for your dressing room?" he asked. They nodded. "Behind catering. Right side."

Shawn Daivari! they gushed as they walked.

The holding area for extras was actually an enclosed tailgate-style tent. Hunter had a good feeling he'd be in the ring that night and started getting ready. He changed back into athletic shorts and a T-shirt, did squats, push-ups, and sit-ups, and then laid back onto a balled-up sweatshirt. Before he could catch his breath, referee Darryl Sharma popped in. "Hunter James?" he asked. "You have a match." Hunter followed Sharma down the ramp, where Jamie Noble, a producer and former wrestler who trained at Atlanta's WCW Power Plant, the same school that passed on Billy Ray, leaned against the barricade.

"Can you work?" Noble asked.

"That's what I've been told."

Noble had slated Hunter and fellow Georgia wrestler Marcus Kross in a tag-team match against the bearded, burly Viking Raiders. The storyline: Two local wrestlers won a lottery for the chance to prove themselves in a WWE ring. "It's Road Warriors all the way through," Noble said. Hunter understood. Popular in the '80s and '90s, The Road Warriors towered over their opponents with painted faces and body armor. Noble's simple directive meant Hunter and Marcus, the undersized outsiders, would lay into The Viking Raiders like toddlers attacking punching bags. The big guys would effortlessly counter their attacks.

WWE Superstar Drew Gulak stood nearby and started dispensing tips: "When you go in, you look at the cam that's on the floor across from you and you give 'em the biggest white-meat babyface smile." Hunter practiced. "Bigger," Gulak said. "You gotta be bigger."

A few hours later, Hunter and Marcus, in gold-trimmed red trunks they brought from home, stepped to the top of the ramp that led to the arena floor.

It was a commercial break. "Look around, take it in," a producer said. Hunter gazed at the crowd. The words of Georgia wrestler Nick Halen, who Hunter spent countless hours training with at Landmark, rung in his ears: "Keep your feet on the ground. It can all be taken away at a moment's notice."

"The following contest is a tag-team match scheduled for one fall," WWE ring announcer Samantha Irvin's voice echoes through the arena. "Making their way to the ring at a combined weight of 590 pounds, Erik and Ivar, The Viking Raiders!"

Hunter and Marcus—wrestling under the names Tommy Gibson and Jim Mulkey, nods to Southern wrestlers Robert Gibson and the Mulkey Brothers—wait in the ring, nervously bickering—an act—about who should make the first move. Over the next minute and a half, the bearded savages, like bored cats, lob their diminutive opponents around the ring.

To the commentators' delight, Ivar drags Hunter by the hair

to the turnbuckle and unleashes elbow after elbow to his cheek. "Elbows to the beautiful young face!"

Ivar climbs to the second rope with Hunter in his arms and belly flops on him in the center of the ring. "Splat!" the commentator squeals before offering his own jab. "I want to be a WWE Superstar, these two said!"

It was another squash match, the kind of match Hunter, angling to make it big, was used to doing; the kind Billy Ray, chasing the same dream, refused. To hell with the gas money and meager payout. This time, the opportunity cost was unmeasurable.

Hunter's too smart to let his ego get in the way of his success. A beginner wrestler's job is to make established wrestlers look good, whether at a VFW or an arena taping of *SmackDown*. In playing along Hunter banks on yet another unspoken acknowledgment of this heartbreak-laced industry: His time will come.

That night he walked the halls talking to WWE Superstars and producers, the very people who will determine his future in the ring. When the bell rang to signal the start of the match, two million people were watching. Two of them were his parents.

It had been two years since Hunter's first match, in Arkansas in 2020. One since he dropped out of Coker University. Now he stood at the doorstep to his dream.

"Damn," Billy Ray said to Jenn in their living room as they watched. "They squashed him."

Billy Ray turned down invitations to play jobber* parts at WCW. "My ego was too big for that," he admits, a flaw he now recognizes may have impeded his success. "Hunter's a politician. I never was."

* Jobber: a wrestler booked solely to make his opponent look good.

After it was over Hunter and Marcus limped away. "My jaw! My back!" Hunter cried out until he was out of sight. At the top of the ramp, Happy Corbin, Ricochet, and six-time WWE Champion Roman Reigns greeted him with fist pumps.

Gregory "Hurricane" Helms walked over. "Have you thanked everyone?" he asked. Hunter had. "Have you thanked Triple H?" "No," Hunter admitted. "I didn't want to interrupt him." "Come with me, I'll tell you when you're good." They watched the TV monitor and waited for a commercial break.

Hunter approached Triple H, who only two months earlier had taken creative control of WWE from Vince McMahon.

"I appreciate the opportunity, sir," Hunter said, offering his hand. Triple H shook it. He asked Hunter about his favorite wrestlers.

"Mr. Perfect and Shawn Michaels," Hunter said. "But I'm named after you." Hunter knew his story and his performance were good. He knew that someday the chief creative officer of WWE would remember the confidence and showmanship of the kid from Georgia who was named after him.

Before his parents knew he was wrestling, Hunter came to Nanny and Pa's house to film promos. Sarah and Robert Noblett kept his secret. "He had my support first," Sarah says. And not surprisingly: The family's wrestling obsession starts with her. She knew Hunter was training long before his parents did, and his secret was safe with her. If they kicked him out of the house, he would always have a place at hers.

Before he left the arena, Hunter hit the catering spread and filled a takeout box with chicken, rice, and potatoes. One slice of Reese's cup–laced cheesecake lay on a platter. "I damn sure took it." Rather than driving all the way home, he stopped for the night at Nanny and Pa's. Standing in their kitchen at 1:30 in the morning, he microwaved a late-night dinner, courtesy of the WWE. And then he ate the cake.

"Were you nervous?" Billy Ray asked the next day. Hunter replied with a confident "No."

"Then I did my job."

Hunter looked at him. "Huh?"

"You know how many high-pressure situations I've put you in?" Billy Ray asked.

Hunter thought through it. All the games and amateur wrestling matches, all the times they'd been at a family get-together and Billy Ray said, "Bet you can't do a backflip." "Bet you I can," Hunter always responded before launching into the air and landing with a grin. The times Billy Ray announced to the gym where they worked out together, "Hey! Hunter's about to set a PR!" He had no choice but to grit his teeth and keep going.

Son of a bitch, Hunter thought. You've been training me for this my whole life.

CHAPTER 11

Carlie Bravo hits Jacob Ashworth with a spinning neckbreaker at a Southern Fried Championship Wrestling show

"Who's gonna make it out of Georgia?" *Georgia Wrestling History*'s Larry Goodman asks himself rhetorically. He quickly arrives at two answers. Hunter James and Carlie Bravo. "There's him, and then there's Hunter James," he says playfully. And then again, for effect. "And then there's him, and there's Hunter James."

It's Monday, August 8, 2022, and Goodman is at home in Norcross, Georgia. The 68-year-old, who works as a licensed professional counselor by day, has been to three wrestling shows in the past 72 hours. By tomorrow, he'll have all three detailed reports posted on the website. He recalls his entrée to Georgia wrestling, at Atlanta's Municipal Auditorium in 1978. "I came from Chicago. I'd never seen that kind of hard-hitting realistic wrestling. It was incredible," he says.

He stuck around. Two decades after his first show review for the website, he still spends his weekends traveling around the state with a notepad. In Hunter he sees an absolute student of the game. A natural. "And he's got the versatility as far as the range of being a really great babyface and being a really great heel."

"I'd say the same things are true about Bravo," Goodman continues. "There's an expressiveness and a way to connect with fans that few performers have."

Carlie Bravo grew up in Queens and Spring Valley, New York, the troublemaking son of Rikers Island corrections officers. When his parents found weed in his closet after he graduated high school, they had him arrested. The judge offered two choices: jail or military service. He chose the latter. It was 2003, less than two years after the September 11 attacks. Carlie turned 18 in boot camp at Parris Island, 19 in Afghanistan, 20 in Iraq. At 24, he took an honorable discharge after eight years as an Infantry Marine.

In the Corps he'd been told he had an abundance of job skills, but out in the real world, the consensus was he was good for nothing except a minimum-wage security job. Instead, he cooked at a TGI Fridays in Myrtle Beach and started a rap career that led him to Atlanta. When the pandemic left him unemployed, he hit the gym and started attending wrestling shows on the city's outskirts. All the up-and-comers performed at Atlanta Wrestling Entertainment (AWE), a show run by Murder-1, a wrestler trained by Billy Ray's trainer, Steve Lawler, who Carlie knew from Atlanta's music scene. Murder was an early Landmark Arena trainee and performer, and well connected to the powerbrokers of Georgia wrestling. He sent Carlie to the Nightmare Factory wrestling school, co-owned by Cody Rhodes, then the executive vice president of AEW. At 34, Carlie was the oldest in the school's first training class. He trained for three months and then, in December 2020, main-evented the student show.

He used his military service to win people over as a babyface when he started performing around the state. "I did that because I'm a Black guy in the South," he says. "The Southern people aren't too keen on confident, strong, Black men, especially Black men from up north who have a little jazz about them."

Carlie figured the way to overcome that was to exploit his background. "White, Black, yellow, or red, the South loves America," he says. "And whether they like it or not, they have to acknowledge that I'm a fucking Marine. They can not like me because I'm Black, or my tattoos or my gold teeth. They cannot deny the fact that I'm America."

Today WWE has more athletes of color on its roster than ever before. But its history shows a pattern of slow trajectory and stereotyped characters. Rather than scripting Black wrestlers as standout stars in singles matches, white writers have typically corralled them into heel stables like the Black Power–inspired Nation of Domination, whose militant, anti-white dialogue was written to stoke fear during WWE's Attitude Era.

Increased media coverage of racial inequality has compelled fans of all walks to speak out against WWE's habit of reserving its most prized belts, largely, for white wrestlers—and of perpetuating offensive stereotypes, like in 2019, when the company sold T-shirts promoting Black wrestler Jordan Myles that evoked "Sambo" imagery.

Popular culture informs society's perceptions of people and

places. All too often, onscreen messages are color-coded, and in professional wrestling Black has often translated as bad or goofy or unworthy. In the indies, wrestlers of all backgrounds create their own characters, bringing amplified or dream versions of themselves to the ring. Unquestionably, there are more Black wrestlers and more Black champions on these lower tiers, where they have freedom of character.

"I love and cherish the indies," the wrestler Effy, who wears fishnets, trunks, and a studded leather jacket in the ring, says from his home in Atlanta, where he makes a living on performances, merchandise, seminars, and running LGBTQ+ shows around the globe. "There's so much creativity and open thought and trial and error and beauty and trying stories." Things you don't see on a commercial show, he says. He's watched wrestlers surrender that creative freedom to wrestling corporations. Sometimes the spirit of the indies calls back to them, he says, and they give up the payday to reclaim control of their character and their story.

Over time Carlie leaned less into patriotism and more into himself, carrying a flag with his own logo to the ring rather than the Stars and Stripes. In January 2023, he battled fellow Georgia wrestler Zicky Dice, in a Crayola-yellow vest and tights and a backward black ballcap. With oval sunglasses and his hair dyed blond, the look was more Dennis Rodman than American Sniper. He approached the ring like the hip-hop artist he once was, all high knees and arms pumping up the crowd. It was a tryout of sorts for the national indie wrestling company Impact. Afterward, producers complimented his look, but with a caveat. When they looked at him in the ring, he remembers them saying, all they saw was a cocky Black guy. They couldn't market that.

It stunned Carlie. The crowd was behind him in the match, chanting his name. Even the announcers were wowed. "He's loud, he's flashy, he's over the top, but he's also got that 'never-say-die' Marine attitude you were talking about," one color commentator said.

"I mean, I'm pretty impressed," his cohost agreed. A few minutes later, when the crowd chanted his name again, she noted, "The crowd here in the Impact Zone really getting behind Bravo."

We move through life identifying archetypes. Our minds are at ease when everyone falls into the category we assume they should.

It's easier to understand human beings as representing one thing rather than to do the work of embracing the truth, which is that we are all complex beings. It's why stereotypes persist, why people from a certain region or with a certain color of skin are viewed as a monolith. By and large the entertainment industry banks on this, and wrestling does too.

Carlie felt like himself in the character he played that day. Now he'd have to devise something that felt authentic and also suited the producers' tastes.

"Do I stick to my guns and say, 'They don't know what they're talking about?' Or do I make a change?" he asked himself. He was proud of who he was and the work that he'd done. "My only stopping block is that people don't understand me because I'm a Black guy with swag." The bigger question being, what's wrong with that?

Hunter arrived at Landmark Arena as a white-meat babyface, wrestling argot for generic, white, good guy, in the form of a high school athlete. Fans didn't buy it. They didn't see Mox from *Varsity Blues*, they saw Biff from *Back to the Future*. Hunter dug in. As a heel he could play into the pompousness of the character, look into the eyes of his fans and tell them with confidence, "I'm better than you."

His trainers, Crystal and Azrael, nicknamed him Zack Morris, after the *Saved by the Bell* character, but steered his personality toward jerk jock. He kept the wrestling gear simple: solid-color trunks, white boots, and his own varsity letter jacket.

There were plenty of examples to study. Two former collegiate amateur wrestlers, Rick Steiner and Mike Rotunda, formed WCW's Varsity Club in the 1980s. Kurt Angle, an actual Olympic gold medalist, wore medals around his neck and harped on the Three I's, "Intensity, Integrity, and Intelligence." Even Griff Garrison, the Bill Behrens acolyte who signed with AEW in 2021, played the part in the tag team The Varsity Blondes.

The T-shirt brand Future Legend offered Hunter discount gear in exchange for social media posts, so he stamped the words on his kneepads. He slapped monikers on himself like bumper stickers. Absolute Wunderkind. Varsity One. Hunter Three Belts. He often told the ring announcer to announce his hometown differently each time, simply out of boredom. Everyone was from Georgia. If he studied Chris Candido that week, he was from Spring Lake, New Jersey. If wanted to nod to Shawn Michaels, San Antonio. He started watching the series *Outer Banks* and saw himself in the protagonist John B, a poor high school kid with a good heart and a plan. For a long time, Hunter James hailed from the Outer Banks of North Carolina.

Todd Sexton paired Hunter with another young wrestler, Luka Daniels, at Southern Fried and they wove their common connection to South Carolina—Luka grew up there, Hunter had been accepted to Coker University—into The Palmetto Express: beachy, carefree, good guys with a Shawn Michaels–Marty Jannetty "Rockers" vibe. "The kids and the girls were supposed to love us, and our wrestling was supposed to get the guys to like us," Hunter says. "Which it did."

"Watch the Southern Boys and Midnight Express," Todd advised them as if assigning chapters in a book. He quickly corrected himself. "Hunter, you've watched it. Luka—watch the Southern Boys and Midnight Express."

Larry Goodman estimates an average of 20 professional wrestling shows take place on any given weekend in Georgia. "Outlaw mud shows," wrestling personality and historian Jim Cornette dubbed them. "It really is extraordinary what's happening right now," Goodman says. At the same time, he acknowledges the difficulty of performing at this level, of chasing the dream. "There's no money in this," he says. "There's never been any money in it. It's strictly for the love of it."

From time to time, Goodman asks himself: "Why do I continue to follow this stuff with this kind of passion after all these years?" He's given up on finding an answer. "It just is what it is," he says. "There's something about it. When I first was exposed to it, I loved it, and there's always been a fascination with it that's never gone away."

In recent years Goodman has watched small-scale wrestling promotions increase in number. "In terms of the indie level, this is as good as it has ever been," he says. "There's never been this many wrestlers who know how to promote themselves."

He credits it to an upswing in the industry overall that trickles down. Aspiring wrestlers see more opportunities and go after them. But there's more to it than that. Wrestling has always peddled escapism. Its call grows stronger in times of fear and uncertainty. In times like these.

—

"A guy we don't want to leave waiting," host Stephen Platinum says after whiling away the first 20 minutes of the *Georgia Wrestling History* podcast he cohosts with Goodman, five days earlier. "Because in my opinion this guy has had to wait way too long." Their guest: 37-year-old Georgia wrestler Slim J, who has just signed a contract with AEW. He had wrestled for more than half his life when he got the call, in the summer of 2022, and had all but hung up his boots. He hadn't even applied for the job.

"For twenty-two years in the business, and thinking it was pretty much over, it was gratifying," Slim says, more recently, reflecting while working out in the City of Cornelia's employee gym. "You never know who's talking about you, who's thinking about you. The business is majority people talking."

Indeed, Slim J's name had circulated among some of wrestling's cognoscenti. AEW manager and producer Sonjay Dutt remembered him from the days they both wrestled with Ring of Honor and wondered if he was still in the business. He called the one person in Georgia who would know: Bill Behrens. If Slim was still working, Dutt said, he'd love to bring him in for a tryout.

Slim spent the bulk of his two-decade career as a babyface but debuted for AEW in the heel stable The Trustbusters. The company paid him $19,000 for five appearances in a year and covered travel. It wasn't enough to survive on, but it was a welcome addition to the roughly $37,000 he made annually in his day job at the Cornelia Water and Sewer Authority. His daughter, Harmony, had just turned 2 when he got the offer.

He celebrated the deal with a used four-wheeler. His wife, Kimberly, got a couple tattoos she'd been wanting, and Harmony, a bounce house. "This will really help us get out of the poverty state that I've been in my entire life," Slim said on the *Tipping Point* podcast that day.

Growing up in Gainesville, Georgia, known as the Poultry Capital of the World for its concentration of processing plants servicing the state's behemoth chicken-farming industry, Slim—who was born Jeremy Boyd—had difficulty focusing in school. He was expelled three times. Kicked out of alternative school twice. He failed ninth grade three times before dropping out at age 16.

His father worked at a Sheetrock supplier. Using his construction skills, Richard Boyd modified the family's mobile home as the family grew. A one-bedroom trailer became a four-bedroom house with a two-car garage and three porches. After their mother died of lung cancer in 1998 when he was 13, Slim and his siblings moved with their dad to Cornelia, Georgia, in search of a new life.

It didn't take him long to find Landmark Arena. Crystal and Azrael were among the people he trained with under a guy from Gainesville named Allen Jones, who would later be recognized by wrestling fans around the world by his WWE Superstar moniker, AJ Styles. It was actually Styles, indirectly, who led to Slim's arrival. When he wasn't training wrestlers at Landmark, Styles delivered drinking water to offices around Gainesville. Slim's sister Jennifer worked at one of them. She learned about Styles, and the arena, through their small talk as he wheeled in 5-gallon water jugs.

Training gave 15-year-old Slim something to focus on. "It made me grow up as a man for sure," he says. He stayed out of trouble—mostly. The folks at Landmark started calling him Slim Shady after he wrecked a car that a girl, eager to see him, had stolen from her mother.

He was running the lights for a show one Friday night when Bill Behrens approached him and asked his name. The boys in the back yelled, "Slim Shady!" It stuck. He adopted a visor—worn upside-down and sideways—a ribbed white tank top, and baggy jeans, and buzzed his hair. He even recorded a few rap albums.

Over the years, he washed dishes at KFC, manned the counter at a video rental store, then worked on a Kubota assembly line, staying afloat with shift work and spending his weekends wrestling. When he moved out of his father's place, he rented a '70s model single-wide owned by his stepmother's parents. The reality of wrestling is that the guy on *AEW Collision* on Saturday night might be the guy descending into a sewer maintenance hole on Monday morning.

Now, he rents a '90s-model mobile home whose maintenance has largely been ignored by its owners. "It's either move out and spend three times what I'm paying for an apartment, or stay in that and stay broke fixing it," he says.

He never stopped learning, training, working out, and viewing himself as a top performer, he told Larry Goodman and Stephen Platinum on their podcast that day in August 2022. "It feels so good that someone sees me as that pro."

With every leap from the turnbuckle, every crash onto the mat, wrestling delivered something unquantifiable: the attention and adrenaline he craved. "It kept me sane."

When he got to AEW he recognized the same kind of camaraderie he'd so easily fallen into at Landmark. "I thought I was part of the family," he says. But Landmark ran on more than profit. AEW is a billion-dollar company. They released him on April 1, 2024.

The next day on X he thanked his fans and AEW. "My gimmick was trash," he wrote. "I get that. I knew that. My work wasn't though. I worked my shoot job through both contracts with AEW. My role there was to act rich. I've always been far from that in real life." His goal in getting signed, he explained, was to "get my wife and daughter out of the shit hole we live in."

"I failed," he confessed.

The company never told him why they let him go. "When it comes to that kind of thing in this business, you'll never know," he says. "Nobody's ever going to tell you."

A little bit of him died that day, he admits. To be hired by the second largest wrestling company in the world and paid that kind of money to do something he loves, to join a family, and then have it all suddenly stop. "Did it kill me? No, because I'm still doing it." he says. "So what motivates me now? My family. And that's really all I need."

He charges a premium now, a quarter of what he got paid in AEW. If promoters pay it, he performs. If not, he'd rather be home with Kimberly and Harmony and go easy on his back—the decades of ring work have left him with eight bulging discs. He's done everything he wanted to do. From NWA Wildside and Anarchy at Landmark Arena to Ring of Honor, TNA, and AEW. He even got cast as enhancement talent for WWE a few times and posed with Michael Phelps after a private show at El Dorado Golf & Beach Club in Los Cabos, Mexico.

He works four 10-hour shifts during the week, comes home for dinner, watches TV with his family, and then goes to the city employees' gym, around 9:30 p.m., after Harmony goes to sleep. At that hour it's empty. He's alone with his body, and the faith that his dedication will pay off. The hope that even if it doesn't, he will have firmed up his reputation as a hard worker. That counts for something. But it's not everything.

"Money doesn't make you happy," he says. "But I promise you, it buys all the things that can make you, your family, and your families to come for generations happier and have a better chance in life."

CHAPTER 12

Hunter at Landmark Arena, June 3, 2022

Thirty minutes before bell time, some 80 people have taken their seats around the ring inside Landmark Arena on Christmas night, 2022. Three industrial-grade kerosene heaters blast hot air from the flanks and stage lights burn above the ring. The song "No Place Like Home for the Holidays" pours from the PA. A fake Christmas tree dressed in blue tinsel stands next to an inflatable Santa, and paper ornaments cling to the walls. A line snakes to the snack bar where a wall-mounted letter-board menu lists prices: hot dog $2, hamburger $3. Landmark's holy nickname, The Church of Southern Wrestling, isn't an overstatement: people greet each other as they find their seats like they're settling into the pews of their small-town house of prayer.

Orange duct tape wraps the posts that rise from each corner of the ring, supporting a huge "X" that towers above it. An oversize golden ticket hangs from the ceiling, a few feet from an array of dried blood splatter. It's a visceral reminder of two intertwined tenets or pro wrestling: opportunity and injury. The first, out of reach for most. The other, all but guaranteed.

Three Black women purchase tickets and then stand by the door, unsure where to sit. Within seconds, the bearded white guy manning a table of "Anarchy Wrestling" T-shirts takes a lap around the ring, returns, and leads them to empty seats.

Cheeks collide with open palms and sweat flies from the ring in droplets that catch the stage lights like glitter. In the main event, The 12 Slays of Christmas, "Angel of Death" Azrael rips into 12 gift boxes, each containing a weapon to use on his opponent Hold My Beer Hanson. Sometime around 7:30 p.m. Hunter appears from behind the curtain. In gold-sequined tailcoat and gleaming white boots, he stands out in this landscape like Marilyn Monroe on the subway grate, right down to the platinum hair. The buoyant and muscled 20-year-old, not yet scarred from a lifetime of punches, soars higher and lands crisper than the rest.

His opponent Nick Halen, the 37-year-old Walmart loss prevention worker who earned Best Match, Best Technician, and tied for Best Overall Wrestler in the 2022 *Georgia Wrestling History* awards, left that night pointed in the direction of the nearest hospital. At least that's what he wanted fans to think.

In their faceoff that night for the Landmark Heritage title Halen went to do a dive on the floor and Hunter dropkicked him midair. Then Hunter did the Kurt Angle belly-to-belly suplex off the top rope. Halen came down hard on the back of his head. He went for the Sharpshooter. Hunter kicked him off. He went for it again. Hunter tripped him, his head struck the buckle. In the end, Hunter countered Halen's finisher, the Gamebreaker, by charging him with a Randy Orton punt to the head.

The next day, Halen shared a fake medical report and composed a message on Facebook, crediting it to his girlfriend, Sabrina. It informed fans that he had suffered a mild concussion and thanked them for checking on him.

It was a work, stolen from Triple H's match against Randy Orton that led to their encounter at WrestleMania 25. The faked concussion was Todd Sexton's idea. He knew only an injury would garner the sympathy Halen needed to lose the Landmark Heritage title without damaging his upward trajectory toward the heavyweight championship. For the next week, Halen's phone blew up with wrestlers and fans asking if he was ok. He had a story, and they wanted more.

Feigned injuries make good stories but real ones threaten the actual health of performers. Georgia wrestler Bryce Cannon incurred his first wrestling injury as a third-grader, when a chair shot to the head on his trampoline led to seven stitches. On March 30, 2024, he clotheslined Randy Reno during a match in Savannah and felt a pop in his knee, the same knee that had bothered him since his foot went between two loose pads four years earlier. After two weeks of icing it, Cannon learned he had dislocated his patella. He was 26, in the best shape of his life, and had racked up gigs at AEW, WWE, TNA, and MLW.

WWE employees get the kind of benefits you'd expect from a major corporation, but its performers, who work as independent contractors but are barred from performing for other companies, do not. WWE covers treatment for injuries incurred in the ring but offers no medical, dental, or vision insurance, no 401K, no disability insurance, or pension.

In a 23-minute monologue in March 2019 John Oliver shamed the company for building its business around full-time performers hired disingenuously as independent contractors locked into exclusive contracts but exempt, by law, from most discrimination and occupational safety laws, and not required to be given benefits.

The NFL player turned professional wrestler Darren Drozdov was 30 years old when he was on the receiving end of a mistimed move that fractured two discs in his neck and left him paralyzed from the neck down in 1999. Five months earlier, Owen Hart, brother of Bret "The Hitman" Hart, fell to his death at WWE's pay-per-view event, Over the Edge, when the harness he wore to ride to the ring from the rafters unexpectedly released. He was 34.

Many independent wrestlers work gig jobs without healthcare coverage and rely on fan crowdfunding to pay for medical expenses. The injuries don't go away after a wrestler hangs up the boots. Koko B. Ware and Jake "The Snake" Roberts are among the well-known wrestlers who've utilized crowdfunding to pay for healthcare expenses. When Kamala "The Ugandan Giant" died, writer Jason King, who profiled the Mississippi-born wrestler for *Bleacher Report*, created a GoFundMe page to help his family pay for funeral expenses. It raised $33,000.

There was some real damage, though, that Christmas night at Landmark Arena when Hunter took the belt from Nick Halen under the guise of a feigned concussion. A day earlier the temperature in Cornelia, Georgia, dipped into the single digits, fracturing the building's plumbing. The freeze was the final kick in the chin for the weathered venue. When the wind blew the roof flapped. For years wrestlers had covered the electronics in the back for fear of a leak. Honeybees lived in the walls. Violent Night, 2022, would go down as Landmark Arena's final showcase, the grand finale of a 25-year run.

To the people who knew the place, it felt like a loved one taking her final breath without the warning of terminal illness. The Landmark family came to pay its last respects by signing the floor with Sharpies. For his part, Hunter climbed the Ultimate X—still towering over the ring from the Christmas show—and autographed his name on the ceiling. He spent the rest of the evening swinging and dropping from the structure like it was a set of monkey bars. Before he left he pulled the framed Hardcore Hell 23 poster from the wall. It was his first appearance on a wrestling flyer, the one that revealed to Billy Ray that Hunter was veering from the path his father had in mind for him. Page one of his story.

Hunter saw Landmark's closure as an opportunity to promote his accomplishments: Fastest win in Hardcore Hell history. Youngest Anarchy champion. Seventeen main events. The last champion ever to be crowned in Landmark Arena. On his way to a match a couple months later, he stopped to cut a promo. In the video he stands in front of the property's padlocked chain link fence. "I had the biggest glow-up in Georgia wrestling in that building." He's thunderous, fast and frantic, moving down the fence line so Landmark, with its rusted roof and unkempt yard, comes into focus. "I went from a nobody on Friday night to one of the biggest stars this state's ever seen."

Two weeks after Christmas Nick Halen and Hunter sit next to each other on plastic chairs before a Southern Fried show, both unseasonably tan. Two years into his career, the teenage softness of Hunter's body has given way to muscle, and his hair is Hulk Hogan blond. He and his new partner Xavier Reyes are tag team champions. Tonight, Todd Sexton has pitted him against a Southern Fried newcomer, "The Blue-Collar Rockstar" Aaron Dallas, a forklift driver by day who pairs his name-tagged work shirt with cutoff jean shorts and plays air guitar to the Pantera song "Cowboys from Hell" as he approaches the ring.

After appearing in *SmackDown*, Hunter took Bill Behrens's advice and emailed WWE creative consultant Gabe Sapolsky to assert his proficiency and willingness to travel. And then, on his 20th birthday, Hunter received an email inviting him to be an extra at the January 9 taping of *Raw* at the Legacy Arena in Birmingham. It would be his third gig with the company, another opportunity to be seen.

"All I'm wondering is what's the catering going to be like," Hunter says to Sal Rinauro, who's also making the trip. "You was talking about Salisbury steak last time and I have not had Salisbury steak in forever and that's all I've wanted since you told me."

"The big trick about catering is loading up a to-go plate," Sal says.

"I loaded up three last time," Hunter replies.

Hunter woke at 6:30 a.m. that Monday. He'd wrestled at three shows in three days, but any inkling of wanting to sleep in dissipated quickly. *It's Raw day,* he thought. He cooked steak and eggs for breakfast and met Billy Ray at the gym. They worked out together. Hunter hit the tanning bed, loaded a cooler with cans of Monster energy drink and caffeine-charged iced tea, and then got on the road.

Being an extra is a crapshoot. There's a payout for your time and travel—$1,000 for Hunter on this occasion—but there's no guarantee you'll do anything more than sit in a dressing room. Hunter understands the opportunity and its cost. He wants to be on TV, in a match, but knows there's value to the experience beyond that: the chance to make an impression on producers and wrestlers, behind the curtain.

He establishes himself as a do-anything go-getter on these occasions. He small-talks. He does what he's told. He doesn't complain. He knows to get to the top you have to start from the bottom. Maybe someone will notice. Maybe they'll offer a tryout, or more extra dates. "Something where I can keep proving that I'm reliable and I want to do this."

He arrived at noon. The sense of panic he encountered at the *SmackDown* taping in Greenville was absent from the Birmingham arena—a sign, Hunter feared, that the matches had all been sorted out.

He found the dressing room, where eight other indie wrestlers vied for spots. Hours went by, no headset-wearing producer came to get him. After the show started he and Sal resigned themselves to the buffet: steak, chicken, shrimp and grits, and the best potatoes he ever had. He ate twice. At the end of the night he walked to his Jeep with three to-go boxes.

On the three-hour drive home, he situated his phone in its hands-free holster and watched his favorite movie, the 1999 film *Varsity Blues* out of the corner of his eye. On the day Hunter met his best friend, Clay, in eighth grade, he quickly nicknamed him

Billy Bob. Clay responded by calling Hunter Mox. They both looked the part. "I love that dog," Clay said, quoting Billy Bob. Hunter responded on cue. "I don't want your life."

He likes the movie for its nuance. The conclusion is spliced with despair: the audience's realization, along with the high school athletes, that their best days are behind them after their final game. "Not every situation has a happy ending," Hunter says. "The good shit ends and sometimes you have to know what you're doing next."

He's young, blind to the cognizance that comes with age. He doesn't regret dropping out of college to pursue professional wrestling. "I could have went there and been miserable for another four years and not been in the ring, but I wouldn't be doing what I'm doing now," he says, driving home from a movie with Christian one night in March 2023, when he would've been close to finishing his second year, if he'd stuck around.

He exists in a world where everything is demanded and nothing is guaranteed. His sights are so locked into professional wrestling stardom there's no room in the frame for anything other than himself in the ring.

With resignation, Billy Ray admits he sees a lot of himself in his son. "I didn't want to."

"He's freaking talented," Billy Ray says a few months later while working out in his basement gym. "The kid knows what he's doing. He's twenty years old with thirty years' experience. But who's to say he doesn't get dropped on his head?"

Only when pressed does Hunter concede to the possibility of a backup plan. He's good at laying out matches, he says. He believes he could work in the industry as a creative, someone in the writer's room—a corporate job that is perhaps even more difficult to come by.

Wrestling promises something different for Hunter than it did for Billy Ray. "It's not a ticket out of town," Hunter says. "I don't think it's a ticket out of anything. I think it's just, I know that I am really good at wrestling. And I know I'm a really good performer. Always have been. When the lights shine, that's when I shine brightest."

When he was little and other kids asked what Hunter wanted to be when he grew up, the answer was always the same: a professional wrestler. Often, they'd laugh.

"At least I know what I want to be," he'd say, and stand tall. "What, you want to be a doctor? You want to go to school for eight years? Fuck that. I'll make more than any doctor when I win the WWE title."

CHAPTER 13

Hunter stands on a scalelike machine called the Evolt 360 Body Composition Scanner in Billy Ray's office at Anytime Fitness, the 24-hour gym where he's worked as a personal trainer for the past seven months. It's the second time in his career at WAM, where he started as a crate builder in 1998, that he's quit to be a personal trainer.

The machine's screen flickers and flashes. Finally it prints a report. Billy Ray grabs the paper. "You have fourteen percent body fat," he says.

He examines his son's numbers. Billy Ray's biceps, quads, and waistline have stretched and retracted over the years, but at 51, he's still compact and powerful.

"You're close to perfect, where you're supposed to be," he says to 20-year-old Hunter. From a man obsessed with physical appearance, the words ring loud.

Hunter's used to this kind of analysis. Amateur wrestling is ruled by weight class, and Billy Ray kept a close eye on Hunter's size all through his school years. "If he told me he weighed in at

181.8 I'd call him a skinny bitch," Billy Ray says. "If he weighed in at 182.1 I'd call him a fat bastard." Hunter, focused on his phone but listening, nods his head. "Yep."

Just twelve hours earlier Hunter came to this gym to film a promo. Shirtless, in sweatpants and Nikes, he did push-up after push-up trying to get the perfect take: his Future Legend ballcap propped in the foreground, the simple exercise that showed off his strength, and a conversation with himself.

"Mirror, mirror, on the wall, who is the greatest performer of them all? Me! The Absolute Wunderkind, Hunter James."

"Mirror, mirror, on the wall, who is the worst tag team partner of them all? Marcus Kross."

It was standard heel stuff, directed at his Southern Fried opponent that night, Marcus Kross, his partner when they were extras on *SmackDown*. By the time Hunter left, it was 1 a.m.

As a teen he took it upon himself to do the work of staying in shape as a competitive athlete, following his father's advice on diet and supplements, and working out in the gym Billy Ray assembled at their house. "This kid became a workhorse when he was like fourteen," Billy Ray says. "He hasn't stopped since."

"People will say, 'Don't have your kids lift weights too soon. It will stunt their growth plates,'" Billy Ray says. "Bullshit."

"Look at him and look at me and Chunk," Hunter says, referencing their heights: Billy Ray is 5'6", Hunter stands 5'10", and Chunk, at 14, is 5'8".

Today Billy Ray wears the shirt he wore at all Hunter's amateur wrestling competitions: black, with the words Future Legend stamped in stars and stripes. It's a quiet gesture of support, but a meaningful one. As they prepare to work out together, Hunter scoops Swedish Fish–flavored pre-workout powder into his water bottle.

Billy Ray twists open a jar on his desk, pops a tablet in his mouth, and offers one to Hunter. "Need one of these?" he asks.

"Nah, I already took one," Hunter says.

The Beta Alanine tabs help with "the pump," the visible, temporary expansion of muscle.

"So that way during my workout I feel like I'm Hulk Hogan," Hunter says.

When father and son are together the conversation doesn't veer far from wrestling and strength-building, subjects that have shaped their lives in every sense of the word. The way they coolly discuss the very industry that has both bound them together and torn them apart belies a pivotal chapter in the family's history, the one when Billy Ray and Hunter didn't talk for months.

"In all honesty, I wanted to beat the shit out him," Billy Ray says about the moment he learned Hunter was wrestling. "It came close to that."

They avoided each other for months. Billy Ray focused on Chunk's amateur wrestling career and repairing his relationship with Jenn. "Maybe he'll go back to school," she said. Billy Ray knew better. Eventually Hunter and Billy Ray's shared interest in body image proved a safe touchpoint. Soon the conversations gave way to where they started: wrestling.

There wasn't a singular moment when Billy Ray came to terms with his son's choice to drop out of college, but rather a gradual wearing down of the frustration and disappointment, a quiet resignation ushered by time and the intimate understanding of the thing that held Hunter in its vice. It was just too powerful.

Today they're working the upper body, Hunter's MO for show days. At Southern Fried tonight, Marcus Kross will quick-defeat him in a singles face-off that tees up a tag team match between Kross with Jacob Ashworth and Hunter's tag team with Xavier Reyes.

"Is Southern Fried Monroe?" Billy Ray asks, trying to remember the show's location.

Hunter affirms.

"I got a bad memory," Billy Ray says. "It's got to be chair shots. I never put my hand up for one of them."

Drugs, alcohol, and adultery coursed through the locker rooms in Billy Ray's day. But Billy Ray had done his hard living by the time he arrived. He quit his bad habits as a way to differentiate himself. He hated being lumped in with "the boys," men so blinded by small-town stardom that they couldn't see up the ladder. He was better than that.

"Now people are proud to be independent wrestlers," he says, fixing his gaze on Hunter. "You're proud to do what you do," he addresses him, cloyingly. "But I never advertised that I was an independent wrestler. Actually, they didn't use that word. It was outlaw wrestling. And the reason it was outlaw was because we didn't get taxed. But . . . I forgot what I was saying."

"He'll tell you the same story three times in a row," Hunter says.

"I will," Billy Ray admits. "Sometimes I'll tell these stories so I can remember them."

The stories are part of the family's identity. One of Hunter's favorites is about the origin of his cousins' names.

"Justin's Justin Credible," Hunter says.

"Nooo, he is not," Billy Ray corrects him. "Justin is named after a pair of boots."

Hunter seems shocked. "That's what I've told everyone for twenty years!"

Billy Ray keeps debunking.

"Jesse James was named after that guy that had the Harley show on television."

"No, he's 'Road Dogg' Jesse James," Hunter smirks. "And Austin is Stone Cold Steve Austin."

Billy Ray shakes his head.

Wrestling's about stories too, and for a while longer, this one seems likely to persist.

"The main reason I stayed in shape all these years is for that one," Billy Ray points to a picture of Chunk on his desk, "and Hunter." He wanted to be a role model for his boys, better than the overweight, unhealthy dads watching their kids on the mat alongside him. One of Billy Ray's greatest joys is running into someone from high school and counting himself as better off. His body is a way to prove to himself—to everyone—that he has ascended from the circumstances he was born into. No one can escape time, but anyone can sprint alongside it. He's prone to reposting fitness motivator memes on his Facebook page and spouting off sayings like, "push-ups are free." He has no patience for people who eat junk food and allow their bodies to balloon.

Billy Ray texted Hunter before every high school away meet. The messages spanned from motivational poster material to brash one-liners. "You're not the chosen one," he typed once. "You chose to be the one." For Hunter's junior-year trip to the state championship, the note was more direct: "Go fuck him up."

A few weeks earlier Billy Ray was in his office when the gym manager came in with her 3-year-old son. He offered to watch the little boy while she had a meeting. Billy Ray pulled up videos of Chunk's amateur wrestling matches on his phone. When those ran out, he typed "Hunter James" into the YouTube search box and then narrated the action and named the moves just like he used to with Hunter when they watched wrestling together.

Afterward, the kid was amped. He wanted to enact what he'd seen on the screen. Billy Ray took him to the workout classroom and showed him an arm drag and a hip toss—the same simple moves he learned when he started training.

Hunter watches his father at the decline hammer press. "Normally this works lower chest," Billy Ray says. "By doing it sideways it works a little more this area," he says, pointing to his upper pecs.

"What you aiming for? Ten to twelve?" Hunter asks.

"Yup," Billy Ray grimaces.

"A little bend in my elbows keeps the pressure in my chest," he says, demonstrating.

"Yeah, you don't want to lock out," Hunter says, repeating advice he learned from his father.

Their physicality and personality most obviously mirror one another at the gym, where they're in pursuit of the same goal: some elusive version of the perfect man. Billy Ray works to look younger. Hunter, to look older.

"One more set, or are you done with chest?" Billy Ray asks, as Hunter pulls 45 pounds on each side.

"Hell no, one more set," he says.

Their conversation moves to a discussion of famous wrestling fathers and sons.

"All us old men can't look like Billy Gunn," Billy Ray says, citing the muscle-bound wrestler, who at almost 60, performs and coaches at AEW, along with his sons.

No other entertainment form breeds fans who feel so closely connected to performers as professional wrestling. Blame it on the lifelike serial storytelling, doled out weekly, for nearly a century. Blame it on the complex emotional dynamic between performers who straddle the line between fact and fiction. Blame it on the heartfelt promos that so often merely fog the truth. Fans often use performers' first names, as if they had just hung out with them last weekend. Because of the volume and frequency of content, often, it feels like they have. Experts credit social media's penchant for behind-the-scenes, so-called "real life" glimpse into celebrities' lives with the rise of parasocial relationships, but in this industry, those have long existed by another name: wrestling fan.

"Dude! Young guys can't even look like Billy Gunn," Hunter says. "His kids can't even look like their dad." "I liked Bob Armstrong," Billy Ray says. And then he runs through the attributes of the ideal wrestler. Women were attracted to him, he entertained kids, and men knew he was a man. They don't make 'em like that anymore, he laments.

"One of the best workers ever," Billy Ray says of Bob Armstrong's son Brad.

Fathers whose ring work inspires their children remains a persistent industry theme. WWE's Bloodline has its roots in an actual family tree of Samoan wrestlers. The stable's on-again, off-again leader, Roman Reigns, grew up watching his father and uncle wrestle as The Wild Samoans. The Rock was trained by his dad, wrestler Rocky Johnson. His maternal grandfather, known in the ring as "High Chief Peter Maivia" also wrestled. All five of Fritz Von Erich's sons followed him to the ring. Brian Pillman Jr. wrestles. So does Charlotte Flair.

"One more set?" Billy Ray asks.

"Sure."

"And then we'll punish the biceps."

"OK."

A garbled mashup of "The Wondrous Boat Ride" from *Willy Wonka and the Chocolate Factory*, Tom Waits's "A Good Man Is Hard to Find," and "Rachel's Song" by James McMurtry tees up the April 13, 2023, episode of *Georgia Wrestling History*'s podcast, two months later.

"We're joined by one of Georgia's top rising stars," Larry Goodman says. "I believe he's still only twenty years old."

"Jumping Jesus!" Stephen Platinum, Goodman's hype-man counterpart says, before Goodman finishes the introduction. "Georgia's Best Male Performer, Hunter James!"

Three months earlier, Hunter stood at a podium inside Southern Honor's strip-mall church venue and accepted his first *Georgia Wrestling History* award. In these parts, the rudimentary website and podcast may as well be the Motion Picture Academy. Its annual awards are its Oscars.

Hunter, along with Carlie Bravo, were up for multiple *Georgia Wrestling History* awards at the end of 2022: both were nominated for Best Male Performer and Most Improved Wrestler. Hunter, in addition, had been nominated for Best Tag Team alongside Scott Mayson and Proc Johnson, and Best Overall Wrestler. Carlie, who teamed with fellow Atlanta wrestler Shawn Dean for his debut on *AEW Dark* in February 2021, took home Most Improved. Hunter won Male Performer.

"Hunter James, my god," Platinum continues, in awe. He tells listeners about the pile of votes Hunter received for the awards. Only people in Georgia's wrestling industry—performers, promoters, bookers—can vote. Many ballots included notes declaring his worth. "It told me people were a fan and a believer in Hunter James in a way that I don't know if I've seen before with anybody else who's got so few years under their belt."

Dialing in from the basement gym at home, Hunter smiles.

Goodman tees up a conversation about Anarchy Wrestling's hiatus and the loss of Landmark Arena. Hunter sees an opportunity to reframe the story through the lens of Hunter James.

"I was the final title change in that building's history," he says, citing his win over Nick Halen for the Landmark Heritage Championship. "I was ready for the next step. Being a singles champion and really trying to raise the value of that championship."

He compares Anarchy's Heritage Champion title to WWE's Intercontinental Championship. They're workhorse titles, given to underdogs rather than the headliners. "I'm a workhorse," Hunter says.

A small new promotion, Ultimate Wrestling Federation (UWF), sprouted up just before Landmark closed its doors, and the Anarchy roster seemed to arrive overnight, to no one's surprise: the same bookers behind the scenes at Landmark were writing the Sunday afternoon shows at UWF, held in a corrugated steel flea market, just outside Athens.

Hunter saw potential in it, and in another off-the-beaten-path show run by Chris Nelms, the veteran Georgia wrestler who drove him to Arkansas for his first-ever public appearance, in 2020. Later that year, Nelms, who works as an administrative assistant for an addiction rehab facility, bought the Georgia Championship Wrestling name from a promoter who hadn't run a show under the banner in a decade. Nelms had a lofty goal: to revive the show once broadcast live from Ted Turner's Techwood Drive studio on TBS every Saturday night at 6:05, the famed Atlanta wrestling program that grew into WWE's No. 1 competitor, WCW.

He took it as far at the Got 2 B Rollin' Skate Center in the town of Buckhead, Georgia, population 183. On show days Nelms hangs two oversized tarps on the wall to create a curtain leading backstage (actually the room where skating rink staff host kids' birthday parties). Hunter earned the GCW heavyweight champion belt, the promotion's top accolade. He was comfortably hovering in that dangerous place Billy Ray had warned him never to be: best in the room.

Goodman probed Hunter to talk about why he spent so much time there. "A lot of those guys wrestled with my dad," Hunter says. "It felt like a home away from home."

"Now it's my show, and I'm going to make it the best," Hunter continues, keeping the shine on himself. Everyone will come to watch him, he predicts. He'll fill every seat, making the show better for the wrestlers and the fans. He's the tide. They're the ships.

Platinum, known for his outsize opinions on the industry, commends him for raising the stock at unsung shows. "So few wrestlers talk about wanting to be a catalyst," he says. "The cliché, 'It doesn't matter if I wrestle in front of fifty or five hundred.' What a load of shit."

A week after Hunter appeared on *SmackDown* as the security guard who broke up a tiff between Happy Corbin and Pat McAfee in the summer of '22, he wrestled Jimmy Jacobs at GCW. Jacobs, whose career includes 10 years with Ring of Honor and a stint in the writer's room of WWE, had recently moved to Morgan County, Georgia, to learn how to live off the land between shows for Impact Wrestling, where he was on the creative team. He soon discovered GCW and reached out to Nelms via Facebook to see if he could work.

Jacobs pinned Hunter, still in his Absolute Varsity era. Before they parted ways, he offered some advice. "Your wrestling's fine,"

Jacobs said. "But what happens in a year when you don't look like a high schooler anymore?" It was a good question, one Hunter, then 19, hadn't considered. "What can it evolve into? And what can you do in your matches so everyone remembers?"

The podcast's hosts press him for the answer. "That's a big-time question," Platinum says. "What's the number one thing you think you need to focus on that you think is going to help you reach that next level?"

Hunter's answer comes quick and confident. "Getting as big as I can."

Hunter keeps a notebook chronicling his matches, diet, and size: A ballpoint-pen history of his growth, paid for by a regimented daily routine that's high on protein and fitness. Billy Ray helps him design workout routines that focus on the arms, chest, and shoulders—"the first thing people notice in the ring."

Every Monday, he records the details of his weekend matches: company, date, opponent, length, and finish. He also keeps a tally: 7 matches in 2020, 85 in 2021, 156 in 2022. The shuttering of Landmark Arena and its Friday- and Saturday-night shows resulted in fewer bookings in 2023 but more regular appearances and increasing popularity at higher-capacity shows like Southern Fried and Southern Honor.

Once or twice a week he comes to work early, puts in his eight hours, and clocks out, so he can work out or get ring time. At WAM he makes $18.50 an hour before taxes. That's between $1,200 and $1,400 of take-home pay every two weeks. A grand of it goes to his car loan and insurance every month. He spends about $250 a week on gym, streaming subscriptions, gas, and groceries, and saves the rest. He usually brings home between $500 and $700 a month from wrestling before merchandise sales. Last year he used his tax refund to buy T-shirts to sell at his merch table.

"All it really takes is to make more money than I am now at my job and I'm done," he says. Making it in wrestling is the only thing in his life he's ever thought, with confidence, *when*, rather than *what if*. "I'm so close," he says. "I need one shot."

But what is that shot and how can he position himself to take it?

According to the docuseries *WWE: Next Gen*, every year more than 10,000 aspiring Superstars apply to WWE. Fewer than 1 percent get a tryout and fewer than 0.2 percent ever have a professional match.

Two years after their faceoff, Jacobs, calling from Jacksonville, Florida, where he works full-time for AEW, remembers Hunter right away. "Yeah! He's a good-looking kid. Young." Jacobs says. He seems surprised Hunter hasn't graced his radar since they met in the ring.

"You know, I haven't seen him in a bit," he says. "Which, I'm a little disappointed." Then, he tempers his statement. "He's young though."

"He's somebody that, if he sticks with it he has the tools to do what he wants," Jacobs says. "He's just gotta keep doing it."

Easy for Jacobs to say, he's done it. After 16 years in the ring, he had a drug-aided epiphany that his true calling in wrestling was on the creative side. He called in a few favors from people he'd met along the way. Bryan Danielson went to WWE's creative department with a good word for Jacobs. "It was a real straight shot in," Jacobs admits. "When people ask me if I believe in manifestation, I go, 'Well, I had one experience.'"

WWE fired him in 2017 for posting a photo of himself with members of Bullet Club, a group of wrestlers unaligned with

WWE who were filming "an invasion" of the company outside the Ontario arena where WWE was setting up to film *Raw*. He then spent five and a half years on the creative team at Impact Wrestling and a year at AEW, making a living off wrestling, but not in the ring.

CHAPTER 14

In 1984, as televised wrestling clawed toward its apex in popular culture, jilted performer Eddy "The Continental Lover" Mansfield got in the ring with ABC News' John Stossel to prove its illegitimacy through a series of staged punches and slams aired on *20/20*. In the latter part of the segment, Stossel takes his cameramen backstage at a WWE show. "I'll ask you the standard question," Stossel says to 6'6" "Dr. D" David Schultz. "I think this is fake." "You think it's fake?" Schultz roars, and slaps Stossel across the face, knocking him to the floor, twice, before Stossel clambers to his feet and rushes down the hall. The infamous "Stossel slap" was as bad as it looked. Stossel later sued the company and settled for nearly half a million dollars. (WWE did not admit wrongdoing.)

The segment didn't smother pro wrestling's fire. On February 18, 1985, 2 million people watched Hulk Hogan defend the World Heavyweight Championship against "Rowdy" Roddy Piper in "The War to Settle the Score," a WWE event aired on MTV. Bob Costas did the ring introductions. Even Andy Warhol was there; he declared it the most exciting thing he'd ever seen. A month later, fans packed Madison Square Garden for WWE's inaugural tentpole event, WrestleMania.

Two years after that, 78,500 people filed into the Pontiac Silverdome for WrestleMania III, touted to be the then-largest attendance* of any live indoor event ever in the world. In 1988, 26.6 million viewers watched André the Giant take the WWF Championship title from Hogan and sell it to the "The Million Dollar Man" Ted DiBiase. By 1993, all of America was snapping into Slim Jims with "Macho Man" Randy Savage.

And though Vince McMahon might like to take credit for popularizing the entertainment form, it predates him by four millennia, give or take. Roughly two thousand years before Christ, some enlightened Sumerian used a reed stylus to write the world's first wrestling match into clay. "Divine King" Gilgamesh versus "Wild Man" Enkidu.

Irked that the pompous, misogynistic Gilgamesh was barging his way into the beds of newlyweds to have his way with virgin brides, the goddess Aruru molds a warrior out of clay and drops him off in the forest to commune with wild animals. Years later, a kind harlot guides the savage Enkidu to the city of Uruk, where he stands in the doorway of Gilgamesh's next victim. The unkempt bulwark of justice ready to defend. Crude, but righteous.

Gilgamesh and Enkidu lock arms and grapple, then Gilgamesh kneels, plants a foot on the ground, and takes Enkidu out with a hip toss. If there had been a ref walking by, he would've dropped to the floor and pounded out a 3-count.

As the story goes, the two linked arms after that. Or, in profes-

* WWE (then known as WWF) reported paid attendance at 93,173, a number that has since been disputed.

sional wrestling parlance, a heel and babyface made the shocking transition to tag partners, the way Mr. Perfect joined Randy Savage to combat Ric Flair and Razor Ramon in Survivor Series '92. The goddess Inanna sends a divine bull to take them down, and Enkidu and Gilgamesh defeat it, together. Wrap these characters in Lycra and you've got yourself a pay-per-view.

Gilgamesh versus Enkidu was more than a fight between two men. It was a battle between supreme divinity and the untamed natural world, channeled through a holy king and a plucky demigod. A clash between right and wrong. This was no bush-league tussle. It had style.

There's something primal about wrestling. Our animal brain recognizes and responds to what happens in the ring. In nature, aggression often starts with some posturing. Elks bugle. Silverback gorillas beat their chests. Red deer stags peacock past one another, sizing each other up before they lock antlers and begin boxing. Now, go watch an episode of *Raw*.

Wrestling's hyperbolic faceoffs resonate with kids, who learn balance and coordination, as well as both verbal and nonverbal communication, through play fighting. Then and now, they recognize the televised roughhousing and mimic it on their living room floors. No one gets seriously hurt, they know, because their favorite wrestlers keep reappearing, show after show. Kids learn not to take it too far.

It's cathartic. Spectators don't see a man in trunks and boots bloodying his opponent's face. They see themselves beating the hell out of the guy who fired them or the kid who bullies them at school. Analog virtual reality, with a splattering of blood. For those living with little, like the Nobletts, when Billy Ray was young, wrestling offered an antidote in a class of its own, a place of attitude and excess they could project themselves into. *Hell yeah. Kick his ass.*

According to SEC filings, WWE pulled in $1.29 billion in revenue in 2022, a record for the company, even when adjusted for inflation, according to industry analyst Brandon Thurston of *Wrestlenomics*. The money the Saudi government has paid WWE to put on shows there since 2018—$550 million—already exceeds the total ticket sales for every WrestleMania ever, adjusted for inflation, Thurston says. Two-night tickets for WrestleMania 41, at Allegiant Stadium in Las Vegas in 2025, started at $1,000.

Professional wrestling knows no match in the television industry. There's no off season. No break between seasons in a series. WWE issues seven hours of original programming every week, all year long, and its shows are among the most co-viewed pieces of content on TV. Nearly a quarter of WWE viewers are Black and Hispanic viewership hovers around 12 percent. Fans can view the company's content library on Peacock. In 2025, *Raw* started live streaming on Netflix. By media standards, televised wrestling is an anomaly. According to Georgia wrestling dreammaker Bill Behrens, no other live, first-run program—besides news—exceeds its longevity.

And yet wrestling's depth has long been overshadowed by its goofiness. It balances on the tightrope between sport and theatre: not quite one, not quite the other, easier to dismiss than to acknowledge. Despite its multitudes wrestling remains the chump of sports, the chunky kid with the stained jeans who's last to be called to the team. And that's because by and large its players and fans are those people too. They know the feeling of being misunderstood, underappreciated, and invisible. Wrestling waits like a messiah with clenched fists, ready to strike down the fear and doubt and chaos of the outside world.

In the chase for professional wrestling stardom, they chase the chance to be somebody that someone adores—or fears. The chance to be seen. In the theatrical warfare of wrestling, they find peace.

"It has something to do with its corrupting of sport," muses sociologist Tyson Smith, who has studied wrestling's relationship with identity and masculinity. We canonize sport because it's wrapped in meritocracy. Wrestling smashes that through a table, Bubba Ray Dudley–style. Anything can happen in the arena. The victor isn't always the fastest runner or leading scorer. We just can't seem to rationalize it, so we scoff at it.

"Part of it is people underestimate the fans," writer Tommy Tomlinson, a lifelong wrestling fan and former *Charlotte Observer* reporter who hosts the podcast *SouthBound*, says. "The people who look down on wrestling don't think the fans get it."

Wrestling is goofy, he admits. The characters and their motives are apparent in a way more "sophisticated" performances aren't. It's garish. It's loud. Obvious rather than avant-garde. "In well-told wrestling angles there are really subtle storytelling lines," he says, "but all of it is told in really broad strokes."

In his seminal 1957 book *Mythologies*, French essayist and critic Roland Barthes spends 52 chapters proving every object and human experience is an amalgamation of familiar images, actions, and sounds. He calls them signs. Things we recognize that trigger our emotions. The signs are familiar. They're borrowed from other places. Barthes himself was a wrestling fan. The book's first chapter is "The World of Wrestling."* It had to be. When it comes to blatant display of signs, no other human experience compares.

* In later editions the chapter name appears as "In the Ring."

From MetLife Stadium to strip-mall arenas, professional wrestling follows a rubric so fundamental that toddlers can follow along (and often do). It's a tennis match of assault and vengeance, a ticket to humanity's oldest show. An eye rake for an eye rake, a backbreaker for a backbreaker.

A wrestler delivers a blow. His opponent tumbles to the floor, stunned. "Come on!" the crowd yells. "Show him who's boss!" He lumbers to the ropes and drags himself up. Good triumphs evil again.

We accept hero and villain are partners in this brutal ballet, that two hearts, bound by trust, pump the blood that spills from their foreheads. The most important detail of a match isn't who wins, it's whether they can get a "pop," that sought after rise from the crowd. Hegel's theory of recognition, stuffed into compression tights.

"There are really only two wrestling stories," Tomlinson says. 'I want what you have,' whether it's the championship belt or the prestige or the adoration of the fans. Or 'I hate what you are.' Most stories, even at the highest level, when you reduce it down, are about those two things. Wrestling makes it more obvious than a lot of other forms of storytelling."

Wrestling appeals to working-class fans, Tomlinson, who grew up in such a family, posits, because it's a show about fighting. "For people who struggle in their lives, who get beaten down and bloodied—literally or figuratively—by their environments, wrestling resonates in a way that other forms of sport don't," he says. "It's symbolic of their lives in a lot of ways."

Wrestling's a billion-dollar industry, but it still carries the stench of sideshow entertainment. In 1982, low- and highbrow culture collided head-to-head in one of the greatest examples ever of wrestling's ability to manipulate emotion.

As a comedian Andy Kaufman excelled in embodying characters: Tony Clifton, Latka Gravas in *Taxi* (preceded by Foreign Man on *Saturday Night Live*), and himself, as Inter-Gender Wrestling Champion of the World. As the latter he infuriated onlookers by doing the unthinkable: facing off with women. (While intergender matches are relatively common in the indies, they almost never appear on WWE.) Kaufman cut chauvinistic promos challenging women to spar with him and offered $1,000 to any who pinned him.

Kaufman wanted to bring his act to a real wrestling ring and approached Vince McMahon Sr., who headed WWE at the time. After the elder McMahon declined, Kaufman spoke to wrestling reporter/photographer Bill Apter, who connected him with promoter Jerry Jarrett and his co-owner and top star, Jerry "The King" Lawler, in Memphis. All agreed: it would be good for business for Kaufman to appear in a show. For Kaufman, a fan since childhood, it was a dream come true.

To drum up interest, Kaufman's promos appeared on Memphis-area TV stations. "You don't have any brains, you're from Memphis, Tennessee," Kaufman said, contorting his face and forcing his words through a rubbery Southern accent. Situated poolside in "Hollywood," Kaufman called Lawler a hick and threatened to sue him. In return, Lawler conveyed pity for the little-boy wrestling fan who dreamed of being a star in the ring but grew up to be a wimp. He promised to shatter Kaufman's dreams "in just about thirty seconds" if he came to Memphis and faced him inside the ropes.

In his first appearance inside Memphis's Mid-South Coliseum, Kaufman invited women to the ring and offered his usual purse. The house was packed and the fans were irate: wrestling gold. To Kaufman's delight, Jarrett booked him for another show. Kaufman did his intergender champion schtick again, but this time, Foxy Brown, a 6'1", 250-pound woman in jeans and a cowboy hat stepped up, and without hesitation, slammed him. Kaufman scurried toward the edge of the mat and gripped the bottom rope as Foxy yanked on him, pulling his shorts down. Eventually she ran out of gas.

Fans wanted more. Next time they met, Lawler played Foxy's trainer and coached her from the corner. When she became visibly exhausted the ref called for the bell, but Kaufman kept attacking. Lawler, in street clothes, climbed over the ropes and ripped Kaufman off her. When Kaufman came toward him, Lawler shoved him to the floor.

"How was that?" Kaufman asked Lawler backstage. And then they hatched a plan for their own match, one that would define Kaufman's legacy as a performer and earn him a spot in the WWE Hall of Fame.

On April 5, 1982, Memphis police escorted Kaufman to the ring. He wore his usual costume: black shorts over a set of white long johns. He baited Lawler then ducked out of the ring. Lawler grabbed a mic. "Did you come down here to wrestle or act like an ass?" The crowd lapped it up. Lawler invited Kaufman to grip him in a headlock. Kaufman seized Lawler's neck in the crux of his elbow, and Lawler sent a signal to the crowd in the form of an outstretched pointer finger out of Kaufman's view. *Just give me a minute here.*

Then Lawler effortlessly lifted Kaufman in a back suplex and dropped him. The fans went nuts. Kaufman sold it, writhing on the floor. Lawler then held him upside down and prepared for a piledriver, an illegal move. The referee rang the bell and deemed Kaufman the winner, by disqualification. Lawler ignored it and served Kaufman another. The fans stayed on their feet, booing and bellowing as EMTs strapped Kaufman into a neck brace and wheeled him out on a gurney. The feud was successful because of all it represented. North and South. City and country. Erudite and refined versus dumb and crass. Kaufman wore the neck brace for months. To this day people debate how much of his injury was real and how much was feigned.

The feud predicated an ongoing era of non-wrestler celebrities entering the ring, from Betty White to Bad Bunny. Cyndi Lauper played Wendi Richter's manager in 1984's "Brawl to End It All," broadcast on MTV, and in the inaugural WrestleMania. She, Muhammad Ali, and Liberace posed with Hulk Hogan and Richter in a promotional photo for the event, and wrestler Lou Albano played her father in the "Girls Just Want to Have Fun" video.

In 2000 the actor David Arquette won a WCW title while promoting *Ready to Rumble*, a film about Georgia-based WCW in which Arquette played the leading role. Wrestling fans read Arquette's far-fetched triumph as an insult. Twenty years later, he sought redemption in the documentary *You Cannot Kill David Arquette*, which follows him as he trains. "I want to clear my name," he says in the film. "And through the process, honor wrestling."

In 1998 Dennis Rodman skipped practice the day after Game 3 of the NBA Finals and flew to Michigan to attack Diamond Dallas Page with a steel chair. WWE lists Rob Gronkowski among its list of Superstars; he first performed on WrestleMania in 2017.

Start looking at life through the lens of professional wrestling and gray, dotted lines become solid black. From politics to music to lengthy academic papers, it abounds. Jamie Lee Curtis lifted Ke Huy Quan in a backbreaker in 2022's *Everything Everywhere All at Once*. Patrick Mahomes and Travis Kelce took turns wearing a customized WWE championship belt as they reveled through

Kansas City after winning the Super Bowl in 2023. That summer, Ryan Gosling, playing Ken, donned a Ric Flair–like coat in *Barbie.*

The Beastie Boys partially credit their rise to employing pro wrestling tactics into their act early on at the behest of their producer, wrestling evangelist Rick Rubin. The 2015 album *Beat the Champ* by the indie folk band the Mountain Goats is front man John Darnielle's ode to his childhood passion. Backed by piano, woodwinds, and organ, he sings haunting lyrics about the passion and sacrifice of wrestlers. In the liner notes, he wrote:

> The situation in my house was deteriorating badly and permanently during the span of my hyper-fandom, which lasted from when I was nine until I was maybe thirteen. My life was chaotic and frightening. I did not cheer the heels. I feared and hated them. I wanted to see them punished. When, in the heat of battle, the good guys would abandon the rulebook in order to fight fire with fire, something inside me responded primally.

In the 2023 book *Ringmaster: Vince McMahon and the Unmaking of America*, the writer Josephine Riesman spends 356 pages chronicling professional wrestling's connection to politics, particularly Donald Trump. She even coins a term, "neokayfabe," to describe Trump's modus operandi: "a slippery, ever-wobbling jumble of truths, half-truths, and outright falsehoods, all delivered with the utmost passion and commitment."

Trump's performances—near and away from actual WWE rings—set the stage for a political era of bombastic, social-media fueled vitriol that echoes the mic work of professional wrestlers. In a 2023 piece titled "How Wrestling Explains America," *Atlantic* staff writer John Hendrickson attends *Raw* with Riesman and ponders McMahon's "profound influence on American culture and politics."*

"Although the symbiotic relationship between politics and wrestling goes back centuries, it is fair to say that Trump exploited WWE tools and tricks better than anyone who had come before him," Hendrickson writes. And later, "Flashy graphics, flying taunts, unraveling democracy: Who could look away?"

"Trump Plaza"—actually Atlantic City's municipal convention center—remains the only venue to host two consecutive WrestleManias, in 1988 and 1989. By attaching his name to a building he didn't actually own, Trump exaggerated his own reach. It was part of the deal he inked with WWE. Trump's actual property, Trump Plaza Hotel and Casino, sponsored the events.

Trump recognized the business potential of the WWE Universe, the company's term for its fans, early on. After that, his was a regular celebrity face in the audience at events. At WrestleMania in 2004, former wrestler and Minnesota governor Jesse "The Body" Ventura climbed from the ring to the front row to interview Trump, then the star of *The Apprentice*. Ventura twice reminded fans of Trump's hosting role in WrestleMania IV and V, and then asked him what WWE's landmark event meant to him. Trump responded by praising McMahon. "It means a lot. I was involved with Vince for a long time. He's a great guy. He's done really an unbelievable job."

Ventura cut to the chase. "If I were to get back into politics, could I expect your moral and financial support?"

Trump smiles. "One hundred percent."

---

* John Hendrickson, "How Wrestling Explains America," *The Atlantic*, March 26, 2023.

A triumphant Ventura turned to the crowd. "You know what? I think we may need a wrestler in the White House in 2008!"

A commentator adds, "And maybe a billionaire as a vice president!"

In January 2007 Trump, in a prerecorded message delivered to the audience on the jumbotron, showered actual cash onto *Monday Night Raw* fans inside Dallas's American Airlines Arena. Three months later, McMahon took on Trump in the "Battle of the Billionaires" at WrestleMania 23 in Detroit. Two years after that McMahon "sold" *Raw* to Trump. "There's no doubt that I have made the right decision to sell *Monday Night Raw*," McMahon said to the crowd in Charlotte. Fans keeled over in laughter. "*Monday Night Raw* will be independently owned and operated with a man who I have, a . . . " McMahon paused. His eyes widened, and he cocked his head to the side, "a history with."

In another prerecorded monologue that foreshadowed the stump speeches he'd give after announcing his first presidential bid in 2015, Trump shamed McMahon for taking WWE fans for granted. "You know, Vince, you never really showed your appreciation for the *Raw* audience. Never once did I see that appreciation. I'm going to do stuff that's never been done before, never been seen before."

Thirteen years later, in 2022, internal board investigators learned McMahon donated a total of $5 million to the tax-exempt Donald J. Trump Foundation in 2007 and 2009, years Trump featured in WWE's programming. In 2019, Trump had admitted to misusing charitable funds and the New York Supreme Court ordered him to pay $2 million in damages to eight different charities for illegally misusing the foundation's money to fund his political interests.

In 2023, Robert F. Kennedy Jr. heckled Joe Biden with shirtless pushups in tight jeans and the caption "Getting in shape for my debates with President Biden!" It had the production level and sophistication of an indie wrestler's promo. The next year, Hulk Hogan ripped his shirt off at the Republican National Convention and promised Donald Trump would save the American Dream.

"I've seen some great tag teams in my time," Hogan roared. "Hulk Hogan and *ooo yeah* the Macho Man Randy Savage! But you know something? I see the greatest tag team of my life standing upon us, getting ready to straighten this country out for all the real Americans." Then, the most recognizable face in all of wrestling referenced the first assassination attempt on Trump to start a story. He removed his jacket, got serious. "They took a shot at my hero." He threw the crumpled garment to the ground. "Enough was enough. I said, 'Let Trumpamania run wild brother.'" He tore through one sleeveless T-shirt to reveal another: a Trump Vance '24 one, in red. Remove the state stanchions and candidate signs and you're at *SmackDown*.

Before winning an Emmy for his role in the Apple TV+ series *Black Bird*, Paul Walter Hauser—who starred as Richard Jewell in the eponymous 2019 Clint Eastwood film alongside Sam Rockwell, Kathy Bates, Jon Hamm, and Olivia Wilde—entered the ring. "I love wrestling. I grew up watching it, and I never graduated from that," he told Stephen Colbert, while wearing his own wrestling T-shirt. "People are like, 'You know it's fake,'" he said. "And I'm like, 'You know what's also fake? Me being a serial killer in *Black Bird*.'"

Players on the exhibition baseball team the Savannah Bananas battle their rivals, the Party Animals. Their head coach Eric Byrnes wears a leopard-print faux-fur robe. Before each game, they practice skits, stunts, and choreography under the direction of an entertainment director. In neon uniforms and cowboy hats, the Animals climb over the outfield fence shooting off roman candles. Players interrupt innings with TikTok challenge dances and sometimes swing flaming bats. A fifth-generation rodeo clown with a penchant for between-the-leg throws is on the pitching roster. The umpire twerks. Before each game, a guy in a suit tees up the face-off with the drama-imbued baritone of a ring announcer. It's a lot like a circus, and a little like a wrestling show.

They're in the entertainment business, not the baseball business, founder Jesse Cole, who draws inspiration from Walt Disney and P. T. Barnum, says. Kind of like wrestlers. "These players are entertainers, first and foremost," Bananas Creative Content Director Ivan Traczuk said in the 2022 ESPN docuseries *Bananaland*. "And if we have really good baseball players and they're not willing to go in on a skit or salsa dance up to the batter's box, then we're not interested in them." A good baseball player isn't automatically a good Bananaball player, just like a good college wrestler isn't always WWE Superstar material. It's athletics, yes, but it's also acting.

Over the years, some people have espoused wrestling as high art, or at a minimum, a form of entertainment worthy of academic study. In 1986 writer Ray Tenenbaum penned "Sleeper Hold," a 22,000-word look behind the curtain, on spec for *The New Yorker*. The magazine turned it down. He tried to sell it as a book. The consensus among editors: "Wrestling fans don't read, and the ones that do, won't buy your book."

Twenty-three years later playwright Kristoffer Diaz's *The Elaborate Entrance of Chad Deity*, which uses the life of fictional wrestler Macedonio Guerra as commentary on everything from race to globalization, was a Pulitzer finalist. Professional wrestlers play the Norse gods Odin, Thor, Freyja, and Loki in *Mythos:*

Ragnarök, a traveling theatre production that's been circling the globe since 2021.

Wrestling may be culturally ubiquitous, but it is, without a doubt, culturally dismissed. Its events aren't covered in the sports or arts section and its players rarely earn the kind of magazine profiles bestowed upon professional athletes and actors. It's a lot like the Dolly Parton of yore, before the intelligentsia recognized her as a beacon of equanimity: unabashed, larger than life, and easy to pick on. And if we allow it, lovable and unifying. A treasure.

CHAPTER 15

Triston Michaels and Hunter

In January 2023 Hunter came home from Birmingham defeated after he hadn't been picked for an extra spot on *Raw*. He'd been eating as much as he could stomach and working out constantly but when he looked in the mirror he wasn't satisfied. Months later he sat in the living room with Billy Ray, at a loss.

"I'll be right back." Billy Ray returned with a little brown bottle. "If you want to get bigger, here it is," he said, handing it to Hunter. "I asked your mother. She's fine with it." Besides, Billy Ray told him, even if Hunter got tested he probably wouldn't get flagged for testosterone because he's young. The hormone runs through 20-year-old male bodies like neon in a Budweiser sign.

Billy Ray felt confident giving testosterone to his son. He knew it would work. His two regrets from his time in the chase are that he didn't utilize steroids and nutrition to their full potential. "Sometimes I wonder what would have happened if I were a *leetle* bit bigger," he says, between sets in his basement gym. He tried testosterone a few times in his career. It multiplied his effort in the gym and masked the pain. But when he stopped he lost everything he gained.

These days, he gets it through an online provider. He was 49 when he took a blood test to measure his levels. The report said he had the testosterone levels of a 36-year-old. *That's pretty good*, he thought. "Would you like to have the levels of a 21-year-old?" the voice on his screen asked. A no-brainer. Once a year he pokes his wrist with a needle, deposits a drop of blood on a lab card, and mails it off. Another year of legal testosterone.

When Hunter was a high school junior taking dual-enrollment classes at a local community college, his English teacher asked the class to write about their favorite murder investigation. Hunter wrote about Chris Benoit.

Over a three-day period in June 2007, the decorated WWE wrestler allegedly killed his wife and their 7-year-old son, and then himself, in their Fayetteville, Georgia, home. Benoit was one of Hunter's favorites—a little guy, a perfectionist, jacked, and pissed off at the world.

Every time Hunter read something that convinced him Benoit did it, he found something else to suggest he didn't. He never arrived at a definitive conclusion. An autopsy showed 10 times the normal level of testosterone in Benoit's body. Most immediately credited his gruesome behavior, which included strangulation and suffocation, to 'roid rage, but a small faction still believe it was a setup. Benoit debuted at 18 and admitted he had suffered more concussions than he could count, many via the impact of steel chairs to the head before WWE outlawed the practice. A neurosurgeon who studied his 40-year-old brain after his death compared it to that of an 80-year-old with severe Alzheimer's disease.

"Even if he did it, I don't believe it was 'roid rage," Hunter says. "I think it was 100 percent CTE—and the depression of losing Eddie Guerrero, his best friend."

Wrestling hitched a ride on the '80s-era obsession with bodybuilding, and then one-upped it. It's one thing to watch unnaturally large men and women stand like oiled statues. It's another to pit them against each other in a wrestling ring. If you can draw upon all manner of inspiration to shape your character, why not mold your physique with the help of synthetic testosterone?

It's impossible to pinpoint when anabolic steroids—synthetic hormones that aid muscle growth—became synonymous with professional wrestling, but history shows it had a lot to do with Vince McMahon. Professional wrestlers of the Golden Era—the late '80s to early '90s—were decidedly herculean. They were human superheroes, and they looked the part.

Terry Bollea was born in Augusta, Georgia, and raised in the roughneck enclave of Port Tampa, Florida. Inspired by "Superstar" Billy Graham, a famously brawny professional wrestler popular in the late '70s, Bollea started supplementing his workouts with steroids around 1978. In a matter of months, the 25-year-old began to resemble his hero, whose bulging neck was nearly as wide as his head. He leaned into it, calling himself Terry Boulder, and soon caught the attention of Vince McMahon Sr., who ran WWE at the time. Vince Sr. promptly insisted Terry adopt the name Hogan to appeal to Irish American fans. The name "Hulk" came when he appeared on a morning talk show in Mobile, Alabama, alongside Lou Ferrigno, who played The Incredible Hulk in the TV series. Seeing them together, the host said to Hogan, "You're bigger than Lou Ferrigno, you're bigger than The Hulk!" Bollea responded: "That's because I'm the *real* Hulk." That night at the wrestling show, the boys in the back, who had seen the segment, started calling him Hulk. It stuck.

While Hogan helped propel WWE to its peak, the Reagan White House fought the War on Drugs. The Anabolic Steroids Control Act of 1990 named anabolic steroids "one of America's most serious drug problems." New Jersey Representative William Hughes led his presentation of the bill not with concern over the well-being of professional wrestlers, but rather teenage athletes, who were seemingly being fed synthetic hormones like Tic Tacs by their high school coaches. As far as he, and the federal government were concerned, the drugs belonged in the same category as cocaine. Illegal possession and distribution of them became a felony.

By then, Dr. George Zahorian, a physician appointed by the state of Pennsylvania to provide ringside care during live events in the state, had become the Santa Claus of the stuff in the WWE, shipping or hand-delivering large amounts of anabolic steroids to homes, events, and the company headquarters in Stamford, Connecticut. Federal agents raided his office in March 1990, and he was later convicted of illegally selling steroids to professional wrestlers. "Superstar" Billy Graham testified to that effect, along with Rick Rude, Tully Blanchard, and The Ultimate Warrior.

Though Vince was acquitted three years later of charges he conspired to distribute steroids to wrestlers he employed, many have since come forward to allege a culture of steroid use. They claim that if it wasn't formally directed, it was quietly expected.

Synthetic testosterone wasn't the only medicine circulating WWE locker rooms. Keeping up often included swilling a steady diet of alcohol, cocaine, and muscle relaxers. Steroids enlarge the heart. Cocaine sets it into overdrive. Painkillers overwork the liver, the organ responsible for clearing toxins from the bloodstream. A lethal trifecta.

Billy Ray's own hero, Lex Luger, first took Dianabol to bulk up before his first season as an offensive lineman in the Canadian Football League, but it was Deca-Durabolin—more commonly known as Deca—that became his anabolic steroid of choice in his wrestling years. By the early aughts, Luger was subjecting himself to a daily assault of pills and booze just to steady himself. Miss Elizabeth, best known for her in-ring wedding with "Macho Man" Randy Savage (who in actuality had already been legally married to her for seven years), overdosed on Luger's couch in Marietta, Georgia, in 2003. She was 42. Luger's turning point came three years later after he nearly suffered the same fate.

Others weren't so lucky. Eddie Guerrero was 38 when his nephew, WWE wrestler Chavo Guerrero Jr., found him unconscious in a Minneapolis hotel room the day before he was scheduled to perform on *Monday Night Raw*. Medical examiners found an enlarged, damaged heart and narrowed, hardened arteries, along with other abnormally enlarged organs.

Heart-related conditions also account for the deaths of 35-year-old Brian Pillman and 33-year-old Eddie Gilbert. Rick Rude died at 40. Road Warrior Hawk at 46. His partner, Animal, was 60. Heart attacks killed The Ultimate Warrior and "Rowdy" Roddy Piper at 54 and 61. New Jack and Randy Savage were 58.

The website WrestlerDeaths.com devotes an entire category

to well-known wrestlers who died before the age of 50. It's 100 deep and includes Andrew "Test" Martin, who overdosed at 33, and Buzz Sawyer, at 32, and Georgia's own Jimmy Rave, at 39. "Mr. Perfect" Curt Hennig OD'd when he was 44. Even Chyna, the female wrestler Billy Ray and Jenn named their daughter after, died from a deadly combination of alcohol, anxiety drugs, painkillers, and sleeping pills, at 46.

A 2014 Eastern Michigan University study of professional wrestlers who performed between 1985 and 2011 showed those aged 35 to 54 were nearly three times more likely to die prematurely than the average American man. It got Benjamin Morris, a lifelong wrestling fan who was then a writer for the statistical analysis site *FiveThirtyEight*, thinking. He pulled up the card from WrestleMania VI in 1990—the year he turned 13—and noticed a third of the wrestlers were dead. He turned out a list of WWE wrestlers younger than 60 who had performed in at least 20 pay-per-view events between 1985 and 2002. Then he used actuarial tables from the Social Security Administration to see the expected death age of an "average" person and compared it to the deaths of the wrestlers on his list. For every age bracket, the wrestlers died at a disturbingly higher rate. WWE wrestlers aged between 35 and 45 years had a mortality rate more than five times higher than the actuarial death rate for those age groups.

At some point one of Hunter's confidants sent a video of him to QT Marshall, the former AEW wrestler and a co-owner—along with Cody Rhodes and the retired WCW wrestler Glacier—of Atlanta's Nightmare Factory training school, where many of Hunter's contemporaries, including Carlie Bravo, have trained. (AEW acquired Ring of Honor [ROH] in 2022, and the next year,

Carlie and his tag partner Shawn Dean made their debut with the company as The Infantry, a military-inspired tag team.) Carlie soon signed a short-term contract and then, in 2024, a full-time deal, with AEW, to perform under its ROH brand. In early 2025 the company moved him to the roster for its primetime shows.

Marshall invited Hunter to come to a practice, the way a chef stages at a restaurant.

The Nightmare Factory is a direct line to the top: Marshall is the Vice President of Show and Creative Coordination for AEW, and Cody Rhodes, having worked for both big companies, is one of WWE's biggest stars.

Soon Hunter got an invitation to Universal Studios in Orlando, where AEW filmed *Dark*,* a YouTube series that showcases matches between up-and-coming wrestlers. Hunter stayed for the full six hours of filming: enough footage to fill five episodes.

The audience, made up of wrestlers and fans, had watched 30 matches by the time Hunter and his opponent, 22-year-old Cole Karter entered the ring.

Karter was well known, by comparison. He'd made it into WWE's March 2022 Performance Center class as Troy "Two Dimes" Donovan and wrestled a few matches in WWE's NXT division, but the company released him three months later. AEW signed him soon after and was still sussing him out.

Their match aired on YouTube on April 18, 2023. The announcers used the first couple minutes to tease the upcoming episode of *Rampage*. Hunter James and Cole Karter were background noise. When they finally gave way to the match, Karter, 6'2" with a sculpted body and a too-white smile, got in Hunter's face. "You don't belong here," he rumbled.

---

* Dark match: one that happens before the official start to a show.

"Nothing! You are nothing."

Tony Khan never called.

Four years earlier, Khan established AEW, the first pro wrestling company to rival WWE since the company bought out its chief competitor, Atlanta-based WCW, in 2001. A year later AEW landed a four-year, $175 million deal with WarnerMedia to broadcast its shows on TNT and TBS. *Dynamite* and *Collision* began exclusive livestreaming on Max in January 2025.

As a teenager in the '90s, Khan built rosters and wrote shows in the world of e-wrestling, something akin to fantasy football. Most were episodes of *Dynamite*, the name he chose for his series. In 2021 he created a second series, *Rampage*. He obsessed. By the time he established AEW, at age 36, he'd written more than 1,000 episodes.

Khan, a lifelong wrestling fan, bestowed himself with corporate titles as if peeling them off a sticker sheet: co-owner, president, CEO, general manager, head of creative. He named AEW's first prime-time shows *Dynamite* and *Rampage*, and added a third, *Collision*, in 2023. (*Rampage* has since been retired.) On August 27 of that year, 72,265 people filled London's Wembley Stadium for the company's version of WrestleMania, an event Khan named All In.

His father, billionaire Shahid Khan, immigrated to the United States from Pakistan at 16 and worked his way up at the Chicago-based automotive manufacturing company Flex-N-Gate, where he started while studying industrial engineering at the University of Illinois at Urbana-Champaign. He eventually bought the company with money he made from launching his own car bumper manufacturing company, and then merged the two. Now, the senior Khan also owns the Jacksonville Jaguars and the West London Premier League football club Fulham FC, as well as part of AEW.

AEW is to WWE what LIV Golf is to the PGA Tour. From the get-go, it aimed to be the alternative to wrestling's omnipresent juggernaut and quickly became known as a place for wrestlers who felt stifled creatively by WWE. "AEW offered this alternative, not only for fans to see a version of wrestling that wasn't being given to them by WWE, but also for an excited talent base that wanted an alternative to do their creative wrestling," industry analyst Brandon Thurston says. That a second, giant, sports entertainment company emerged and persists tells the story of professional wrestling's perpetuity. As wrestling creeps into major streaming services, its audience only grows.

Hunter felt the pangs of rejection in Birmingham when he didn't get called up for an extra spot on *Raw*, but he was able to quiet them. Now the dread and frustration radiated through his insides. He still believed opportunities like *AEW Dark* were the way to his dream. But some of the lines he told himself—"You're gonna get ninety no's before you get a yes"—felt hollow. *Why isn't anyone taking a chance on me? I look better. Physically, I can do ten times more than they can do*, he thought. He talked to himself as he drove home from Orlando. *Why is he signed and I'm not? Why are they getting more time than me?* No answer arrived.

Weeks passed, and his repetitive schedule—and the shine he received in his local locker rooms—healed him. "I don't regret it," he decided about traveling to Orlando.

Hunter had a hunch his prime-time appearances had spurred a change in his parents. The big-name performances had come quickly and frequently: *SmackDown* in August 2022, *Raw* and Impact in January 2023, now AEW. He was a pro wrestler now, not someone trying to be a pro wrestler. Hunter texted Billy Ray as soon as he found out he'd be on TV in *SmackDown*. Billy Ray wrote back: "You may have been born for this, but you aren't the chosen one. You chose to be the one." The words were the same ones his father used to send before amateur wrestling tournaments. Billy Ray was back in Hunter's corner.

Slowly Billy Ray indulged his own curiosity about his son's career. "Where you at this weekend?" he'd ask Hunter Friday at work. And on Monday: "How was your match?" Eventually he started watching Hunter's matches on YouTube. More texts came through. "That match was awesome." "You look ten times bigger on TV." "You look like a star."

By now Hunter had grown close enough to Rick Michaels, another Georgia dreammaker, that he'd been a groomsman in his wedding at Landmark Arena.

Anarchy wrapped its annual Christmas Day show in 2021, and wrestlers and referees busied themselves in the locker room, undressing and packing up.

"We got one more present," Rick, Anarchy's showrunner, said to his fiancé, Triston, still in his referee stripes.

Someone covered Triston's eyes. His mother, Menette, in from Opp, Alabama, approached with a box wrapped in red and white paper. "Mama!" Triston yelled, slapping the gift aside and pulling her close.

Triston, a manager at a Dollar Tree store, opened the box and unfolded its contents: a striped referee's shirt stamped with the word GROOM. Tears ran down his face. Rick approached and dropped to one knee, his reading glasses propped on the crown of his freshly shaven head. "We're getting married tonight, honey," he said. Security guard Rodney Hix, a large man with a soul patch, wrapped his arms around them and kissed their foreheads. Joyful applause filled the locker room in Cornelia, Georgia.

"We gotta get the cage down, and—" Rick looked at his watch, "we gotta get this wedding underway."

Gary Lamb, Southern Honor Wrestling's promoter and the pastor of Action Church inside the wrestling show's venue, walked with Rick to the ring, where the attendants—nearly all wrestlers, in coordinating T-shirts—waited with clasped hands. Triston escorted his mother to the ring. At the steps, he stopped to lift her portable oxygen tank.

Lamb started with a verse from Song of Solomon, Chapter 8. "Many waters cannot quench love, rivers cannot sweep it away." He wore jeans and a black blazer. His Southern preacher's voice a dead ringer for Danny McBride's character in the HBO series *The Righteous Gemstones.*

"Friends and family, I've done some crazy shit in my life," he continued. "I have never went to a wrestling show on Christmas Day and married two men with blood at my feet." The room broke into laughter. Lamb got serious. "We are gathered here today in this wrestling ring to celebrate the joining of this man and this man." Hunter stood on Triston's side in shorts and a backward hat.

"People will talk, people will criticize, but only you two know what you have," Lamb said, before getting to the important question.

"Do you Rick, in the presence of God and all these witnesses, promise to love and cherish Triston in sickness and in health, prosperity and adversity, as long as you both shall live?" Rick, in a shiny bomber jacket, delivered a quiet, "I do."

Triston paused and looked around when Lamb posed the same question to him. "We're in a wrestling ring, I gotta do it right," he said before inhaling the air required to deliver a Stone Cold Steve Austin–style "Awww hell yeah!" They looked at each other and buckled in laughter.

"As if this moment couldn't be any more perfect," Lamb said, acknowledging the eccentricity of it all. "I will ask for the rings to be brought to the ring."

Color commentator JJ Johnson appeared at the curtain with Charlotte, the couple's dog, named after Ric Flair's daughter, the wrestler Charlotte Flair. The rescued lab-pit mix wore a red Santa vest.

"Friends and family, dog, as crazy as it is, you've literally just witnessed one of the most beautiful acts of love there is," Lamb said. "According to Holy Scripture, according to the law of the state of Georgia, I now pronounce you husband and husband."

"Hell, I don't know who the groom is but you both can kiss each other."

The couple and their attendants filed out. Hunter took Charlotte's leash and walked her to the locker room.

Soon after his AEW appearance, Hunter got a text from Rick, who now worked for NWA as a tailor. "NWA wants you in North Carolina."

The CW show *Billy Corgan's Adventures in Carnyland* follows the Smashing Pumpkins front man as he attempts to revive the 75-year-old National Wrestling Alliance—the company he purchased in 2017—while planning a wedding, parenting two young children, and touring with his band. The first and second episodes follow Corgan and crew as they put on the Crockett Cup, a tag-team championship filmed in front of a live audience in Winston-Salem, North Carolina, in June 2023.

In one scene, Corgan addresses the mass of wrestlers, producers, and others required to pull it off. In the far left of the frame, in a hoodie and backward cap, a nameless, faceless figure stands: Hunter James. Still showing up.

In Winston-Salem he'd get in front of Corgan, head producer Billy Trask, and talent relations director Pat Kenny—his chance to prove himself to decision-makers at a company keen on signing lesser-known talent. Hunter didn't know what would happen, but he trusted Rick. "I've never seen him not get his way when it comes to working magic."

His confidence waned as the day wore on. Hunter wrestled Jackson Drake, a slim but muscled 19-year-old from Greensboro, North Carolina, for a camera check. It didn't even count as a dark match.

He grazed the catering spread, introduced himself to people around the room, and talked shop as much as he could. Sometime that day, former wrestler Austin Idol, 73, who plays a manager in NWA, approached him. "What about changing your name to Gorgeous Georgie Graham?" he said.

In Hunter's boyish face, blond hair, and blue eyes, Idol saw a canvas that could be painted to echo the pompous and bouffanted Gorgeous George, the sequin-and-velvet-draped 1940s wrestler whose flamboyance inspired Muhammad Ali to aggrandize himself in interviews and trash-talk opponents. Idol himself looked to "The Sensation of the Nation" when developing his own character, known for bulging biceps and platinum locks tucked beneath a newsboy cap and an '80s-era feud with Memphis's Jerry "The King" Lawler (the man who famously defeated comedian Andy Kaufman in the ring in 1982).

The towering Southern Fried fixture and NWA wrestler Judais, who houses Idol's wrestling school behind his Greenville, South Carolina, gym, stood nearby and heard the advice. "That's fucking stupid," he said, ribbing Idol. Hunter had earned the respect of the giant.

It got Hunter thinking, though. "Why not Hollywood Hunter

James?" It rolled off his tongue, and he liked the way it sounded. "Lights always on me, cameras flashing, girls on the red carpet." As the producers grew increasingly interested in other performers, Hunter spent the day running through the possibilities.

Hollywood could be anything. It's whoever you wanted to be, whoever the crowd *needed* you to be. The name, what it conjured, reflected Hunter's versatility in the ring. He wasn't any one thing, he was lots of things.

"Dude, you're starting to look really good," Nick Halen said to Hunter early in the summer of 2023.

Aging into his twenties, aided by the extra boost of testosterone, his body rapidly came to resemble a man's. "I finally feel like a wrestler," Hunter said to Halen.

That year he did three cycles. "I feel ten times better off of it, but sometimes you gotta get bigger. You gotta risk it for the biscuit, if you know what I'm saying."

Rick suggested Hunter stop shaving his body hair. Hunter heeded the advice. "It gives the illusion of you being a little bit thicker," Hunter says. Besides, three of his favorite wrestlers—Shawn Michaels, Mr. Perfect, and AJ Styles—sport chest and stomach hair. He looked more like the persistent, textbook image of a man, the image that, history proves, promoters want in their rings.

In July he drove straight from the family vacation in Panama City Beach to defend his GCW Heavyweight Championship belt against Kerry Morton, a promising young performer with a respected pedigree. He's the son of Ricky Morton, one half of the '80s-era babyface tag team, The Rock 'n' Roll Express. Just a year older than Hunter, with a body far less chiseled, Kerry had already been named World Junior Heavyweight Champion in NWA. In the locker room, Rick doled out more advice: Stop shaving your face too. Hunter adopted a stubble beard. An easy way to add a few years to his age in the ring.

In June, a fan of Hunter's brought his daughter, off for the summer from the University of Georgia, to the show. After Hunter's match he climbed the ropes with his towel and dramatically wiped the sweat off himself, Rick Rude–style. "I'll take you home!" the girl yelled. He was used to heckling, but it caught him off guard. He tossed the towel into her hands.

They texted. He took her to dinner. They spent most of July 4 weekend together. The next weekend, after his usual three straight days of training and wrestling, she texted him: She didn't want to see him anymore. It proved what he already knew: He didn't have time for a girlfriend, especially one who didn't respect his passion. He was right where he wanted to be.

CHAPTER 16

Judais and Hunter

"Southern Fried Nation! It's going to be a Southern-fried Saturday night!" ring announcer Rick Richards shouts into the mic on July 1, 2023.

The song "Outlaws and Outsiders," with Cory Marks's vocals backed by Travis Tritt, kicks up, and David Manders and Bill Behrens, back-office characters well known enough to fans to earn an applause, climb into the ring. Manders, the owner of Southern Fried, hypes the crowd. "This is what I like to see. This is what we built!" For his part, Behrens speaks like he's Scott Pelley teeing up an episode of *60 Minutes*. "Tonight is going to be an amazing night. I can guarantee it."

A few weeks earlier Judais—the 6'5", 270-pound NWA wrestler with a soft spot for Southern Fried—defeated heavyweight champion CT Keys in what *Georgia Wrestling History* called "the greatest SFCW title match in company history." It was his fourth time winning the belt.

Tonight, kids line up near the curtain, miming Judais's entrance with straight-armed fists. The cathedral horror sounds of *Carmina Burana* mixed with Metallica's "For Whom the Bell Tolls" fill the room, and The Priest of Punishment appears. Southern Fried's most affecting figure—with full beard and long dreads flowing from the crown of his otherwise shaved head—moves slowly. He scans the crowd with a calculating eye. His entrance music shifts to a hammering headbanging rhythm and he jogs around the ring bumping fists. He's a big bad menacing guy, but he's their big bad menacing guy. So what if he looks like he's a character from *The Walking Dead*?

He praises SFCW and its fans and defines himself as their defender. He won't tolerate any disrespect. It's a prologue for the show, with some creative direction for the crowd. He circles the ring, belt in hand, and proselytizes its significance, his broad biceps in view via the armholes of his cutout Southern Fried Championship Wrestling T-shirt. "This represents all the wrestlers on this roster. This represents everyone sitting in these seats tonight." They're here for it.

He foreshadows. "And when I walk to the ring as a Southern Fried Champion I will not tolerate anyone—" his voice goes full tough-guy—"being disrespectful to this company."

And then extends a promise. "If you're honorable and you're

strong and you're worthy and you just happen to pin me for this belt, I will shake your hand." Honor.

Rick Richards lays out the rules of the gauntlet match. Two competitors will enter the ring. If one can't defeat the other within five minutes, both men are disqualified, and the next two are up. "The winner of the gauntlet match gets a shot at the Southern Fried heavyweight championship title against Judais, July 22, right here in Monroe, Georgia," he bellows, hyping the crowd.

He calls them up. By minute 15, two compact, high-flying, big-energy performers—Hunter and Najasism—battle like territorial songbirds.

Back body drop, boot to the face, European uppercut, elbow drop. A pause. Hunter jumps up, kicks forward and lands with a flying elbow. They waver. A somersault kick to Hunter's head, a frog splash. Kick chop, kick chop. Hunter hammer lock–clotheslines Naja, as he's known to friends and fans, into submission. One minute, then 30 seconds to go. Naja keeps his head up. Double elimination. No contest. The crowd boos.

"We're not going down like this!" Manders interrupts, flexing his control. "We're taking this to sudden death. I want a winner tonight." Another swell.

Naja bounces in the corner, 5 feet 7 inches of tightly bound strength, a windup toy ready to rip. The next pinfall or submission wins. Referee David Weakley's 15-year-old son Hayden moves around the ring with a Steadicam.

Hunter attacks with a double foot stomp. Naja kicks out. Dodges Hunter's splash. A plant. A pinfall. Too short. Hunter goes for a springboard moonsault. Hand to the sky. Naja pins him with a lights out. He kicks out. Naja to the penthouse. Hunter follows. Superplex. Naja on Hunter's shoulders. Buckle bomb.

Corkscrew spear. A missed springboard elbow drop. Triston Michaels, playing the role of Hunter's manager, distracts the referee. Hunter rolls Naja up. Cheap victory.

"Absolute varsity, absolute garbage," JJ Johnson says into the microphone recording audio for YouTube.

"Let's face it, was there any other option than Mr. Absolute Wunderkind?!" Hunter yells at the crowd. "It's my God-given right to become the youngest Southern Fried Heavyweight Champion."

The lights go out and Judais's music shifts the tone. Hunter will pay for this. Judais, all bare chest and honor, creeps toward the ring. He raises his balled fists, stares Hunter down. "Look who's all growns up," he says, mocking him. Then he gets serious, extends his arm for a handshake. "Good luck." Hunter looks around. Smirks. Judais grows impatient. "Shake his hand!" someone yells from the crowd. A simple act, redolent with meaning.

"Shake my hand, boy." Judais grumbles. Hunter lifts a hand, but changes course and then, in a split second he will later edit to slow motion and post on his Facebook page, slaps Judais, hard, on the cheek. *Oh no he didn't. Oh yes he did.* If there were a guillotine in the back, the fans would've wheeled it to the ring.

The slap was showrunner Todd Sexton's idea. He suggested Hunter run in fear after the impact, but Judais didn't agree. "I feel like he should stare me down," Judais said. His explanation reflected Hunter's character. "He's not scared. He's dumb, but he's not scared."

Hunter steps toward Judais, inches away from the rise and fall of his bare chest, and waits. They linger in the collective unease, the fans strapped into the roller coaster, nearing the crest of the hill. Judais grabs Hunter by the neck, pushes him toward the ropes.

Five days later, *Georgia Wrestling History* posted its top 12 wrestlers in Georgia. Judas, as he was known in Georgia before changing his name to Judais for NWA, No. 1. Hunter James, No. 5. Anywhere near Judais is a good place to be—on a list, sure, but even better in the ring. The slap became a teaser for the summer blockbuster between Georgia's most irresistible David and Goliath. At home, Billy Ray watched. "You stood toe to toe with a giant," he told Hunter. "And then slapped the shit out of him." He was proud.

Judais was born Michael Cole in 1974. He played football and baseball in high school, then pitched for Furman University, a private liberal arts college in his hometown of Greenville, South Carolina. A sinewy 6'5", he was the kind of athlete coaches noticed. Wrestling promoters too. An entire category of performers known as Big Men persists in wresting, and for good reason. A towering presence sends signals that need no dialogue. Add moves that appear effortless and you've got an intimidating character that can play heel or baby. André the Giant spent most of his years as a lovable, gentle giant. The town of Ellerbe, North Carolina, where he lived out his final years, held a celebration after his death called "A Giant Tribute" in 2023. Mark Henry, Ted DiBiase, and Haku came to sign autographs. Vendors sold memorabilia, and a local wrestling promotion put on a show.

Judais graduated from college with a degree in exercise science and was working as a Pepsi account executive when he went to see his cousin in a show at Brodie Chase's wrestling school in Greenville, where he'd been training.

A security guard approached Judais and brought him to the locker room. "Ever thought about being a wrestler?" Brodie Chase, a decently well-known performer in the South since the early '80s, asked. Judais demurred. Brodie played it cool. Come to training tomorrow to check it out, no commitment, no charge.

Soon Judais was training 12 hours a week. He was tall and athletic, but not heavy. Brodie's ball of clay. "We've got to put weight on you," he said.

Judais ate 12,000 calories a day and gained 50 pounds in a year. "You have to be Goliath, so they can be David," he says, sitting on a weight bench in the gym he runs in Greenville, 23 years later. "Because that's what people want to see. They want to see David and Goliath, and they want to see David win sometimes. Whether you're the babyface or the heel, you're always Goliath."

Judais discovered a world of goofball physicality in Brodie Chase's wrestling school, far from the pressure and rigidity of traditional sport. "It felt like I was having fun," he says. "It still feels like that."

Brodie initially assigned Judais a character that forced him out of his shell: a Chippendales-style dancer. Five years later while wrestling in Puerto Rico, his hotel roommate Flash Flanagan helped him devise "The Priest of Punishment," borrowing elements from Vampiro and The Undertaker.

While doing massage therapy and exercise tech work at a doctor's office, he was hired for a six-show series at a fairgrounds in Nashville. It paid more than he made in a week at his "real" job. It was a turning point, a win at the roulette table that convinced him the payout was there if he kept going.

In 2004 he started as a mortgage broker at Countrywide, just as the company neared its peak as a $500 billion subprime home loan lender. It was a good setup: They had no problem with him leaving work early on Thursday and missing Friday for shows. Then one day he got a call. The office was shutting down. He signed the NDA and allowed the severance payout to keep him afloat while he lived and wrestled in Puerto Rico. When he came home, he started working as a personal trainer, and then eventually bought the gym.

And then in August 2021, just as Judais, 47, was winding down his wrestling career, the call came from NWA: a per-appearance contract and the freedom to evolve his character. One crinkle: they'd spell his name Judais rather than Judas and pronounce it Jude-eye-is rather than Jude-us. He adopted dreadlocks, wore zombie-rocker pants. In his words, "I went full Bruiser Brody." He doubled down on his workouts, ate until he felt sick, and gained 40 pounds in six months.

What he loves most about wrestling is the challenge of blurring the line between reality and entertainment, for the fans. "When people go watch *Avengers* they know they're not watching Robert Downey Jr. fly across the ocean with lasers coming out of his hands, but they don't sit there and say, 'This can't really happen.' They're immersed in it," he says. Using his body—his character—to get them to this point provides a thrill he never experienced in sports, or anywhere else. Then he rattles off his injuries like a third grader identifying states on a map. Multiple broken noses. Dislocated shoulders. Broken ribs. Hand. Fingers. Foot. Ankle. ACL. Quad. Groin.

Wednesday, his family's Catahoula puppy, bites at a pulley, then leaps over weight benches like obstacles in an agility course. "Wednesday, stop," Judais says firmly. She settles onto a treadmill and sighs.

Between the two of them, he and his wife, Allison, have four daughters ranging in age from 6 to 11. They've been married a little over a year. It's his only relationship wrestling hasn't wrecked.

If she was going to run, she probably would've done it on day one. Camera guys from the Puerto Rican wrestling company International Wrestling Association were filming a promo at his gym that involved a bucket of fake blood pouring over him, *Carrie*-style. After the shoot, he walked from his office to the open gym, black gear from head to toe, face painted white, covered in fake blood. Allison, a gym member, stood, mouth agape. "I'm a pro wrestler," Judais said flatly. Allison, a nurse turned competitive bodybuilder, was unfazed. They started dating.

Hunter made his mark on Judais early on when a Survivor Series–style elimination match on Thanksgiving night in 2021 ended with a dogpile pin on Southern Fried's gentle giant. Wrestlers jumped onto the heap one after another as if they were trying to seize a fumbled football. Hunter's knee landed smack on Judais's nose.

After the match, Judais grabbed a paintbrush from the Boys & Girls Club's supplies and manually shoved it back into place. It had only been a week since a doctor had surgically repaired his nose from its most recent break. "He's a little heated," Nick Halen warned Hunter. Hunter was only a few months into his Southern Fried career. He wanted to apologize but feared a face-to-face encounter. Instead, he slipped out of sight and sent a Facebook message from his phone: "Sorry I knee-dropped your nose." Two years later David and Goliath would vie for the show's heavyweight championship. The face-off was Judais's idea. He'd been watching Hunter and felt he deserved the main event.

Three weeks after the slap, Southern Fried fans young and old line up along the barricade leading from the curtain to the ring. They know who's coming. Inside the ropes, Hunter smiles as Judais appears. Only here would a 5'10" 20-year-old stand so confidently as a towering man more than twice his age, with a motive, lurches toward him. Perhaps only in wrestling would that younger, smaller, man smile and smirk.

Judais pounces on Hunter with the belt, smashes it on the back of his head, knocking him to the floor. Hunter points to his chin, yells. "Hit me!" *The nerve.* He dodges a right hook, scoots behind Judais and nails him in the back of the head. "What on earth?" play-by-play announcer Adam Vance asks. Before Judais can turn around Hunter's behind him, showing off by gleefully running in place. "Look at the cockiness, the arrogance of this young man," Vance says. "He has no idea what he's doing."

Vance's counterpart, Rosario Grillo, riffs. "You know what? As stupid as he is, I almost kind of respect it. You gotta take it to the giant's face. That's the only way you're going to win."

Judais punches again, misses. Hunter knocks him in the chin. Judais kicks. Hunter slides out, slugs him in the cheek. Finally Judais catches Hunter's wrist. Time stops. He stares. Judais slaps Hunter in the face. Hunter leaps backward, feet over head over the ropes and out of the ring. Judais descends. Hunter flees. *A coward.* Slides back in the ring. Dropkicks Judais. Gets him in the corner and attacks his head like a speed bag. The giant, steadied by his hands wrapped around the top ropes, barely flinches. Hunter goes until he's winded. Then, in true Goliath mode, Judais marches toward him, picks him up, throws him into the turnbuckle, and slugs him. Hunter reacts like Wile E. Coyote after running into a wall.

"His one punch did more than Hunter's twenty," Grillo notes.

Hunter's reduced to a pile. Judais ascends the ropes. Leaps. Hunter jumps up, dropkicks him in the chest midair. "This is his shot, man. This is what he believes he was born to do is be champion, and he's trying to fulfill that prophecy here tonight."

Hunter pushes Judais's neck into the middle rope. Gives him a boot to the face. The play-by-play continues. "I have no doubt that Hunter is the future world champion of this company and of this industry. Every time we see him he's in better shape."

Judais delivers another: a hard slap to Hunter's face. Hunter grips Judais in a scissor lock, talks trash and knocks him in the head as he's positioned behind him. The fans start to chant Judais's name. He's got them.

He launches Hunter in a high back body drop, then a fallaway slam. "Threw him out like yesterday's trash!"

Judais pounds the turnbuckle. Hunter kicks him between the legs—cheap heel heat—and then rebel-yells, "Brainbusta!"

He slings his arm over Judais's shoulder and bends Judais over, setting up for his finisher. He tries to lift him. Again. Judais holds strong, yanks his arm backward, wraps his hand around Hunter's neck, lifts and chokeslams him. Then the Priest of Punishment gets to work setting up his own finisher, El Crucifijo. Triston stands on the ring apron and tries to distract him. Hunter, disheveled and glossed with sweat, pants in the corner and gives him two middle fingers. Judais attacks, then assesses the damage. Hunter lumbers to his feet, spits at him. An audible "ooooo" surrounds the ring. The referee tries to stop the carnage. Judais knocks him out of the way, disqualifying him and giving Hunter the win, but not the belt. After the dust settles Behrens takes the mic and announces a rematch on August 6. Southern Fried's fans, he knows, will show.

Fifteen miles away, Billy Ray and Jenn sat on their deck, sipping peach moonshine and lemonade to ease the sticky summer heat. Billy Ray scrolled through his Facebook feed and stopped on his friend Mary's live stream of the match. It was straight Shawn Michaels and Undertaker. A match that didn't belong on the indies. It moved the boulder inside him. He'd already resigned himself to Hunter's pursuit of wrestling. Now Hunter had earned his respect as a performer.

A month later an unusual post appeared among the fitness motivator quotes on Billy Ray's Facebook feed:

"HOLLYWOOD is coming to Winder GA. Come see Hunter James do what he does, and what no one else can do."

The message appeared above a flyer for Hunter's upcoming show.

Talking to Hunter about his matches was routine now. At work, Billy Ray would descend the stairs from his office to the warehouse floor, where Hunter worked, phone in hand with one of Hunter's matches pulled up on YouTube and a question about it. Hunter always had an answer. A conversation between father and son that began two decades ago, continued.

"Breaking hearts and winning belts. Really?" he said to Hunter one day. Hunter laughed. He was guilty. He'd used the phrase in an in-ring promo. Billy Ray had coined it when Hunter was five.

"I would love to see that match in reverse," Billy Ray said after rewatching Hunter's match against Judais.

"With me as the baby?" Hunter asked. "Oh yeah, it'll happen."

CHAPTER 17

On November 19, 2005, 31-year-old Dave Wills left his home in Marietta, Georgia, and drove almost 200 miles north to Spartanburg, South Carolina, for a wrestling fan fest called Tribute to Starrcade, a celebration of the 1983 event held at North Carolina's Greensboro Coliseum on Thanksgiving night. Dusty Rhodes, Tully Blanchard, Mick Foley, and Jerry Lawler—middle-aged men who could still draw a crowd—were scheduled to appear.

In his black NWA T-shirt, Wills sat three rows up on the bleachers of the Spartanburg Memorial Auditorium, which looked more like a middle school gym, and stared at some of his heroes. "Beautiful" Bobby Eaton, "Loverboy" Dennis Condrey, Terry Funk. In jeans and windbreaker pants, their faces bore the lines of age and theatrical combat. They leaned back in folding chairs and waited for questions from the audience.

Wills took the mic.

"I just want to thank each and every one a y'all for all you've done to your bodies," he said, his voice quavering.

His cartoonishly round face pressed against wireframe glasses and his right hand gripped the journal he'd brought along for autographs.

"It's still real to me, dammit!" he blurted, before breaking down.

The video made its rounds on the internet. The clip appeared on *Jimmy Kimmel Live!* (Wills declined the invitation to appear on set because of his day job at a maintenance and janitorial company). Daniel Tosh got wind of it and, almost six years later, flew him to LA.

"Wrap it up, crybaby," Tosh barked at the screen airing the clip. Then he delivered a barrage of one-liners.

"Girls love a man with sensitivity. They just don't want to bang a chubby one in a tight T-shirt."

"Rasslin's like Broadway for hillbillies. It's the third favorite white trash pastime, behind incest and NASCAR. Probably because it's the last sport where honkies dominate."

"Wrestling's a billion-dollar industry. Do you know how many rednecks it takes to get a billion dollars? More than billion."

The show cuts to a confused-looking Wills sitting on a chair in a wrestling ring as Tosh, in orange trunks and Ultimate Warrioresque armbands, runs the ropes. Tosh sits down next to him and peppers him.

"You think Arn Anderson's a pussy?"

"Is Brooke Hogan a man?"

"Did you ever masturbate to Miss Elizabeth?"

Finally, Tosh asks. "Do you know that wrestling is fake?"

Wills remains stoic. "Regardless of whether it's predetermined or not, they make it look great, sacrifice their bodies in the ring, no doubt about it."

Wills was emotional that day in 2005. Eddie Guerrero had

died five days earlier. Other wrestlers—Chris Candido, Big Boss Man, Miss Elizabeth, Curt Hennig, Road Warrior Hawk—had died recently too, all before turning 50. Wills understood the risk involved in wrestling. He couldn't bear to think about the next generation of talent falling into the same life-threatening habits.

"I will never use the word fake," Wills says, calling from his home in Acworth, Georgia, nearly two decades after the event. "Nobody wants to see Darth Vader and Luke Skywalker hanging out drinking coffee. You've got to suspend your disbelief." Consent to the artifice is an act of respect.

Dave used his internet fame to promote himself and started attending fan conventions as a guest, not a fan, and selling T-shirts and stickers. Frequently, strangers approach him to say, in all sincerity, "It's still real to me too."

Sixteen years after Dave Wills broke down, wrestler CM Punk returned to the ring after seven years away.

The fans in the seats of Chicago's sold-out United Center had a hunch Punk would choose his hometown for the site of his return. They started shaking their fists and chanting his name. "This building hasn't shook like this since Michael Jordan was here!" an announcer cooed.

Punk appeared and kneeled on AEW's catwalk, looked back at the crowd, and then jumped into the air with clenched fists, taking it in with a guttural "Yeeeah!"

The camera panned over screaming fans and stopped, for a moment, on a face covered in tears. Crying CM Punk Fan was born.

When the arena quieted Punk began a monologue about his needing to take time off to become mentally and physically healthy. He then transitioned his narrative with magic words, words that resonate with viewers of any age. "Can I tell you guys a story?"

Inciting incidents. Culmination. A third-act twist. The suplexes, the powerslams, and the piledrivers replace lines in this violent soap opera. A wrestling story is a hero story that plays out week after week, year after year, sometimes for decades. We love these long-running hero-villain tales. Indiana Jones, Star Wars, the Marvel Cinematic Universe. When you scrape away the cinematography, side characters, and subplots, they're reduced to the same fundamental composition, the vibrant jewel inside the geode of professional wrestling: a battle between good and bad. In film as in wrestling, a few stand the test of time to form a canon of cherished tales. Hogan versus Savage. Flair versus Sting. Austin versus McMahon. The Bloodline.

Hunter had chosen wrestling over college and his father knew he had no intention of changing course. Billy Ray started to think about the story he could tell in the ring: a match that would signal his own exit from the industry and his acceptance of Hunter's entrance into it. Hunter had proved himself. He was destined for WWE, and once he signed, he'd no longer be free to perform outside it.

Billy Ray got to work on his body and created a glory-days playlist. "I Want Action," "Look What the Cat Dragged In," "Talk Dirty to Me," and "Unskinny Bop," of course, but also songs by Shinedown, Saliva, Drowning Pool, Godsmack, White Zombie, and Kid Rock. He titled it "What a Ride," an ode to his days in the ring. Some nights, he'd push himself so hard in the gym his vision went black.

Now, on an August afternoon in 2023, almost two and a half years after he came at Hunter with a wrench, he stares down the 16′×16′ square that made him who he is, the rock that both strengthened and bludgeoned him, the thing that, for a while, severed the ties between father and son. He can't stand still.

Hunter walks by with Triston. "Is that the guy taking your ten percent, Hunter?" Billy Ray jokes. Triston looks his way. "Fifty," he says with a smirk.

Three hours before Southern Fried's show the concessions area bustles with people carrying in coolers of canned soda and boxes of chips and candy bars. At 3:40 p.m. a woman enters with a slow-cooker full of pulled pork.

Billy Ray walks toward the merch table where Chunk, who's been riding with Hunter to his shows, arranges T-shirts, stickers, and autographed photos. In one, Hunter, bare-chested in golden trunks and the gold sequin tailcoat, peers out from a pair of wayfarers, his bleach-blond hair gathered in a gold headband.

Billy Ray recognizes the man sitting next to him: Triston's husband, Rick. "National Guard Armory. Lawrenceville," he says. Billy Ray had once teamed up with Rick's then-wife in a match against Rick and another wrestler.

Hunter's in the ring now, practicing forward rolls. Billy Ray stands on the ground watching. "They did those rolls in amateur wrestling," he says, arms crossed.

With the year of college credits he earned in high school, Hunter would just be starting his final year of college if he had stuck around. The time has gone by fast. Billy Ray knew it would. It's the reason he insisted Hunter wait.

In Billy Ray's mind, the same derelicts that populated locker rooms when he was wrestling now surround Hunter. But Hunter has established himself as different, better, the way Billy Ray, in his mind, did. It's evident in the way he takes care of his body and executes his moves in the ring. Hunter's paying his dues in these spaces now because he has to, but he'll graduate beyond them. He's going to do the thing Billy Ray didn't. He's going to make it.

In December 2021 WWE launched its NIL program, branding it "Next in Line," and signed Olympic gold–winning amateur wrestler Gable Steveson, 21. The company visits major colleges and universities in a highly publicized effort to recruit college athletes. "The problem is, most of these kids have never watched wrestling in their life," Hunter says, defending his decision. Perhaps he's right about skill coming not from college sports but from a life of fandom. Two years later, Steveson, or any other NIL signee, had yet to debut on a televised WWE program.

Billy Ray wasn't getting any younger. He knew he'd never look as good or be as fast as he was in his prime. But he could tell a story. First, he needed to practice his powerslam. So he met Hunter at the Boys & Girls Club that day before the show.

He stands for a moment in the ring, uncertain of himself. Hunter doesn't let him linger. They lock up, and Hunter gets right to the first move, a clothesline. Billy Ray flips, throws a dropkick and lands on his tricep. The ring magic that once numbed his body from pain has lost its potency. He feels the tear right away.

He keeps going, hits Hunter with his powerslam. Hunter pops up and gives credit where it's due. "That's where I got it from," he says to the guys sitting on the ropes, watching.

Billy Ray's work is done. He lays in the ring on his back, the weight of his age and the heft of the moment more than he can carry. He looks at Hunter. "I'm getting out of here." Eventually he climbs out and steadies himself on the floor. He watches Hunter practice and his son's moves ripple through him as he stands, leaning into the mat.

Billy Ray was stiffer in the ring than he thought he would be. Hunter could tell he was nervous because he didn't call any of the moves. It was like he expected Hunter to know what he was thinking, to anticipate their next position—a skill Hunter had gotten very good at over the years, as he played out his life the way Billy Ray wanted him to.

Billy Ray is gone before the Reverend Joseph Brock, the real-life pastor of Living Hope Baptist Church in Baxley, Georgia, introduces Hunter, "the youngest Southern Fried champion of all time!" to open the show with a celebratory in-ring promo complete with cardboard party hats and confetti cannons.

Hunter's new Brainbuster shirts—black with D-Generation-X-style neon green lettering—arrived this week. Chunk arranges his brother's merchandise on a table. Above him, the Boys & Girls Clubs of America's motto hangs: Great Futures Start Here.

Sarah and Robert Noblett, wearing matching Hunter James T-shirts depicting their 20-year-old grandson in heroic graphic-design form, sit in folding metal chairs next to the table. Robert sips from a can of Diet Mountain Dew. Three empties, plus two drained Diet Cokes, stand safe between his feet. He's been collecting them for scrap.

Hours before the show, Angie Hinton, in a Hunter James shirt, has claimed her usual seat in the front row. Her boyfriend Billy is on Southern Fried's security team. "The short, chubby, bald-headed one," she says cheerfully.

She likes the way Hunter interacts with the crowd and hangs out in the ring to talk to kids. "I mean, he can't do it as much being a heel, you know."

One of Southern Fried's top fans, she knows just about everyone in the seats. "I've seen fans leave and come back. They don't stay gone, not from here."

Jason Maddox sits on the bleachers on the other side of the ring. Maddox used to play softball Friday nights but gave up running bases to wrestle in Georgia rings after a teammate, the wrestler Curtis Coleman, recruited him. "We got a show in Colbert tomorrow," he says.

Being here reminds him of coming to shows with his dad and grandfather. "Every now and then we'd go down to the Turner station," he says, recalling the times they went to WTBS studios in Atlanta for live tapings of GCW.

Edward Haley, another former softball teammate, sits next to him and shares similar memories. "I used to go out to the wrestling in Athens, used to be at the J&J," he says, of the long-running flea market, before roll-calling some of his favorites of that era: El Mongol, The Assassins, Mr. Wrestling, and Mr. Wrestling II.

Around the other side of the ring, Kenneth Cason of Barnesville sits near his adult son. "He loves wrestling. He kind of got me back into it, since my wife passed away," he says.

Cason recalls watching wrestling at the fairgrounds. His parents couldn't afford tickets for all the kids, so one would enter and then sneak under the tent flaps to hand theirs to a brother or sister. "As a kid, it's just so big," Cason remembers and smiles.

Tonight, before he leaves, Robert Noblett will shuffle to the concession stand with a plastic grocery bag and ask to sift through the trash for more aluminum cans. At home, he deconstructs motors, air conditioners, washers, dryers, and other equipment and takes the metal components to recyclers who pay by the pound. Once he made $1,000 in a week.

"People will call him and say, 'Hey I got junk for you, you want to come get it?' He's like a kid in a candy store," Sarah says, in their living room two months later.

Sarah and Robert have lived in the same trailer park since the late '80s. "It was supposed to be a fixer-upper but we ain't fixed it up yet," Sarah says of their singlewide, from her velour recliner near the front door. She wears an AJ Styles shirt.

When Billy Ray started training with Steve Lawler in 1992, Sarah drove him. Once, Billy Ray's sneakers were so worn out Steve said, "You don't have to pay me this week. Go buy yourself some new shoes." It's a story Billy Ray likes to tell too. In Sarah's recounting of it, she swaps Hunter's name for Billy Ray's—a mistake she often makes. Maybe it's a simple slip of the tongue, or maybe it's because the two are so alike.

Sarah and Robert married in 1971. Billy Ray was born in '72. It was Sarah who introduced the family to wrestling. In between the prime-time shows—now on seven nights a week, between both major companies—she watches Hunter's matches on YouTube. Hunter recently bought her a smart TV so she could watch his matches on a bigger screen.

Sarah spends nearly all day inside. The trailer's windows are covered by drapes or makeshift curtains. A towel is stuffed into the diamond-shaped window of the front door. Sunlight gives her headaches and she suffers from persistent back pain caused by a car accident in 1999.

"My daddy always told me he was going to wrap me up in bubble wrap," she says, before recounting various injuries she's suffered over the years and persists through. Once she got a call that her brother had passed out in the bathroom at work. She got him into his car, a straight shift. "You can't drive that car," someone said. "You're not going to sit there and tell me I can't do it," she said. She proved them wrong. "That's the way I was raised," she said.

"Just like Hunter," Robert says from the couch, and laughs. Last year he retired from Progress Container & Display, "finally, for the last time," Sarah adds, where he drove a forklift for 43 years.

Sarah's parents moved in in 2003, after her father's heart attack, and then her mother fell and broke a leg. Dementia set in soon after. "She'd cuss me out. Wanted to get my brother to whoop my butt. And I was Daddy's girlfriend and just after his money. I knew it wasn't Mama, but it still hurt anyway," Sarah says. Her parents died soon after one another the next year. "I've got a lot of anxiety about all that," she says, "Mama had Parkinson's and she couldn't eat good. Why didn't I help her eat? Why didn't I feed her? And Daddy, he would ask me if I knew how to cook so and so, and I'd say yeah, but I never did cook it."

"What if, what if, what if..." She trails off and shakes her head.

She pulls out a stack of photographs. "That's Robert and Mister Wrestling Number Two." They took the picture at a show in Buford, Georgia. "First time we ever had front-row seats," Sarah says. "Abdullah the Butcher stepped on my foot."

When they first moved here, "there were so many druggies," she says. She stopped taking the kids to the playground at the church around the corner when she found needles there. There used to be an office with a general store where kids could buy drinks and snacks, and a shelter to stand under while they waited for the school bus. One day it was gone. Neighbors would knock asking for pain meds or food. Domino's drivers got robbed three times in a year, delivering pizzas on their road. "It's gotten better," she says.

In the next photo, Billy Ray kneels wide in the center of a ring, hair brushed in a side part, shirtless, beckoning his opponent with extended arms. Jenn's brother, Jerry, stands in the foreground next to the ropes. They pose again in another photo, soft young faces with belts draped on their shoulders, a Holiday Carpets truck in the background.

"We're proud of all of them," Sarah says before explaining the next photo. This one's in a decorative silver frame. Billy Ray's chest, with pronounced pectorals, peeks out from a denim jacket. Above the waist of his jeans he wears a red-metal belt. "This is him winning international TV champion," Sarah says. "I don't know where."

"We got all kind of pictures of them in yonder on the wall," Robert says, pointing toward the hall that leads to their bedroom, the edges of his words softened by his aphasia.

Newspaper clippings from Hunter and Chunk's high school wrestling careers, mixed with nearly three decades of pro wrestling flyers and portraits, create a collage that takes up one entire, wood-paneled wall of their small bedroom. Justin, as Chop Top, standing on the ropes in black trunks inside Landmark Arena. Hunter in gold aviators and sequin jacket, posing with a belt. Chunk, in his high school wrestling singlet. Billy Ray with baby Justin in one arm, the other drawn up to accentuate his bicep.

"There's Number Two, Dusty Rhodes, and there's Hunter," she says. "The white one that's just got words on it, that's Billy Ray's," she says, pointing to a flyer for a little league benefit show in 2007.

A few rows of photos hang next to the bedroom door. "These are all the grandkids here, all boys," Robert says proudly. And then he points to the girls. "And these are all the—" he stops, searching for the word. "What are they?" he asks Sarah. "Great-granddaughters."

"Some days I feel fine," she says, shuffling back to the living room. "I do this, I do that, no aches, no pains. And then some days I can't move at all." Her voice quiets to a whisper. "I make myself go to them," she says of Hunter's wrestling shows.

Robert chimes in. "When she wants to go to wrestling, I'll take her."

CHAPTER 18

Hunter and Billy Ray

"You tell what you want to tell," Hunter had said to Billy Ray when they worked out together in February. They rib each other constantly but for a moment, both were still. Sincere.

"I'm letting him tell what needs to be told," Hunter explained. "It's not my match. It's his match."

"And it might be my last one and it might not," Billy Ray said. "I don't think I'm ever going to use that word 'retire' because I hate it when people say, 'I'm retiring,' and then . . . "

He envisioned an in-ring promo to tee off a 20-minute match

against Hunter, with his nephew, Chop Top, as referee. He'd say he's handing over his title—the greatest light heavyweight on the planet—to Hunter, get a pop from the crowd, and then Hunter would tell him to shut up. "You've never handed me anything," he'd say, and then get in Billy Ray's face. "You made me work for everything." Their story.

But their match had been scheduled and delayed more than once, thanks to scheduling mishaps, and then Billy Ray had torn his tricep practicing with Hunter. Now it was September. The injury had tamped down his workouts. The nerves had curbed his appetite. He'd lost 11 pounds in the last two weeks. They were wrestling 90 miles from home on a holiday weekend in a place where no one has a clue who they are. This was not how Billy Ray had pictured it.

The two-story Macon Arts Center, a windowless event space that provides a stage for regional comedians and R&B acts, stands six miles from Macon's city center, its cracked parking lot ensconced between a Pepsi bottling plant, a heavy equipment rental yard, and an auto auction. A coterie of men carry steel cables, wood boards, and metal posts through the building's heavy metal doors. Around 4 p.m. the pieces and parts become recognizable as a wrestling ring.

The bar sinks have been scrubbed clean. Sunlight pours through propped-open doors, illuminating warm bottles of liquor and empty plastic pitchers. Wrestlers arrive and climb the stairs to the mezzanine overlooking the ring. They sling their bags into corners and giddily descend upon the pool tables, a rare luxury for passing the time until their matches. As far as wrestling venues go, this one is plush.

Hunter grabs a cue from the rack. Justin leans into the table next to him and watches the shot, his red wrestling tights peeking through wide holes in his jeans.

TJ Trigger, a 19-year-old Landmark trainee with a svelte rock-star look, sinks the eight ball. "This is the first time you've ever beat me in something," Hunter says.

They head down to the ring to warm up their bodies but also to test the tightness of the ropes and sturdiness of the mat. Others soon join, drawn to the siren song of the ring racket. Hunter backflips from a post and lands perfectly in the center of the mat. "The ultimate test," he says. "It's good."

Crystal Rose and her trainee Brittany "Taurain" Canup lock up. At 20 minutes before 5 the "Ultimate Pusher" Tyreke, a 5'3" used car salesman, climbs to the corner turnbuckle and poses, in red faux-fur robe and plastic crown. Tonight, he'll be named the King of Macon.

Hunter carries in plastic bins of T-shirts, stickers, and photos and unfolds his merch table. Tonight Billy Ray will do the thing he said he'd never do: attend another of Hunter's shows. And then he'll do something even more unthinkable only a few short years ago: get in the ring with him.

"Where we stashing our stuff at?" he asks when he arrives, a duffel bag slung over his shoulder. It's been a long time since he's arrived to a venue as a performer. He's nervous but tries to play it cool.

Billy Ray had another plan for his dream match with Hunter. When it was time to wrap it up, he'd whisper in his son's ear, "Pin me." He'd never let his kids beat him at anything. They triumphed at a board game or footrace or arm-wrestle only if they were truly better. In the world of professional wrestling storytelling, the words were Billy Ray's way of saying, "You did it. You won. You're better than me."

The culmination of this universal father-child story was one only wrestling could tell, not in words, but in movement. It needed to be felt. Pounded into the mat. It was time.

When he tore his tricep, Billy Ray and Hunter had to rethink the whole thing. Instead of going head-to-head, where there'd be too much pressure on Billy Ray as a solo performer, they'd pair up as a babyface tag team against Chop Top and Jerry Nelms. The match would have meaning: Chop Top was Billy Ray's nephew. Nelms was the guy who, with his brother, Chris, secretly drove Hunter to his first-ever match, in Arkansas. The Nelms brothers had wrestled since Billy Ray's time in the ring, and never left.

Billy Ray and Hunter hatched a new finish: Hunter would powerbomb Billy Ray and roll off him. They'd lay prone alongside each other for a 10-count. An even more perfect ending: Nobody wins.

Billy Ray ran through the match in his head over and over again in the weeks before the show: not just the moves, but what they meant, what wrestling could communicate that words couldn't. Hunter was less concerned. "We're marking something off the list but it's not a passing of the torch," he says before roll-calling the fathers and sons who've shared a ring: Cody and Dusty Rhodes, Ric and David Flair, Dory Funk Sr. with Terry and Dory Jr. "This is our time to have fun." He'd take the heat, send Billy Ray in for the hot tag to hit the shining points, and they'd go home. Not just another gig, but not the match of his life either. It was more for Billy Ray than him.

Sarah and Robert Noblett put on matching Hunter James Brainbuster shirts and drove the two hours to the show. She brought her iPad, her pain patch, and warned Robert not to speed. At the venue, she climbed the stairs to the mezzanine to greet her son and grandsons. “Can one of y’all tie my shoe?” she asked, out of breath.

“I’ll let you do it, babyface,” Justin says. He was happy to let someone else do the bending. He’d been gritting his teeth through the pain of a bulging disc in his lower back, the same condition that forced his father out of the ring.

“Hey, I gotta get over,” Hunter says, and kneels down.

The music is loud and the vibe expectant, like the early hours of a party. The idleness has Billy Ray’s empty stomach in knots. Hunter notices. “How’s the dragons?” he asks.

“I think they’re breeding,” his father says.

“I don’t even remember being this nervous my first match,” Bill Ray says. Reflecting in the days after, he’d correct himself. “I’ve never been that nervous.”

It’s the Saturday of Labor Day weekend, the national champion Georgia Bulldogs have their season opener, at home, and Nelms’s show, which usually runs 70 miles north, is in a new venue in a new territory—all factors that predict a poor showing of fans. Nelms delays the bell in hopes more people will arrive. At 6:20 p.m. some 50 people sit around the ring in a venue with a maximum occupancy of 550.

“Are we ready for some wrestling?” Nelms’s wife, Ricki, tries to hype them.

The crowd, heavily weighted with the friends and families of performers, seems tired. “That’s the worst sound in the world,” Billy Ray, watching from above, says, before disappearing to the bathroom again.

He peers over the railing to the ring below and the memories flood in. Himself as a kid at the Omni. As a 21-year-old in the ring. He knew how to work the crowd because he knew what it felt like to be in it. "What a ride," he says, finally, his eyes focused on the ring.

Soon, it's go time.

Billy Ray spits the nicotine pouch he's had tucked in his bottom lip into the trash. "Don't blow up,"* Hunter says to him.

The staccato snare drum and guitar licks of the Poison song "I Want Action" take over the space and Hunter descends the stairs to the ring. Alone at the top of the mezzanine stairway, Billy Ray jumps in place, shakes his hands like they're wet, paces back and forth, and eventually lets out a primal whoop. Then he smiles a knowing smile. He's back.

The small crowd gets loud as Hunter preens around the ring in green tights, gold-sequin tailcoat, and title belt.

"I may not be the nicest guy all the time," he says into the mic, acknowledging his bad-guy character for anyone here who knows him, and there's at least one: "Oh my god, we know all about that!" a woman yells.

"But tonight's a little different," he continues. "Because for the first time in six years," he slows down, gets louder. "Somebody's coming for a fight in Macon, Georgia!"

The match hadn't even started and already it had departed from the plan. Typically heels come out first. The plan was for Chop Top and Jerry—the bad guys—to wait in the ring for Hunter and Billy Ray. But Hunter's music came on first. And when your music hits, you move.

A wrestler relies less on storytelling and more on moves and blatant displays of character when he performs in road shows.

---

* Blow up: become visibly exhausted during a match.

But tonight there's a story that doesn't need months of exposure to understand, a universal tale of a father and son.

"My tag team partner tonight, weighing in at 190 pounds," Hunter yells, inflating Billy Ray's weight. "The guy that raised me, the guy that, well, put me in these boots," he says, speaking to the crowd not as Hollywood Hunter James, but as a 20-year-old about to wrestle the person who taught him everything he knows. And then he crescendos. "My dad, Jamey Dean! Play his music!"

In jeans and a decade-old Superman "S" shirt, Billy Ray raises his arms and showboats around the ring as the party-rock anthem of his life obscures everything around him.

Jenn and Sarah stand next to each other near one corner of the ring, following him with their cell phone cameras as he fist-bumps fans who have no idea who he is. Robert stands, smiles, and claps.

Billy Ray turns the corner and mimes a bow to Sarah. He hugs her, kisses Jenn on the cheek, and eyes the ring. In one swift move he catapults himself up, sliding feetfirst beneath the bottom rope, a standard entrance that was second nature three decades ago but now proves difficult. He wobbles, steadies himself, and smiles, then locks eyes with Hunter. Hunter smiles, shakes his head. "Grab a hold, old man," he says. In wrestling, the words mean slow down. "Aww hell," Billy Ray says. This won't be as easy as it was all those years ago.

Hunter leans toward his father. "How does it feel?" he asks.

Everything was right where Billy Ray had left it. He answered with the first words that came to mind. "Like home."

Chop Top and Jerry deliver a sneak attack before the bell rings. Billy Ray and Hunter send them out of the ring with a double hip toss, then celebrate with a synchronized strut, a nod to the '80s era tag team The Fantastics.

"Y'all done playing dress-up?" Hunter ribs, loud enough for them to hear.

He swivels his hips, Ravishing Rick Rude–style, toward Chop Top and Jerry. Billy Ray throws his head back, laughing.

"They scared!" Hunter yells. And then again, from the other side of the ring. "They scared!" the audience yells back.

Hunter directs the crowd like a dolphin trainer, starting chants, throwing his arms in the air, and stomping his foot to set them in motion. It works.

He locks up with Chop Top, then delivers an armbreaker. "Break it, Hunter! Break it!" someone yells. Hunter twirls his cousin around and then snaps his bicep over his shoulder. Justin reverses the move.

"Let's go Hollywood!" Billy Ray hollers from the corner.

Free from his cousin's hold, Hunter addresses the crowd again.

"We want to see Dad in here, don't we?" he yells.

Hunter tags Billy Ray in.

"Still got it, old man?" Jerry asks out loud before they lock up.

Hunter climbs to the top of the turnbuckle after starting another chant, this time for Billy Ray. "He's still got it!" he yells, setting off the crowd again. Billy Ray toe taps from side to side like a boxer, raises his arms into the air and asks for more. Hunter cues the fans once more.

"Jamey Dean! Jamey Dean!"

In the ring, in blue jeans, that's the place he feels the most alive, the most valuable. The throb of his tricep, the pain of his 50-year-old body slamming onto the mat, momentarily disappears.

Billy Ray delivers a stinger splash and a spot where he pretends to grab a handful of Chop Top's chest hair, then tags Hunter in. Hunter carries the rest of the match. Again and again Hunter reaches across the ring for Billy Ray's hand and gets blocked—a charade to protect his injured father.

It was the dropkick that did it. Billy Ray pushed himself up from the floor after delivering the move and instinctively reached for his arm in pain. For most of the match's remaining minutes, he stood outside the ropes, his left arm hanging limp by his side. He watched his son revel in glory, alone. It was all he could do.

Student becomes master. Son becomes caretaker. Hunter's goal had been to make sure his father left the ring as healthy as he could be. He took the heat. Hunter gives Chop Top the brainbuster, the ref counts him out, and the announcer declares Hunter and Billy Ray the victors.

Hunter hangs the belt over his left shoulder and sits on the bottom rope beneath the turnbuckle, panting. Chop Top lies prone in the other corner. It's Billy Ray's turn now. Shirtless, glistening with sweat, his chest rising and falling faster than the beat of the music, Billy Ray paces the ring with mic in hand and waits for the crowd to quiet. Hunter bows his head.

"Twenty-eight years ago I started wrestling," he says, still breathless. "And then came along this child."

"I never made it to where I wanted to be," he says, laying himself bare. "I never had my moment! My WrestleMania moment." Hunter watches, shakes the hair out of his eyes, lays a hand over the belt.

"But you know what I did get to do?" Billy Ray asks, circling the ring.

"I did, one time, get to tag team with the future of this business!" His voice is loud now. He points a finger at Hunter.

"He is the hardest working man I've ever seen in my freaking life," Billy Ray says to his son. "I see what he does every day. Am I jealous of him? Hell no! Am I envious? Yes. Because I wish I was as determined as him."

Hunter, still sitting in the corner of the ring, lays the belt between his boots and then returns his gaze to his dad.

"Son, there aren't going to be a lot of times I get to see you in these small places anymore," Billy Ray continues. "But when you main-event 'Mania my ass will be in the front row. Kid, I love you more than anything in this world," he says, his voice cracking.

Standing on tiptoe, he wraps his arms around Hunter.

It was a wrestling promo, each word forcefully delivered and propped up by pathos. No piano-driven sports-movie score played in the background. No camera zoomed in on the tears welling in Hunter's eyes. Every day of their lives, Billy Ray tells his sons he loves them. But wrestling imparts something a perfunctory sentence can't.

Hunter climbs to the top of the turnbuckle, sends his hand, with two fingers up, toward the sky, his go-to victory salute. Billy Ray falls to his knees in the opposite corner, sits back on his heels and lowers his head as if he were next to a grave. Rendered immobile by emotions only wrestling can unlock, he breathes it in. This breath could be the last he has inside a ring. He takes another.

CHAPTER 19

Billy Ray completes Hunter's sentences as they break down their match in the living room eight days later. Two Band-Aids on Hunter's forehead cover the razor-blade slice he self-inflicted last night at Hardcore Hell 25. Hunter shies away from blading,* for the most part. "It's cheap," he says. A skill-less way to get a crowd reaction. It's another Billy Ray–ism he perpetuated from father to son. "You know why people do all the highflying shit?" Billy Ray is known to say. "Because they can't wrestle. You know why they do the hardcore shit? Because they can't wrestle."

Hunter opened the show by defending the Anarchy Heritage Championship belt in what *Georgia Wrestling History* later reported fans had named the "the show stealer," only to be told, in a perfect tee-up, he would defend it again in the main event, "Azrael's Steel Cage of Violence Gauntlet Match." The melee uti-

* Blading: intentionally cutting oneself in the ring, usually on the forehead and with a razor blade tucked into wrist tape.

lized a two-by-four, a pizza paddle, wood skewers, and a metal trash can lid. Billy Buck threw Azrael through a barbed-wire-wrapped table from the top rope, eliciting a coveted "Holy shit" chant from the crowd. In the end, Landmark's longtime babyface hero, Jacob Ashworth, took the belt.

This morning, Hunter soaked his white trunks in cold water to remove stains from the blood that trickled down from his forehead, and from the foreheads of other wrestlers. "I refuse to not wear white when I'm gonna bleed," he says. "Because I'm going to show it off."

Hunter leans back in a recliner and pulls up his and Billy Ray's match on the wall-mounted TV. On the screen, he wiggles and flips like a fish at the end of a hook, trying to free himself from his cousin's grip. "I just try to move around and create space, like we did in amateur wrestling," he says, narrating the action. "You have to move to create the opening. Space is the—"

"Enemy," Billy Ray interjects.

On the screen, Billy Ray chops Jerry in the chest. "Where the hell did that come from?" Hunter asks.

"I told you," Billy Ray says. "It's instinct. That's all I can do now."

In the days after the match Billy Ray ruminated as he watched his injured arm turn purple. He wasn't satisfied. "I owe him that match," he says. "And I owe me looking better so I can close that book." He won't be satisfied until he, in top physical shape, locks up with Hunter in the ring.

After the show that night Billy Ray swallowed some pain pills, got in the passenger side of the Jeep, and rode with Jenn to Tybee Island.

The fans wanted dives in Hunter's match against Chop Top, later in the night, Hunter says, but he didn't deliver. "Because I didn't get paid that night," he says caustically, jiggling crushed ice in an oversized Styrofoam cup from Sonic.

Billy Ray and Hunter return to commentating their match, roll-calling the origin of each move like sommeliers sniffing out terroir.

"Shawn Michaels," Hunter says. "Kerry Von Erich." "Bobby Eaton." "Mike Tyson, WrestleMania 14."

Billy Ray chimes in. "Some Dusty Rhodes punches."

"I guess The Rock too, if you think about it," Hunter says.

On the TV Hunter climbs the turnbuckle, preparing to back-flip into a superkick. Chop Top comes at him. "He always comes in charging so quick when I get into the corners," Hunter complains. "Let me turn around, then come at me," he says, as if his cousin can hear. "Then I can give you an elbow or something." The moves must come in a logical order. When the action is rushed, it doesn't appear real. "Why am I throwing an elbow if I don't see you coming?"

"I need nicotine," Billy Ray says and goes to the kitchen counter for a pouch.

Hunter continues his critique. "I wish one of those guys would have been more vocal," he says. "You threw me in the post and then put me in a headlock. If you throw me in the post why aren't you working my shoulder?"

"Jerry puts the Master Lock in."

Billy Ray laughs. "You call it the Master Lock?"

"Hey! It is the Master Lock!"

"*Pfesh.* The full nelson's been around forever."

Same story, different title.

Billy Ray looks lost in the match. "Your enzuigiri kick's really good," he says to Hunter.

They watch as Billy Ray pushes himself up from the dropkick.

"That's when I knew you were hurt," Hunter says. "Your voice changed."

The injury dictated the tenor of the rest of the match: Hunter would lead, taking the brunt of the heat to keep Billy Ray from getting further injured. "I did the best I could to copy his powerslam," Hunter says.

Through subtle differences in its form and velocity, the powerslam conveys a wrestler's style and personality. It's the little black dress of wrestling. There's a million ways to wear it. Hunter's is more of a quick-snap move, the way Randy Orton does it. Billy Ray's looks more like Buzz Sawyer's. Or, as Billy Ray puts it, "Mine is like a Ferris wheel. His is like a quick car wreck in NASCAR."

They watch Ricki Nelms come to the ring with the microphone.

"No idea what I was going to say," Billy Ray says.

Then Billy Ray watches himself direct words at Hunter that two years ago he couldn't fathom. For a few moments in the living room, father and son say nothing at all.

Billy Ray breaks the silence. "That was my favorite moment in wrestling," he says. "Ever."

CHAPTER 20

The first weekend in November, Hunter drove to Nashville with Triston's husband, Rick, and another up-and-coming star, Alexander Lev, for an NWA taping.

Rick uses his gig with NWA to promote his own protégés. On this occasion, he brought his two most promising performers, Hunter and Lev. Both blond, under 21, regulars at the same Georgia promotions, and increasingly good friends, thanks to the many hours they had spent training, talking, and texting. Lev wears eyeliner and runs with a straightedge emo/goth gimmick, calling himself The Messiah and shaming fans and wrestlers for being "addicted" and "unfaithful." Hunter keeps a running tally of monikers—Absolute Wunderkind, Varsity One, Future Legend—all aligned with his straightforward persona, the cocky, pretty-boy jock.

Lev, the son of Polish immigrants who moved to America when he was 2, didn't grow up in sports and lacks the institutional knowledge of a lifelong wrestling fan. He graduated high school in 2022, a year after Hunter, and spent two weeks at

Georgia's Kennesaw State University before dropping out. He trained with QT Marshall at the Nightmare Factory and found his way to Landmark Arena. Now he lives with Rick and Triston in the guest bedroom that has, over the years, housed many a wayward wrestler.

"We know something is going to happen for one of us or both of us," Hunter said, before the trip. "I know this is going to sound egotistical, but I think he's crazy if he doesn't sign me," he added, about NWA owner Billy Corgan.

Lev had a look but lacked organization and experience. Rick deputized Hunter to keep him in check. "Make sure he eats and tans," Rick said when Hunter dropped him off at Nashville's Skyway Studios, where a live-audience taping of *Powerrr* would start in a few hours.

For months fans had speculated on rumors of a network deal for NWA that would bring its content beyond its YouTube channel. Finally the company announced *Powerrr* would debut on The CW app early the next year. Its reality series, *Billy Corgan's Adventures in Carnyland*, would join it in May.

Hunter and Lev arrived at the studio around 11:30 to a confident Rick bearing an urgent message: "Y'all have a match." Hunter would pair with another indie wrestler, Adrian Thomas. Lev would team with Jackson Drake. Rick's connection to the company had worked. His top acolytes would go against each other in front of NWA's top brass.

Theirs was number No. 2 out of 18 filmed that day. Hunter hit a nice dropkick, jumped as high as he could for the elbow drop, and tagged Thomas in. He and Drake kick-fought, the tempo picked up. Lev cut off Thomas, bringing the heat, Hunter threw a hard clothesline, then his powerslam, and signaled for his brainbuster. Drake charged him to the corner, Lev tagged in. Hunter went upside down in the double suplex. As soon as his feet touched the ground he picked Lev up for his finisher. Lev wasn't ready, didn't jump. Hunter hoisted him again, dropped, and pinned him.

The way Hunter remembers it, NWA's heavyweight champion at the time, EC3, was impressed. So was director Billy Trask. Multiple wrestlers complimented him. "And it wasn't just, 'Hey guys, good stuff,'" Hunter says. "I know that's bullshit." They commented on specific moves. "Your powerslam's too pretty for someone to kick out of," Hunter remembers EC3 saying, watching from his post next to Billy Corgan. Hunter left feeling confident.

Two weeks later, the trio packed up and road-tripped to Sarasota for NWA's "Return to Robarts," a *Powerrr* taping in an arena fans would recognize as the site of countless Championship Wrestling from Florida (CWF) shows in the '70s and '80s.

There'd been some confusion in the weeks leading up to the event. In his texts to Rick, Corgan used Hunter's name but described Lev. Rick brought them both.

On the way they stopped in Tampa for an NWA affiliate show put on by NWA wrestler Bryan Idol. For the second time, Lev tagged with Drake. Hunter sipped an energy drink in the locker room, trying to push through the drudge of an oncoming cold.

The next morning, in Sarasota, they got their assignment: Lev and Drake would appear as tag partners again, against Hunter and the NWA-rostered wrestler Chris Silvio. Silvio would take the lead.

They hung backstage and awaited further instructions. Lev got called up for another match. Hunter didn't.

Three days later, Hunter reflected. "I'm not really sure what's going on with NWA. People like Sal and Judais say it should be a no-brainer that I should be there. I don't know if Billy Corgan just doesn't see it?"

Lev and Hunter's gimmicks couldn't be farther away on the continuum of wrestling tropes. "Billy Corgan is in love with the weirdness of Lev," Hunter speculates. "That's the only thing I can think of."

It's about who you know but also what they're after.

In the days after, Hunter grappled with the reality: Lev was rising in NWA's ranks. He was getting left behind. "I know what I'm capable of and I know what Lev's capable of, and Lev's nowhere near the level I am."

Frustration set in again. "The problem is that everyone always hypes me up when it comes to AWE, WWE, Impact, whatever. They're always like, you're gonna get signed from this. And then nope, I'm on my way home back to my Friday to Sunday gigs and nothing happens."

Hunter wouldn't give up entirely on NWA, but he'd take it into his own hands. He emailed NWA's head of talent relations, Pat Kenny, links to three matches that reflect his versatility. The one where he took the title from Judais with a dirty finish. "A gimmick match, with intensity." His 8-minute match with "The Flying Fro" Michael Walker. "Screech and Zack Morris going at it. Smooth, no wasted motion." Hunter James v. Marcus Adams. Nearly 30 minutes long. He hits all his favorite moves.

And then he returned to what he does best, working hard, now with even more intensity. *They don't want me now,* he thought. *They will.*

"Sir.

Son.

Superstar.

Hollywood,"

Chris Nelms wrote in a message to Hunter, a few weeks later.

Hunter knew right away that Nelms had seen the Nashville NWA match, which meant NWA had put it online. He hadn't heard anything from anyone at the company. Nelms sent a photo of him and Hunter in the ring and asked him to autograph it. Hunter agreed, with a cry-laughing emoji. It was the ego boost he thirsted for, a tiny slurp of success to push him another hundred miles.

"A Hollywood Premiere at 25:30," Hunter wrote on Facebook with a link to Episode 135 of *NWA Powerrr.*

Nelms used the news to hype GCW. The little show with the big name he ran inside the skating rink suddenly had star power, times two. "GCW stars Hunter James and Alexander Lev make their NWA debut! Check it out and see them both in action Dec 23rd!" he wrote on GCW's Facebook page, above a link to the video.

Hunter turned 21 the next day, went to work, then legally bought a bottle of tequila. That weekend his parents took him to Harrah's Casino in Cherokee, North Carolina. Billy Ray drove and Hunter sat in the backseat designing a magazine cover–inspired flyer on his phone, situating his accolades—GWH Best Male Performer, Sponsored by Future Legend Apparel—below gold script of his name, Hollywood Hunter James. He peers from behind a pair of aviators in a black-and-white photo, the top half of his tightfitting, short-sleeved button shirt open, dollar bills tucked into his belt. As they traveled north, Hunter tweaked the design.

He later posted it on Facebook, along with photos of his new illustrated shirt design in four colorways and a link to purchase them from *prowrestlingtees.com* for $24.99 each.

New "HOLLYWOOD Red Carpet" and "HOLLYWOOD Magazine" T-shirts available in the link below! Walk Across

HOLLYWOOD Boulevard and Strut on Down the Red Carpet with a New Hunter James shirt Today!!

By now, Billy Ray and Hunter watched wrestling on TV together at home, with Billy Ray critiquing and Hunter taking mental notes. In the between times Hunter asked for body advice. "Does my back need to be wider? Does my chest need to be bigger? Do my shoulders look like I work them? Are my arms coming along?"

What he really wanted was to ask those questions to someone with power. "I can do whatever," he says, driving to the gym and speaking about his body as if he were a carpenter considering a piece of cherrywood. "I just don't know what to do. So I always just assume get bigger because we're in the wrestling business." Bodies matter. He learned that from Billy Ray.

A month earlier he succeeded in pulling off the complicated act of turning babyface in one of his regular shows, PCW. Heel turns are easy—one heinous act and it's done. Becoming a babyface takes more convincing. In wrestling as in life, you have to build the audience's trust.

It goes back to that unspoken agreement between the people in the ring and those around it. If a wrestler is convincing in the execution of his job, the fans will follow his cues. It's part of the deal, an invisible handshake. Real-world injuries are the easiest path from bad guy to good. Nobody's going to boo someone who's been out for six months with a broken tibia.

When Triple H returned to the ring on January 7, 2002, eight months after a brutal quad tear, the sold-out crowd inside Madison Square Garden got to its feet. America still shivered from the September 11 attacks. Wrestling fans were unmoored by Stone Cold Steve Austin's heel turn and The Rock's departure to Hollywood. And then, on that fateful night, Triple H made everything right. In jeans, leather jacket, denim vest, and soaking-wet, shoulder-length hair, he was Perseverance. Brute American Strength. If the roof was vibrating during his triumphant entrance, it blew off when he ripped off his shirt and pummeled Kurt Angle.

Teaming with a babyface is another way to win hearts. The warming of the Cold War had diminished the potency of Russian villains by 1986, when Nikita Koloff paired up with Dusty Rhodes to take on The Four Horsemen. Or, a heel can turn on his bad-guy backers, as was the case in 1999 when The Rock disbanded The Corporation, a heel faction eerily headed by the McMahons.

Hunter always pictured himself as a heel, not a babyface, but he knew he could incorporate some bad-guy moves into his good-guy character. He learned that from Billy Ray, too. Their hero, Shawn Michaels, balanced the act. So did Eddie Guerrero ("Lie! Cheat! Steal!") and Hulk Hogan.

"I haven't had an adrenaline rush like that in so long," Hunter said of making the turn. There's the feeling of satisfaction when you leave the ring knowing you had an outstanding match. This was different, better, the thrill of opening a whole new box of toys.

A babyface can be creative on offensive moves. Heels are straight to the point, no ducking and dodging. The babyface's rubric is built on fighting back.

"Babyface Hunter in my eyes is still going to be cocky," Hunter says. "He's going to cheat a little bit."

"Babyface Hunter James is dangerous."

CHAPTER 21

Some 200 people fill the Boys & Girls Club by 7 p.m. on December 16, 2023, for Southern Fried's holiday show, Season's Beatings. A short, round man in a Santa suit and beard stands in front of a fake tree dressed in white ribbons and lights and jingles bells between photos with wrestling fans. The sound meets the smell of warm nacho cheese and popcorn wafting from the concession stand. Wrestler Nick Halen's girlfriend, Sabrina, and their kids sell homemade cookies in one corner of the gym. "Rockin' Around the Christmas Tree" fades into "Fancy Like" on the PA.

The last time fans gathered here it was Thanksgiving night. Hunter teamed with Triston to kick his partner, Xavier Reyes, out of JBE, the tag team named for their spitfire preacher manager Dr. Joseph Brock.

Tonight he's booked for a spot—a brief appearance to move a story along—rather than a match, so rather than tights or trunks Hunter wears snug white jeans and a light-blue button-up shirt, still creased from its packaging. White threads bind the back flaps of his navy blazer, a garment he's never had the occasion to wear.

In the locker room, Triston sports Hunter's newest shirt. It depicts him shirtless, six-packed, and blond, arms hanging over two high-heeled women on a palm-flanked red carpet.

"Be sure to take the tag off before we go out," Triston says, noticing the price tag on Hunter's jacket. Hunter lifts his arms, looks down, searching. "It's on the sleeve," Triston says. "See? If I was an asshole I'd let him go out there like that."

Jacob Ashworth, a welder by day and one of north Georgia's most beloved native sons of wrestling, who has consistently performed around the state since starting his career at 16, in 2005, sits in the corner with his girlfriend, Lacey, who uses the idle time to knit a blanket out of camouflage yarn. In the same way a song and its singer can reflect a place and its people so too can a wrestler. Jacob Ashworth is Northeast Georgia. Honorable and hardworking, weathered hands, soft heart.

Ashworth's big break came at WrestleMania 27 in 2011, when he stood in a row with a dozen other shield-wielding performers who made up Triple H's gladiator-themed entrance to face The Undertaker in a no-holds-barred match at the Georgia Dome.

When Ashworth comes to the ring in Monroe, fans stand in reverential applause as if he were a wounded soldier coming home. In a way, he is. The ring has injured him over the years. So has his work as a welder, a trade the wrestler Slim J taught him when they both worked at a commercial door supplier.

Ashworth's belly is rounder, his hair thinner than it was in 2011. None of that matters. Wrestling's about respect, and he's earned it.

Ashworth's father raised him, in Royston, Georgia—birthplace of baseball legend Ty Cobb and consistently listed, along with Monroe, among the poorest places in the state. Until he met Lacey, he too was a single father.

"Hey, I love how the shirts look just like you," he says to Hunter. "He looks like Buc-ee Beaver though," Hunter says, ribbing Triston. They all laugh.

"I hope you trip getting into the ring, you fuck," Triston says back to him, deadpan.

"This is the shit I put up with, and that's my best friend," Triston adds, for the entire room to hear.

It's the kind of affectionate insult volleyed between people who love each other, and it echoes the reason why they're all here: to be roughed up to the point of endearment, not annihilation.

Hollywood Hunter James remains a heel at Southern Fried. Problem is, over time people come to love wrestlers they see at every show. It's hard to hate someone who puts in the work. Appear enough times, consecutively, as Hunter has at Southern Fried for the past two-and-a-half years, and no matter how mean you are people will eventually cheer for you, seeing through the gimmick to the person who, weekend after weekend, spends his Saturday night entertaining you.

In their performance, Hunter and Triston deftly navigate a complicated human phenomenon: balancing multiple versions of the self. Every day we decide which gimmick to bring to the show. We play to the crowd. Amp up one part of us while silencing another. We present the version of ourselves the crowd wants to see, the one they react to, the one they want us to be.

Fans have a lot to do with shaping a wrestler's gimmick. "It's so hard to be able to keep all the heat you've gotten when everybody loves what he does," Triston says. "And no matter if I try to be the biggest dick in the world, there's gonna be people cheering for him. He's fun to watch."

"Hard to keep heat when you're fucking good," Triston concludes. He looks at Hunter, feigning annoyance. Hunter gloats. "Faggot," Triston says, lovingly dismissing him.

Triston grew up outside Houma, Louisiana, running wild with three cousins and a brother.

"I'm gay," he said to his family as they sat around the table one Thanksgiving when he was a teenager. Then he picked his mother's cigarettes up off the table and went outside for a smoke. His grandfather gave him a knife to protect himself with. "If you have to stab somebody do it three ways," he instructed. "Deep, wide, and continuously, to make them bleed out."

"Cajun mentality," Triston recalls. He's home on a rare week off from his day job at Dollar Tree. An openly gay wrestler in the South, he's never had to use it.

Triston's biological father, Elvis, left his mother when he found out she was pregnant with him. "Really, truly, he's a bastard," Triston says. His stepfather, David, overdosed when Triston was 20. "He was a good man when he wasn't high," he says.

Triston grew up in the '90s renting VHS wrestling tapes from the local video store. He loved watching referees like Joey Marella, Earl and Dave Hebner, Mike Chioda, and Danny Davis. The power they possessed captivated him. So when he started training at 19, after moving in with a man in Mobile, Alabama, he knew he wanted to referee. Eight months into it he was working main events, overseeing matches between wrestlers like Glacier and Brutus "The Barber" Beefcake. The first time he got in the ring, he felt like he had arrived at the place he was destined to be. "It's really truly an addiction," he says.

Triston moved to Andalusia, Louisiana, where his mother

managed a motel, then later to Pensacola, where he honed his craft. One day Rick Michaels called. Another openly gay Georgia wrestler, Simon Sermon, had told Rick about Triston, thinking Triston would be an asset to the Georgia scene, and also that Rick might like him. After a few conversations they lost touch. And then, after a Florida promoter offered to pay Triston with a handful of Somas, Triston headed north.

He got a ride to Atlanta and stayed with a friend. Within minutes of announcing his new home on Facebook, Rick messaged him. If you can get to Peachstate Wrestling Alliance, I can get you a spot, he wrote. Triston met Rick for the first time at the show. "March 13, 2013," Triston recalls without hesitation. "We've been inseparable ever since."

In Georgia, Triston found a much more professional scene. To explain the difference he borrows a line from manager Bobby "The Brain" Heenan. "Comparing the Georgia scene to the Alabama and Florida scene is like comparing ice cream to horse manure."

Sarcastic, with a bone-dry sense of humor, Triston grew up on insult comedy—Don Rickles first, and then Bianca Del Rio. "It was a natural fit for me to become a manager and antagonize people and get them riled up, so I can transfer the heat to my guys—to Hunter."

"People are starting to like him more," Triston explains. "But now that he has me, anytime they start cheering for him, I can shut that shit down."

Controlling people's emotions is an amazing feeling, Triston says. "I will look at somebody, pick out their faults, and just mercilessly attack them."

If a fan uses Triston's sexuality as an insult, he *will* fuck with them. He is so good at drawing heat that more than once, Rick has asked him to step back from managing because he worries about fans retaliating.

"Rick hates that I did this," Triston says, laughing, before he tells the story. A 5-year-old kid at a show kept calling him a faggot. "Good parenting, you toothless bitch!" he said to the kid's grandmother. "She got hot, tried to come after me," he says. He laughs again. "It was around Christmastime, and this kid . . . , 'faggot, faggot, faggot.' Finally, I had enough."

"Hey kid," Triston said, inviting the child to come close. "I got two secrets for you. One, you're adopted and your mama don't love you. Two, Santa Claus isn't real." Power.

Playing a character prevents him from taking it too far. Instead of stabbing someone out of anger, he goes after them verbally, insulting their most visible characteristics: extra pounds, a gimpy leg, an oxygen tank, a lazy eye. "You pick on me, I'm going to find out what really ticks you."

The worse his week goes, the more aggressive he becomes in his role. "Everything is transferred out of my body, thanks to wrestling," he says. At 13, he was diagnosed with bipolar disorder. His mother stopped administering the prescribed lithium when he became disturbingly lethargic. Triston credits wrestling with helping his mental health.

"Everywhere I turn, there's wrestling. Everything we do, there's wrestling. And be honest with you I wouldn't have it any other way. This is my life," he says.

He met Hunter when Hunter came with Chop Top to Landmark Arena. Triston and Rick watched from the wings. "The kid's just doing everything, bebopping around," Triston recalls. Rick watched, then looked at Triston. "That's our next AJ," he said.

Hunter's quick wit matched Triston's, and they became fast friends. Triston approached Todd Sexton about teaming up with a heel at Southern Fried just as Hunter started his ascension. The straight young stud and his bombastic gay manager premiered together early in 2022.

Hunter asks Triston to give his outfit a look. "You like the color scheme?" he asks. Triston approves.

"I was going for North Carolina Tar Heel vibes," Hunter says.

"Oh yeah, you look like a douche."

"You didn't wear it last night so it works," Ashworth chimes in, picking up his singlet and giving the crotch a whiff.

Hunter laughs. "That's the most wrestling thing I've ever heard."

"I'm not getting in the ring with someone with stinky gear," Ashworth says. "It's disrespectful."

"We don't do stinky heat," Triston says, shaking his head.

Thirty minutes into the show Hunter delivers a different kind of cheap heat to his old tag teammate, Xavier Reyes, who he unceremoniously dismissed at the last show.

"Ladies and gentlemen, would you please welcome, accompanied to the ring by the Guiding Light Triston Michaels, he is Georgia Wrestling's 2022 Male Performer of the Year, here is Hollywood Hunter James!" announcer Rick Richards says. Poison's "I Want Action" competes with the cheers, squeals, and boos.

Hunter struts toward the ring, ignoring the fans along the barricade like a horse with blinders on, stopping only to showboat in front of amateur photographer Bob McAteer's camera. Phyllis Britt, a school bus driver who grew up watching wrestling with her mother, is on her feet next to her daughter and granddaughter. Another regular named Jeff Mooney, in a faded SFCW wrestling T-shirt and wrestling mask, pushes an industrial trashcan on casters around like a dance partner. Chunk, in Zubaz and his letter jacket, stands up behind Hunter's merch table, iPhone up, capturing it all.

Hunter moves quickly around the ring with Triston trailing him. He holds an all-but-finished glass bottle of Cheerwine—echoing the prop he used in the James Dean–inspired photo he turned into a faux magazine cover.

Triston takes the mic. "Hey, stupid! I'm going to give you an early Christmas present on how to introduce somebody," he says. "Ladies and gentleman, from the Outer Banks of North Carolina, I give you Hollywood Hunter James!"

Hunter opens his coat to reveal chest hair above his half-buttoned shirt. Triston has a mustache and a Joe Exotic–style bowl haircut, except natural brown and missing the mullet. He hands the mic to Hunter.

"When a plot twist happens they always ask, 'Why, Hunter, why?'" he bellows. He explains the reason he turned on Xavier: He's not in his league. But really, it's because fans were starting to cheer for Hunter and Xavi. Having him turn on his partner reaffirmed Hunter's role as a heel and set Xavi on a new path as a babyface. "Xavier Reyes is just a star on my walk of fame," Hunter growls. "And it's my footprint that's keeping him down!" Triston scuffs his feet in the ring. Hunter pivots to address the camera. "And it will keep him down until the day that I end up on the grandest stage of them all."

The crowd spots Xavi staring Hunter down from the curtain. Hunter throws off his jacket and squats, fists up, fight-ready. Xavi dives into the ring, Hunter leaps out—a cowardly heel move. Xavi blows his nose in Hunter's jacket. "That thousand-dollar sport coat!" color commentator Adam Vance says before Hunter retreats.

Alone with the crowd Xavi asks the fans, "You want me to kick his ass?" They affirm.

Tetchi Makuji, bare-chested with a painted face and the words Merry Christmas Matha! painted on his chest, meets him at the curtain and beats him back to the ring. Makuji breathes his blinding green mist into Reyes's face and presses him to the mat with a Shiranagi lock, his version of Haku's Tongan Death Grip.

With Xavi in submission, Hunter climbs to the ring. Triston hands him a set of hair clippers. Tetchi lifts Xavi's lifeless body up by the shoulders. A partially retired sanitation worker named Robert Mathews leans into the barricade and watches, nodding his head in satisfaction as he dips a hand into a bag of popcorn.

Reyes, a chemistry teacher and amateur wrestling coach at a high school 15 miles away, has allowed for the scalping. His last day teaching, before Christmas break, was yesterday.

Hunter carves rows into Reyes's head. Clumps of dark brown hair fall to the mat.

"Who knew Hunter James went to the Ed Leslie School of Haircutting?" Grillo asks from the commentators' table.

"Absolute trash," Vance says.

Haircutting and head shaving demand their own wing in the library of wrestling stunts. Grillo's Ed Leslie reference is to Leslie's career as Brutus "The Barber" Beefcake, who brought a pair of oversized haircutting scissors (actually garden shears) to the ring. Brutus may be the most popular trimmer in professional wrestling, but he's not alone.

It's one of those undeniably authentic feats of professional wrestling. You can't fake cutting someone's hair. Donald Trump and Bobby Lashley shaved Vince McMahon bald after Lashley beat Umaga in 2007's Battle of the Billionaires. Rey Mysterio scalped CM Punk in 2010. Furious fans pressed up against the chain-link cage inside Memphis's Mid-South Coliseum after the 1987 steel cage hair match between Austin Idol and Jerry "The King" Lawler.

So in an instant, inside the Boys & Girls Club on a Saturday night in December, Hunter is affirmed as a heel and Xavier is christened babyface. Hunter's music—Billy Ray's music—plays again, and he raises the clippers to the sky like a sword.

A security guard shuffles to the ring with broom and dustpan to clean up the mess. Xavier, delirious, shuffles off, his arms supported by two other guards.

Georgia Wrestling History's Larry Goodman clutches his notepad and watches. "They're bound and determined to get these people to boo Hunter," he says. "They don't want to boo Hunter." Goodman wears a T-shirt he got more than two decades ago, a souvenir from a Christmas show at Nashville Municipal Auditorium in 1999. Bob McAteer, the photographer, stands next to him. A metro Atlanta resident since the early aughts, he works in the Supreme Court of Georgia's IT department but grew up going to wrestling shows at Los Angeles's Grand Olympic Auditorium. He recently discovered the *Georgia Wrestling History* website, connected with Larry, and got involved.

Run-DMC's "Christmas in Hollis" opens another match. Rob Adonis, the high school drama teacher who trained WWE Superstar Xavier Woods, and fellow Southern Fried regular Bobby Moore wait in the ring. Sal Rinauro and Sunny Daze, in a Santa T-shirt, walk toward them. Sal offers exaggerated handshakes to the kids along the barricade. A Santa chant erupts. It's a community that transcends walls. Referees, security guards, fans, wrestlers: everyone plays a part.

Chunk sits alone behind two rows of autographed Hunter James 8×10s. A rack of Hunter James T-shirts hang behind him.

At 9:30 he starts packing the merchandise into a One Hour Tees box, carefully slipping the photos into a flex binder.

Billy Ray's been making him lift, a punishment for not doing well at school and motivation to improve his rank on the wrestling team. He worked his biceps so much recently he couldn't lift a 5-pound weight. Another tough love story for the family's tome. Billy Ray's been watching him at practice and driving him to and from tournaments across the state. Chunk quiets. Stares at the ring. "In a couple years I'll be doing this," he says, at last.

CHAPTER 22

Hunter wears a pink oxford shirt beneath a white sports coat and stands on the deck of his parents' house early in January 2024. His address to Jacob Ashworth, who will attempt to take the Landmark Heritage title Hunter's had for a year, unfolds over tintype-filtered footage of his triumphs. "The Landmark Arena's gone," he says, while images of its locked chain link fence populate the screen. "I'm taking this championship for my personal collection."

Ashworth's social media address—all legacy and grit—

unfolds in a dark room next to the "10 Commandments of Why We Wrestle" and a Church of Southern Wrestling sign. "It's not going to be a wrestling match, it's gonna be a fight," he threatens.

The famed promotion, which had been without a home since frozen pipes took out the beloved Landmark Arena the year before, would return, temporarily, to the Boys & Girls Club in Monroe, Georgia, on the first Saturday of January. The ramshackle building is as much a character in Georgia wrestling as the people who performed in it, and now it would return to the story. All its championships would be on the line. Nick Halen and Judais would vie for the heavyweight title in the main-event ladder match. Hunter would attempt to win back the Landmark Heritage Championship from Jacob Ashworth. Other familiar faces of Georgia wrestling filled out the lineup, from 5′7″ Najasism to 6′8″ Geter.

A few weeks ahead of their match, Hunter sent Ashworth, in loose order, a list of moves he thought would work well in the match. It read like a cross between court stenographer shorthand and a pro golfer's yardage book.

Chain

Shine

Heat→work the back (make a post and tell commentary to mention the post about Jacob carrying the landmark arena on his back.)

—Jacob seated in corner. Close talking. No yelling. Big facial expressions and body language. Chop. I take punch (big bump sell) charge back in him

—again but Jacob moves as I charge

Double down: chin lock, escape, sleeper, almost pass out, throw me off and take a back drop for the double down (maybe to the buckle into HbK in the corner into backdrop)

Comeback

Falsies in no order

Wasteland. Flip to feet. Enzi. AJ. Nope. Ashes. Roll. Keep arm. Pepsi twist. 2 like with no bump. Duck third into O'Conner German.

Brain bustaaaa. No. Gorred buster. Ashworth roll. 2 count. Into roll the dice.

Hard buckle from the middle of the ring. I take it like a splash and stick to the ropes. Kick the stomach. I pop up and land of Jacob's shoulders. Wasteland

Jack knife, bridge, Jacob slides me. No hitch. Up kick. Kip up. Knock me down. Trailer hitch

Ref gets him off. Ref talk. Ref talk. Discuss punch. Miss euro. Slide to the apron. Enzi, Hit shot. 450.

On the night of the show, the crowd exalts Ashworth, 34 and paunchy in a black singlet, as he lumbers to the ring. Hunter appears in a neck brace. It's a prop, something to trick his opponent. "At Southern Honor last night I got brainbustered on a stage," he says. It's true. Chip Day delivered the searing move at the top of the catwalk. But Hunter's fine. "I'm not medically cleared to compete tonight," he says to the crowd.

"You're a fake! You suck!" they yell.

"Hunter James, I didn't expect this out of you," Ashworth says. "It ain't my problem you went to another promotion and got your ass handed to you."

"How's that neck?" Ashworth taunts.

Hunter, fed up, rips the brace off, along with his blue-sequin-trimmed vest, and grabs the belt from where it rests in the referee's hands. "This is going home with me!"

Ashworth takes the lead in the match until Hunter pushes his neck into the rope. Six minutes in, Ashworth retaliates with an electric chair drop. When done correctly, the receiver of the move tucks his feet behind the aggressor's back to stabilize himself and lands on the center of his back as they both fall backward in a crowd-pleasing thud. It's not beginner stuff, but they aren't beginners.

Hunter sits on Ashworth's shoulders like a toddler. Ashworth grips Hunter's shins. As the conjoined bodies fall backward Hunter's legs go forward, tilting his body backward. Hunter's neck, rather than his back, takes the impact. Referee David Weakley knows right away. So do the fans. It gets quiet.

Hunter instinctively reverse somersaults out of the landing, sits up, wobbles, and tips over. Then he lays breathless on his back. A fan in the front row holds a nervous fist to his mouth. Rick Michaels watches the match on a screen in the back. "Tell them to take it home!" he says via radio to the earpiece in Weakley's ear. The ref scurries over and whispers the message to Hunter. "Fuck no." Hunter whispers back.

The opponents lay next to each other. "One!" Weakley yells, holding his fingers high in the air for the entire crowd to see.

Ashworth, still prone, lifts a leg and slams it down hard once, and then again. "Two!" Weakley yells. Ashworth rolls over and starts toward his feet, banging on the mat to rile up his fans.

In the opposite corner Hunter, breathless, steadies himself. Within 15 seconds, he flips over the turnbuckle and ricochets back to meet a high back body drop from Ashworth, then springs from the turnbuckle in a 450 splash—an impressive rush of moves for someone who just landed on his neck and had the wind knocked out of him. For the finale, Hunter takes the neck-based Roll of the Dice finisher, an on-point conclusion for a match that started with a feigned neck injury but now seems especially cruel and dangerous. Hunter insisted on it. He's a performer and this is the story he wrote. He'd sent some daggers in that promo. Ashworth needed his payoff. As Ashworth raises the belt Hunter slings himself onto the shoulders of two security guards, who carry him away from the ring.

In the locker room afterward, Ashworth was almost in tears. Wrestlers surrounded him. "Nasty fall." "Are you ok?" Todd Sexton's wife, Kelly, asked if he remembered what happened and instructed him to follow her finger with his eyes. Hunter felt fine, but he knew the adrenaline would wear off, unmasking the injury. After the show he drove to meet his parents at their friends' house. On the way home, his neck stiffened.

Earlier that day *Georgia Wrestling History* had released its 2023 award nominees. Hunter was up for two of the most coveted: Best Overall Wrestler and Best Male Performer. The next day, Larry Goodman posted his show report. Mega Clash brought in 500-plus attendees, according to Goodman's count, twice what Landmark Arena could hold and the third-largest crowd Southern Fried had drawn, anywhere. "Solid match. The babyface/heel dynamic was strong," he wrote. "Ashworth had the crowd behind him, James's star power notwithstanding. The bump James took on the electric chair was super scary. Nobody's fault. Just one of those things. Landed right on his head and he was A-OK. Ahh, to be young, dumb and flexible."

Hunter left knowing Ashworth was worried sick. The next

day he drove to Colbert, Georgia, where he knew Ashworth was booked on the afternoon show and gave him a hug. "I can't wait for the next one," he said.

Hunter got on the forklift Monday at work and realized he couldn't turn his neck. Later, he could barely lift a stack of boxes that didn't total 20 pounds. He went to Billy Ray's desk for advice. "You need to go get checked out," his father said. It was one thing to let a tricep heal on its own, but you don't mess around with neck injuries.

Hunter drove to an urgent care center. He had always heard professional wrestling injuries weren't covered by insurance, so he didn't offer all the details. "I was goofing off with some buddies." True, but not the whole story.

The nurse asked if he heard a pop when the injury occurred. "No," Hunter said. "The adrenaline was going. The room was loud. I didn't hear anything."

They instructed him to get a ride to the emergency room for a CT scan. Billy Ray arrived to drive Hunter's Jeep home and Jenn took him to the hospital. On the way he advised his mother not to give too many details. Jenn seemed overly calm, a sign, Hunter knew, that she was really worried.

Instead of Googling "neck injury outcomes" as they waited for the results, Hunter thought through ideas he could pitch to promoters to keep him relevant while he was injured. How can I keep me and Xavi's story alive? How does me and Chip's story evolve? He canceled an appearance in Swainsboro, but he wasn't going to miss PCW, where he'd recently turned babyface.

He was hurt, not injured, he was sure, and you can wrestle hurt. He'd done it in August after smacking his knee on the stairs at Southern Honor's Royal Rumble. He wrapped an Ace bandage around it, slipped a knee sleeve over it, and strapped on a kneepad.

The next night he hit a 450 off the top rope in a 25-minute match with Judais.

A nurse practitioner arrived to deliver the news: Hunter's C1 and C2 were jammed, and his neck muscles were so inflamed they were preventing the vertebrae from returning to their normal positions. The tightness and reduced range of motion would resolve themselves with time, and muscle relaxers.

For the moment, Hunter was spared the fate that has interrupted the careers of so many wrestlers. Big E broke his neck in a belly-to-belly suplex during a 2022 episode of *SmackDown*. Hardcore Holly in a botched powerbomb from Brock Lesnar in 2002. Darren Drozdov lost use of his arms and legs after a running powerbomb went wrong. His was the case Billy Ray used to warn Hunter of the danger that threatened even the most well-trained wrestlers.

Hunter and Jenn picked up dinner on the way home, and the next day Hunter slept in and stayed home from work. In the aftermath, he didn't give much thought to how it happened. He could've injured himself anywhere in the ring, doing anything. It just so happened this was the move that did it. It wasn't that Ashworth didn't know what he was doing—he was a veteran, after all. Sometimes, things just happen. The fault belonged to no one. He'd do it all over again. By Friday, he was back in the ring.

As he began to heal, Hunter thought about where he'd been and where he was going. He had now worked for four major promotions: WWE, AEW, NWA, and Impact. This year he wanted more. But how to get there? He noticed the wrestlers with the biggest social media followings, not the most talent, had been booked at NWA's show in Sarasota. Maybe he should pay to boost his posts or get more active on X. Somewhere along the line someone had told him, "Everyone knows you're a wrestler, that's what they pay to see you do. Show them the person inside." Maybe he'd start creating vlogs documenting his life as an independent wrestler. Build the following. The gigs will follow.

The fans loved him, he could feel it. "They know there's something there and that something's going to happen in the future, like, I'm going to be on TV one day. I'm going to be a big star and I'm not going to be around anymore. They know something is in their presence." It was the suits at these big promotions that couldn't see his talent. Eventually, he knew, someone would take that chance.

CHAPTER 23

An 8-year-old named Mason Andrews sat in the audience the night of Hunter's injury with a framed poster of the event flyer. Mega Clash, it promised, in red, white, and blue script above 14 Georgia stars, rendered in black and white. By the end of the night every one of them had signed it.

Mason is a Georgia wrestling superfan. When it's not Little League season, he attends multiple shows in a weekend. With the help of his dad, Alex, Mason keeps tabs on his favorite wrestlers via Facebook. On their birthdays, he arrives to shows with gifts. He creates baseball card–like sports cards for them.

In return, they toss him relics from their matches—kneepads, wrist tape, a sweat towel, a bandana. He and Alex crafted a replica Hunter James gold sequin jacket for him. He dressed as Nick Halen for Halloween.

Mason met Halen at Landmark Arena when Halen returned to wrestling after seven years away. A few weeks later, Mason and Alex spotted him looking at wrestling figures at Target. Mason so badly wanted to talk to him but was intimidated. Alex messaged Halen on Facebook. Halen had left the store already but turned around and met them in the parking lot. Squatting down on the paved walkway in front of the store, they posed together for a photo.

In 2023, Mason issued a Top 100 list of Georgia wrestlers. Nick Halen was No. 1. Hunter, No. 2. "He was scared of hurting anyone's feelings," Alex says. "He added number one, Nick, and number two, Hunter, and then he took the next eight that he knew were his top ten but he couldn't figure out which order he wanted to put them in. So we put them in a hat."

"I remember how they wrestle," Mason says about the process, sitting in his parents' shared home office. Alex interjects. "And how they make you feel?" "Yeah."

He printed a certificate for the Top 10. Alex designed a T-shirt and promoted the purchase link on Facebook. Nick and Hunter were first to place an order.

Mason met Hunter at Landmark when he was part of the heel stable The Program, with Scott Mayson and Proc Johnston. "They were bad guys but they came out and talked to him after the show," Alex says.

Scott Mayson (No. 4 on Mason's 2023 list) reached out to Alex about putting together an appreciation show for him. Mayson booked the venue and put together a roster. They called the show Mason Wrestling Federation's Rasslin' in Royston and scheduled it for March 23, 2024. Alex and Mason got to work personalizing Party City title belts and perfecting Mason's gear: a feathered robe, sunglasses, gold-studded ballcap, and a Money Mason Andrews singlet. "He went bedazzle crazy there for a little bit," Alex says with a laugh. He wanted to be flashy, like Ric Flair and Hunter James.

The night of Mason's show, a line snakes through the parking lot to the entrance of the Royston Dome, another timeworn building wrestling moved into when the rest of the world was done with it. Inside, vintage posters from similar spaces around the South decorate its walls. Red metal rafters bear the weight of a tired plywood ceiling. A giant jar of dill pickles glows neon green on the snack bar set up in the corner. Bright stage lights illuminate the ring and the American flag behind it.

A bulletin board by the door includes an evacuation plan and some handwritten notices. One informs entrants that the building's owners are not responsible for any accidents or incidents. Another warns them not to cross the barricade, and a third notifies them the show is rated PG-13 but "curse words may slip out." A glossy, full-color 3×5 card advertises tonight's show: Money Mason himself, with gelled hair and a Hunter James–inspired gold sequin jacket, peers out from behind aviator glasses below gold letters spelling out his moniker.

Inside, Billy Ray and Chunk are already setting up Hunter's merch table. It's been four years and four months since Hunter bounded down Jamie's driveway that November night after high school wrestling practice. Three years since Billy Ray watched his son perform at Landmark Arena. Six months since father and son teamed up against Chop Top and Jerry Nelms in Macon. Tonight Billy Ray broke his own rule—again—about showing up. "The only reason I'm here is what they're doing with the show," he says, in defense. "I don't care if they get out there and throw water balloons at each other." He came because he recognized the sincerity of it. It may be a bunch of hack wrestlers in the ring with Hunter, but they're doing it for good reason: to make the crowd, and more importantly, a kid, feel good. He wore a Hunter James T-shirt and invited a dozen friends.

For his part in the show Hunter works himself toward the ring, stopping on every side to twirl in his bright white sleeveless denim jacket, hands in the sky, trailed by Triston in his gold bomber. The ring announcer introduces their partners, "Georgia Grown" Scott Mayson, in jeans, kneepads, and full beard, and Mason's favorite wrestler, Nick Halen. A dream team. Hunter stops to coronate Mason with a plastic gold crown and then throws his hands in the air to hype the crowd.

"All hail!" Hunter yells. Billy Ray harmonizes with the crowd's response. "Hollywood!"

In the ring, Rick Michaels and Azrael wear full-body blue Lycra suits with matching *luchador* masks. Xander Seabolt, the Landmark trainee who unexpectedly delivered the affecting promo three years ago, stands on the ring apron outside the ropes, waiting. Hunter squares off with one of The Grapplers, as the duo is known, and then shoulder tackles him to the mat.

Billy Ray reacts with a gravelly "Yeeeah!"

Hunter's in the ring with Seabolt now. "You scared?" Hunter goads him, shuffling his feet hard on the mat for sound. "He scared!"

It's a call and response. Billy Ray answers. "He scared!"

"Let's go Hunter!" a chorus of child voices starts up.

The main event is a Royal Rumble–style elimination match. Hunter's sitting behind his merch table with Billy Ray and Chunk when his entrance music comes on. He looks confused but reacts in an instant the way any wrestler would: he leaps into the ring.

One after another, wrestlers take on Tower, standing 7′ tall in a black jumpsuit in the center of the ring. In the end, 4′-tall Money Mason Andrews triumphs. The ultimate David and Goliath battle.

Two of Billy Ray's friends and their young children stop to say goodbye. Hunter gives the kids a souvenir: a T-shirt for the little boy, a crown for the girl. The kids are reticent.

"Give him a fist pump or something," someone says.

Hunter smiles. "No, it's fine. Hope y'all had a good night."

"Thanks, Billy," the dad says.

Hunter enjoyed the liberation of a standalone show. There were no limits or mandates on what you could do in the ring, no brand warfare. It was for the fans, for Mason. Billy Ray complained Hunter didn't showcase all his signature moves. "Just the discus punch," Hunter says. "And in the Royal Rumble I hit my brainbuster twice."

The final bit is a grand finale. The wrestlers—Black, white, short, tall, bearded, wearing everything from button shirts to a unicorn headband—follow Mason to the ring, clapping. Nick Halen grabs the mic. "All these people here. Everyone here. People selling T-shirts, people selling concession, they paid to see you," he says, bent over and pointing to Mason. Scott Mayson hoists Mason up on his shoulders. It feels like a community theatre cast applauding their star. Later Mason will confirm: it was better than Christmas.

For Scott Mayson, who hatched the idea of the show, it was one of the most fulfilling experiences of his life. "There was a lot of crying that night because I was so happy how everything came together and how it made him happy." Mayson thought of himself as a kid, watching wrestling with his dad.

William Darryl Wilson died of diabetic coma at 38, two days after Christmas, when Mayson, whose real name is Eric Wilson, was 12. "Our thing was wrestling," Mayson says. "I'd sit in his lap and we'd watch all the time." He stopped after Darryl died. It brought back too many memories. And then one night he rode with some friends to Landmark Arena. He was lost without his father. He dropped out of high school. "It was a really dark period in my life," he says. At Landmark he found a place he could exist away from the dismal reality of his real life. He parted the ropes in 2009, he says, thinking maybe he could help someone in the crowd the way the wrestlers he watched had helped him.

Mayson grew up poor, and lived with his brother, father, and uncle at their grandparents' house in Habersham County, Georgia, 5 miles from Landmark Arena. His mother left when he was little, and Darryl struggled with alcoholism and diabetes. Mayson went through a period he defines as "not being a productive member of society." He doesn't credit wrestling with pulling him out of that, but he says it did open his mind. At Landmark, for the first time in Mayson's life he was around people who are gay and who held different religious views than he grew up with, or none at all.

"I grew up in a Southern Christian family. There were a lot of closed-minded beliefs. I'm not a bigot," he says, with a chuckle. "I do have wrestling to thank for that."

Backstage before Mason's finale, Mayson helped the boy into his robe. Mason put his sunglasses on and started toward the curtain. Then he stopped and turned around. "I gotta get my hat!" he said. "I want to give it to my best friend when I entrance." To Mayson, it demonstrated the unseeable power of wrestling, the thoughtful kindness that courses beneath the violence. He dried his eyes again.

CHAPTER 24

At Southern Fried's February 3, 2024, show, a girl in the audience caught Hunter's eye as he circled the ring. Petite, blond, button nose, laughing. They locked eyes.

"I'm gonna get her," he whispered to Triston.

He "sold" in her direction during his match—wrestlespeak for directing his best moves and biggest emotions to the area where she was seated. After, he sat inside the barricade at the bell keeper's table, next to her seat.

He introduced himself. They made small talk. Finally, he asked, "What are you doing tomorrow?" She trumped him. "What are you doing tonight?" After the show they drove to Applebee's in her Tesla and spent the next 21 hours together. At one point they parked at Waffle House but were so deep in conversation—about family, religion, music—they never went in. In the predawn hours, they drove to Walmart for energy drinks, candy, and a blanket, and as the sun rose, cuddled at a city park. He put the Eric Church song "Hell of a View" on. Everything felt right.

The butterflies didn't disappear. His heart beat faster around her. His mind thought quicker. Wrestling, for all its thrills, was nothing compared to the adrenaline of being in love. In the days that followed they spent nearly every nonworking moment together. They watched movies, danced in the kitchen while cooking blueberry pancakes. He fell asleep while she gently scratched his head. She gave him a toothbrush. He called her Bailey Grace. She called him Hunter James.

Another time, they were dancing in the kitchen and he got an idea for a move set he could use in a match. When the song was over, he used her as a body double to play out the spot. She couldn't stop laughing. Within a matter of weeks she figured out the antidote to a beleaguered or bored or fidgety Hunter: "Why don't we watch some wrestling?" A girl had never spoken such beautiful words.

In early February Hunter booked a reservation for them at an upscale Italian restaurant in Atlanta. He noticed the clean, bright lighting in the parking deck and stopped. "Hey, I don't want to be too much, but can I shoot a promo?" he asked. In the clip, she assumes the role of paparazzi photographer. He walks into the frame, pretends to be caught off-guard, and then teases his upcoming match in Savannah.

They ate duck prosciutto that night. Hunter ordered a pasta he couldn't pronounce. He even drank a glass of wine—his first.

The next morning they deadlifted together at her gym. Bailey, 21, lived in Winder and worked in Atlanta as an account manager. She insisted they alternate paying for dinners.

He spent hours thinking about what to get her for Valentine's Day. They'd only been dating for two weeks, but he'd never had a connection like this, not this natural, not this fast. *What was too much? What wasn't enough?* He caught her eyeing Dove chocolates when they were at Walmart. "Thank God for wrestling. I'm very good at noticing little things," he says. He picked up the chocolate and ordered wallet-sized pictures of a photo they took together the night they were all dressed up for dinner.

The pandemic struck in Hunter's junior year. He never had a high school sweetheart. His weekends were stacked with amateur wrestling tournaments, and after he graduated, with professional wrestling shows. He didn't have time for dates and never went out of his way to find them. But now Bailey shined brighter than the ring. If he had an open date on his calendar, he spent it with her rather than trying to find a gig. Some weekends, his life actually resembled an ordinary 21-year-old's. If he had shows, she rode with him. They stayed an extra two nights after a Savannah gig and laid on the beach. "We're gonna make it in the wrestling business," she said one night driving home with him.

The open dates gave him more time to think. He had an honest conversation with Rick Michaels. "Why Lev and not me?" he asked. The question had throbbed inside him since Lev inked a contract with NWA. If Hunter couldn't get on NWA, a midsized company, how would he ever make it to WWE? Rick provided a frustrating, but truthful answer: It's not always about talent and hard work. It's about timing. Hunter had heard that before, but with Bailey around to fill in the space between matches, workouts, and work, it was easier to accept. He stopped putting his name out there to be an extra. Instead of booking every show, everywhere, he was purposeful. In his eyes, it raised his stock. He leaned into posting vlogs on YouTube that documented his life—with Bailey—as an indie wrestler. Weekends out of the ring when his body had time to recover made him realize, at 21, that he'd been living in a constant state of subtle pain. But after two weeks off, he couldn't wait to get back.

That spring his and Billy Ray's employer, WAM, invited Hunter on a trip to the company's headquarters in Italy. He stood out at work, he surmised, and they were grooming him for a promotion. "The first thing I told them was I'm not missing a wrestling show," he says. He insisted they fly him out Sunday night and back Friday morning.

He hated every second of it. He was used to having the freedom to create his own schedule. In Italy he was beholden to a heavily planned group agenda: watching PowerPoint presentations at the factory all day, then group dinners. "It was awful," he says. "Nonstop people talking about work. I don't even watch football but pretended just so I could talk about something other than this fucking warehouse job."

There was no time to work out. The food was oily. The abundance of carbs made him sick. "What was your favorite part about Italy?" a higher-up asked him on his last day. "It's going to be in three hours, when I leave," Hunter deadpanned. The best part about being away from home, he realized later, was recognizing what's important in his life. He missed everything. Bailey. Wrestling. Working out. His Jeep. His parents. It was all he knew, and it was all he needed.

CHAPTER 25

Wrestlers pray before a show benefitting the Barrow Community Crisis Fund after the Apalachee High School shooting in Winder, Georgia

Hunter's Apalachee High School letter jacket hangs from a nail on his parent's front porch. "Sunday, Sunday, Sunday!" he says to camera, from behind a pair of mirrored aviators. And then his tone shifts. "Professional wrestling comes back to Winder, Georgia, for a cause. And it's not about Hollywood Hunter James," he says, despite wearing a shirt stamped with the James Dean–inspired photo of himself. "It's for those who were affected by the tragedy that happened on September 4, 2024, at Apalachee High School." The school he graduated from three years ago.

Scott Mayson was the first to text him that day. "You went to Apalachee, right?" "Yeah, why?" he wrote back. "Did you hear about the school shooting?" At work, Billy Ray approached, holding his phone. "I just heard from Chunk there was a school shooting." The gunman had not yet been apprehended. Schools in the surrounding area, including Chunk's, were on lockdown.

Hunter shared a series of photos on Facebook that conjured up a high school career untouched by tragedy: him and the Apalachee wrestling team on senior night; at state his junior year; in his letter jacket holding Landmark Arena's NCW title belt in his original gimmick, The Varsity One. "I back the CHEE" he wrote, above a barrage of hashtags.

Matt Westlake, a ring announcer for some area wrestling promotions, reached out within a few hours. He and wrestler Chris Del Ray, who attended Apalachee as a freshman and graduated from Barrow County's other high school, Winder-Barrow, were planning a show to raise money for affected families. It was well-known within the wrestling community that Hunter was an Apalachee grad. He was their first call. They named the show Battle for Barrow, a play on the sports rivalry between the county's two high schools, known as Battle of Barrow. Chris Del Ray and Hunter James, representing the rival schools, would headline it.

Hunter signed on, with one caveat. If he and Del Ray faced off, Hunter wanted to make sure his opponent's alma mater, Winder-Barrow, wasn't villainized. Opposing forces are elemental to professional wrestling, but this was about a community coming together. No hometown boy could play a bad guy, not now. Del Ray could be the aggressor, but he couldn't be a heel.

The crowd at Edged Events in downtown Winder, Georgia, numbered 175 on Sunday, September 22. Westlake had hoped for more, but other fundraising events had been scheduled for the same day. It had been nearly three weeks since two students and two teachers were killed by gunfire at Apalachee High School. It was the 385th mass shooting, defined by the Gun Violence Archive as four or more people injured or killed, in 2024, according to the nonprofit, and the 218th time a gun was fired or brandished at a school, to date, that year, according to the K–12 School Shooting Database. Apalachee was the 32nd school shooting that resulted in death and/or injury so far that year. The accused: 14-year-old Colt Gray, who pleaded not guilty.

Chris Del Ray's daughter, a kindergartner, and niece, in sixth grade, were released early that day from schools in the district. At home, they described how their teachers used tables and chairs to block the windows.

The town bore the mark of tragedy. Apalachee Strong signs decorated front yards. Church billboards spelled messages of encouragement in block letters. Inside the venue—the lower level of a brick office building—people in the seats wore AHS and Winder-Barrow T-shirts. Veda Barnard, recognizable from her near-perfect attendance at Southern Fried shows in Monroe, sat in the front row in a shirt that said STOP THE HATE.

A pile of wrestling figures zipped in sandwich bags and priced at $15 each lay next to a stack of foil-wrapped hotdogs at the concessions stand. Tickets to the show, along with the sale of anything else, would go to the Barrow Community Crisis Fund.

Barrow County Commissioner Alex Ward, whose district includes Apalachee High School, stood alone in an Apalachee polo shirt near the table where color commentators Christopher "CDub" Clavell and Michael Gentry had set up audio equipment on a folding plastic table. That morning he stood at the starting line of a charity ride that drew a thousand motorcyclists. Tomorrow, he'd help fill backpacks with soft blankets, stress balls, and stuffed animals for AHS students on their first day back to school.

Ward thanks the audience for showing up to support the community. And then something unusual happens. The wrestlers and referees emerge from the locker room in single file and snake through the crowd toward the ring without a word. Leatherface in bloody apron, Nicky Hyde in Victorian tailcoat, Sid Ellington in Danhausen-esque face paint. They frame the ring and lay their palms on the mat. They're neighbors, not enemies, in a community that's been attacked.

"Looks like we have a few local heroes here," Westlake's cohost, Jason Maddox, says.

"I think we do have a few local heroes here tonight," Westlake says.

"Looks like we have a puppy?" Maddox says.

"We do have a puppy! Hunter James has got a puppy, people!" Westlake says. A reticent cheer warms the room. Hunter and Bailey broke up in July, five months after their first date, and he missed her goldendoodle so much, he says, he got his own. On the way to pick up the 13-week-old puppy, he and Chunk batted around names. "C.C. pick up that guitar and talk to me," Bret Michaels's voice in the Poison song "Talk Dirty to Me" interrupted their conversation. C.C. now travels with Hunter to shows. He hangs out in the locker room and rests in Hunter's arms when he's at his merch table. When it's time for Hunter to walk to the ring, C.C. goes too. The dog has become part of his act.

Westlake calls for a moment of silence. "Those affected need our love more than anything right now." The room grows silent, except for the sound of a crying baby.

A pastor from a local Baptist church leads a prayer. Wrestlers and refs lean into the mat and bow their heads. Hunter places

C.C.'s paws on the bottom rope. In his AHS letter jacket, he presses his forehead into C.C.'s fur.

"We know that love prevails and we know who provides that," Pastor Duke Forster says. He implores God to rain down on Apalachee, to keep sending heroes, like the ones standing around the ring, who have donated their time to raise money for people affected by the shooting. "Father, we will, with your help, prevail. Amen."

The room is quiet for a few seconds, and then Westlake breaks the silence.

"Who wants a shirt?" he crows. Westlake and Maddox heave rolled-up T-shirts, printed with the event flyer, to the screaming crowd. They're ready to have fun, ready to forget, for a few hours, the awful thing that happened just six miles down the road.

The wrestlers retreat to the locker room. A gray-bearded man wears a USMC sweatshirt and tentatively holds an American flag behind the last row of fans. Now, he works his way to the ring holding it high. "Real quick, If I could have everybody stand, take their hats off," Westlake directs the crowd. An instrumental recording of the National Anthem plays, and 31-year-old Apalachee alum John Wayne Maddox sings.

Jeff McCarty holds a Nikon camera and slinks around the room in an Apalachee football shirt. His son, Noah, a junior, is one of the team's quarterbacks. When Noah made the team, McCarty, a warehouse manager and amateur photographer, offered his services. Since then he's been shooting games and player portraits. When parents asked for more dramatically styled shots of their student-athletes, McCarty brought in colored lights, a fog machine, and props, including a length of extra-large galvanized chain and a sledgehammer he sometimes sets on fire before pressing the shutter.

Two years ago he was taking head shots for someone in downtown Winder and noticed wrestlers walking the streets in show gear. He followed them to the ring, set up in the middle of a blocked-off street, and started shooting. Now, he photographs wrestling shows too.

"Ladies and gentlemen, are we ready for some wrestling tonight?" Westlake, clean cut in sequined shoes and well-fitting sportscoat, crows.

Poison's "I Want Action" interrupts him and Hunter appears in sneakers and his Apalachee jacket. As if being the hometown hero weren't enough to get him over, he cradles C.C. in one arm and slaps outstretched hands with the other. When he gets close to the ring, he passes the puppy to Billy Ray, in the second row. For a fleeting second, between handing over the dog and jumping into the ring, father and son hug. Hunter runs toward the ring, slides under the bottom rope, and hops to his feet, hyping the crowd.

"Coming to the ring, Hollywood Hunter James!" Hunter helicopter-spins around the mat, Shawn Michaels style, and then hangs from the corner post, basking in the adoration. Billy Ray and Hunter exchange a knowing look, and Billy Ray takes a photo. After the match, he posts it on Facebook along with a caption—"of course he won the battle royal."

The music stops. "Such a great song though, Hunter." Westlake hands over the mic. "I know, it's a great song. I hear it every time I walk out and perform as HOLLYWOOD HUNTER JAMES!" The crowd approves. Now he has to do the complicated character work of all-at-once being the pretty-boy, cocky wrestler Hollywood Hunter James, and Hunter James Noblett, the Apalachee High School grad, whose presence today represents a school and a community entrenched in the grief of wanton violence. At first, he struggles. "Tonight, not only do we make a memory happen . . . ," he says, stumbling over stoic words, "we make a tragedy . . . better."

And then he speaks from the heart. "I brought a lot of trophies back to Apalachee High School. I brought a lot of medals back to Apalachee High School." Like all the most impactful wrestling promos, it's true.

"That heavyweight championship is coming back to Apalachee High School tonight!" he yells, to the crowd's delight. A championship, the healing of a community—tonight they're one and the same. I'll see you guys later on, he promises. And then a threat, in the form of Hunter's opponent, Chris Del Ray, appears. "If you want this belt," he says, holding it high. "I'll give you a chance, under one condition."

"Name it," Hunter says.

"If you win the battle royal you'll be main event for this title."

"Woah, woah, woah, let me get this straight," Hunter says. He's along for the ride, and so are the fans. Hunter sees it as an opportunity to set himself up as the more-decorated wrestler, also true. "You mean the guy that's been on WWE, the guy that's been on NWA, the guy who's been on TNA, the guy who's been on AEW . . . " he roars, his voice quickening and growing louder with each accolade, " . . . has to win a battle royal to get a shot at *your* championship?!"

Del Ray affirms. "Challenge accepted." A Hollywood chant begins.

"Ladies and gentlemen, your first match, a good, old-fashioned Barrow County Battle Royal!" Westlake yells.

—

Early in my reporting I sat down with the sixth-grade social studies teacher who performed in Georgia rings as the wrestler Justin Legend. He'd soon introduce me to Jamie Holmes, who invited me to his backyard, where for the first time, I met Hunter Noblett, a 16-year-old with a dream. In the 5-year span of my reporting, Legend would hang up his boots and create, with former Drive-By Truckers tour manager Cole Taylor, Classic City Wrestling, a pro wrestling show backed by live music in Athens, Georgia.

I arrived to the interview, in September 2019, eager to take notes on the subculture I sought to disrobe. I left with inklings of the revelations that would wake me from sleep many nights in the years that followed.

"If I wanted to see two people have a legit contact sport I would've grown up loving boxing," Legend said, from across a round metal table outside a strip mall coffee shop. Instead, he grew up body-slamming a giant teddy bear on his bed and casting his parents and siblings in matches on the living room carpet.

Justin's father, Bill, was a pastor. The church got a PA system in 1990, when Justin was in third grade. After the crowds cleared from Sunday services he took the mic and echoed the words of his father. And then he'd mimic another profound voice in his life: ring announcer Gordon Solie interviewing wrestlers before their matches. He'd lean side to side, switching roles in the theatre of his imagination.

Justin parroted two seemingly disparate voices in his life, but in truth, Gordon Solie and Bill Burnham had the same job. They were storytellers. They captivated people in the audience and persuaded them toward an uncertain truth. For Bill, that truth was the gospel. For Solie, it was kayfabe.

When Bill took Justin to Atlanta's Omni Coliseum for Starrcade '86, Justin was years from navigating the complexities of life outside the ring, where heroes aren't who they seem, where people you trust abandon you at your weakest, where the very institutions that hold society together crumble in your mind. He was transfixed—smitten by the action in the ring and by the rare alone-time it afforded him with his father. Justin had Bill to himself that night at the Omni, and he had him every Saturday night at 6:05 when a tradition more sacred than sermon unfolded in the Burnham living room.

Bill sat supine in the recliner. On a couch kitty-corner from the TV, Justin lay belly down, chin on the armrest, eyes glued to Georgia Championship Wrestling on WTBS. Between commercials, father and son watched injustice served and avenged, moral duality stuffed into skintight leggings. Justin sucked down the spectacle like Kool-Aid, but it didn't quench his thirst. He needed to be in the ring. He would be a divorced father of two before he'd pull on a pair of black compression pants and part the ropes as "Pretty Boy Killer" Justin Legend for the first time.

When he was 35, he sat in a chair as a tattoo artist etched the timestamp "6:05" above his left bicep. I met other Georgia wrestlers with the same tattoo. It's the time Georgia Championship Wrestling started every Saturday night. More than that, it's an ode to professional wrestling at large. The one constant in his life that's been there for him since he was a boy, the thing that's never let him down, the thing that makes him truly happy.

That day, I asked Justin to describe the feeling of being in the ring. "Complete tunnel vision," he said, and "oddly emotional."

"You're putting your life in someone's hands. And then when you're done you just want to do it again."

If he could rewrite his own story the way he writes his character's, he'd make just one change: he'd start sooner.

"I think back to when I was a kid," he explained. "I didn't know a lot of things for sure, but I knew that every Saturday night I was going to be able to watch wrestling." As a child, Justin could identify the depth of comfort professional wrestling provided. Now, as a father, a wrestler, and an educator, he could put it into words.

"The lines are very clear," he said. "In wrestling you know who the bad guy is. Unlike in real life."

My pen stopped. I looked up from my notes.

"And even though the bad guy might run on for a while you know that eventually . . . ," he paused. "The bad guy gets taken down."

Real life lacks such certainty. Over and over again after we talked, I watched the world shrink to the size of a 16′×16′ square and reached a conclusion anyone in the ring already knows: Obsessions are everywhere, but wrestling's different. It demands strength and vulnerability. It's powered by sleight of hand.

Justin pounded his demons into submission every weekend of his career. Costumed opponents, yes, but also, the stuff of life. The girlfriend who left him alone in the hospital with a deadly infection. *Powerbomb.* The church that pushed his dad out. *Legdrop.* The best friend who killed himself. *Piledriver.*

Justin found his own church, one with rites and vestments, idols, adoration, and ceremony; and at its core, the Bible's principal contest: good against evil. But more than anything, he found comfort. A voice that whispered through the chokeslam, you're safe.

When I hear about a school shooting, my mind goes to wrestling. I wish the person holding the gun had instead climbed into a ring. I wish they could've felt the tingling symbiosis of the performance. I wish they would have found a community where they were seen, even celebrated. Wish they could've pounded their opponent and then sat across from him at Waffle House. Wish they could've gone home, sore and soothed, safe. Self-mythologizing is self-preservation, but it's acceptable in very few settings. A wrestling ring is one place—maybe the most valuable place—to feel exceptional, no matter what you look like or where you came from. It's not a coincidence that grief, poverty, and trauma are more prevalent in people in and around the ring. It's what brought them there.

And so, on a Sunday afternoon 18 days after the unthinkable, some small-town wrestlers use violence to heal a community. Fans watch to be entertained. To remember, but also to forget. In the face of true evil, the thrill of violence swaddled in performance offers comfort. Around the globe, fans watch injustice avenged in wrestling rings. In the merciless arena of real life, that's a hope, not a guarantee.

"Hot dogs are ready!" Westlake, ever buoyant, announces. Chunk jumps up and returns with one.

Billy Ray can't sit still. He's nervous about the show. The ceiling's too low. The other wrestlers on the card aren't as good as Hunter. He just wants it to go well. He goes to the back to find his old friend, Leatherface. He talks to Jerry Nelms. Finally, he sits, and pulls a nicotine pouch from the tin in his pocket.

Billy Ray watches silently, his face bare of emotion, as wrestlers throw each other out of the ring. Next to him, Jenn's foot, in a flip-flop, bounces in nervous cadence.

Butch Magarian, the color bearer, stands behind the last row of chairs with the US flag tucked in his left arm. Its post never touches the floor. Ward, the county commissioner, sits in the front row.

The announcers draw attention to someone else in the front row: a little girl. It's her first wrestling show. Billy Ray pops out of his chair, beelines to Hunter's merch table, grabs an autographed photo, and delivers it to her. Another Hunter James fan.

The roster tonight represents Georgia wrestlers old and new, not the most muscled or decorated, to be sure, but accomplished in the number of years they've spent in the ring and valuable in their personal connections to the place. It also represents the cross-section of Billy Ray and Hunter's lives, a gritty, living tableau of wrestling's perpetuity. Jamie Holmes, who started training Hunter in his backyard when Hunter was 14, left his boots in the ring in January, had his ACL and meniscus surgically reconstructed in February, and laced them up again for a street fight in June. He knows Billy Ray from the days they worked the same rings, sometimes facing off inside the ropes. Terry Lawler, 54, has faced off against Hunter multiple times. His brother, Steve, trained Billy Ray. Leatherface, well into his third decade as a Georgia wrestler, starts up his chainsaw. "Nicest guy I've ever met in the business," according to Billy Ray.

The smell of gas-powered equipment fills the room. Leatherface slams Jamie into a chair in front of Butch, holding the flag. Eventually the old man pulls out his phone and films the action, smiling and cradling the flag in the crook of his other arm. CB Suavé, a 2005 graduate of Winder-Barrow High School,

Apalachee's hometown rival, carries an Apalachee flag signed by all the wrestlers. Georgia wrestling superfan Veda Barnard will make the highest silent-auction bid and take it home.

The time comes for Westlake to hype the main event. "Weighing in at 215 pounds, the Apalachee alum, Hollywood Hunter James!"

Poison's "I Want Action" kicks on and Hunter, the star of this show, appears again. Varsity One trunks, letter jacket: the gimmick he started his career with is the one that serves him now. A T-shirt bearing the Apalachee "A" hangs from his trunks like a sweat towel and grazes the top of his boots. He smiles, proudly tugs at his lapel, and shoots his right arm to the sky. He weaves through the seats, and then leaps beneath the bottom rope, sliding into the ring and landing on a bent elbow in front of his parents. They're proud. Of course they are. The goal of this show is to make fans feel, for a few hours, that the score is settled, that everything is as it should be. For a few minutes in a wrestling ring, it is.

While his opponent—"Your champion from Winder, Georgia, weighing in at 205 pounds!"—makes his way toward the ring, Hunter hangs his jacket on the post where it will stay for the length of the match, like a talisman.

"If you've never seen what Hunter James has done before . . . " One of the commentators repeats the type of line that has fueled Hunter's confidence since he started his career. "You're in for a treat." The type of line that keeps him in these small-town rings, that makes him believe he'll make it beyond them.

The reaction to Chris Del Ray is a mix of boos and cheers, soon drowned out by a chant: "Holly–wood! Holly–wood!" Hunter soaks it up, leans left and right, grinning and holding a hand to one ear and then another. "All hail!" he yells. They answer: "Hollywood!" And then he starts a cadence to remind everyone why they're here, why he's here. "App–a–la–chee! Ap–a–la–chee!"

They lock up. For a few slow seconds Hunter balances in a headstand between Del Ray's legs. They go after each other's necks. Hunter dropkicks Del Ray in the back of the head. Del Ray rolls. A Hollywood chant starts again. Hunter mimes the act of buckling a championship belt around his waist, then scuffs his feet like he's kicking dirt in Del Ray's direction. An arm wringer, a kick to the chin. Del Ray kicks off the middle rope and reverses the move to Hunter. With his opponent still gripping his arm, Hunter fluidly moves from a one-armed cartwheel to a backbend to a somersault. They clasp hands. Del Ray jumps from the top rope to the mat, back to the top, then to the floor, taking Hunter's arm with him and cracking it on the top rope. Hunter crawls to the corner.

Del Ray goes after the injured shoulder. Hunter rears up and right-hooks him in the face. Del Ray gives it back. Hunter falls to the ground. Del Ray suplexes him, holds him to the ground by the neck. He tosses Hunter off the rope. Pins him. The ref counts to two.

In every match there's a period when the babyface strains, when he's at his weakest. He can't possibly go on without help. He looks toward the fans. The people in the seats, whether they know him or not, supply it. It's their job. Today, the Apalachee High School community sees itself face down in the ring, panting, trying to pull itself up from an undue attack. It sees itself in Hunter as he struggles to stand.

Hunter rebounds, injured but strong, punches rapid-fire with his right arm. Unhinged, angry, he gives his opponent the beating he deserves. The attack, requited. An Apalachee chant starts again. Now they're calling for his finisher, the brainbuster. Hunter heaves, red-faced, draws an arm up and points to the guy who called for it as if to say, "Yup, just wait." He tries. Del Ray kicks out. They're both on their knees exchanging slaps. Hunter uppercuts. Backflips from the corner, lands on Del Ray's back. Hunter falls to the floor, tries to catch his breath.

And then the swerve. Hunter's cousin, Chop Top, and the wrestler Pat Roach watch from the flanks. With both Hunter and Del Ray down and the crowd's eyes fixed on the action in the ring, they advance toward it. Chop Top dives below the bottom rope and attacks Hunter's face. Roach gets to work on Del Ray. The announcers frantically ring the bell. Surprise attackers coming at innocent hometown boys with intent to kill.

"Nooo!" Westlake cries. "We are not having this night end like this!" The carnage continues. Hunter and Del Ray lay helpless on the floor. The villains kick them in the chin, again, again, again. *Someone make it stop.*

Westlake grabs the mic. "Back off! Y'all gonna come in here and mess things up? Why don't y'all do a little tag team action tonight. How's that sound?" And then he addresses the fans. "What do y'all think?"

Hunter reaches for the mic. Laying in the ring, the lowest rope propping him up from under his arm, sweaty, disheveled, he says, "I'm not waiting for another one of your shows. I am doing this right now."

"Let's go Hollywood!" someone yells from the floor.

Hunter looks at Del Ray. "You ready to whoop that ass right there?" Del Ray considers it. Looks at Hunter. "I'm all in, baby." Rival high schools, wrestling opponents . . . They'll do it. They'll see through their differences and come together, for Apalachee.

The fight spills out of the ring, into the crowd, right in front of Hunter's family. Jenn and her mother move out of harm's way. Billy Ray stays, planted in his plastic chair with a knowing calm.

Hunter dropkicks Roach and slams his forehead into the mat. Roach goes after him with a chair. Hunter rips it out of his hands and slams it on his back. He follows up with a high kick to Roach's chin then follows Chop Top out of the ring. Chop Top collides with the cinderblock wall. He writhes on the concrete floor, steps from his uncle. Billy Ray ignores him. The action is fast, unflinching, like an action movie. Live, in-person, performed by actors who do their own stunts.

The bookers wanted Hunter to bring the whole Apalachee package—the trophies, the medals, a fresh-faced, high-flying symbol of triumph. "I'll wear the letterman," he said. He wouldn't carry the awards. "It's not me."

In the end, he felt the spectacle was too much about him. He shouldn't have won the battle royal and the tag-team match. Don't overexpose the star. The shooting hadn't even affected him. He went to Apalachee, but that was three years ago. He was too many degrees of separation away. But a wrestler's role—a person's role—is often to be the person everybody wants you to be. He played the part.

Roach uses his body weight to pin Hunter in the ring. This flabby, aging wrestler is no match for Apalachee High's 2021 Wrestler of the Year. Del Ray comes to help. Then Hunter lifts 305-pound Roach into the air and suplexes him. In wrestling as in life, anything is possible. Apalachee will persevere. Chop Top sends Del Ray out and then it's down to Hunter and his cousin, working through life with wrestling just as they always have. They're older now but the dance that both breaks and mends is the same. If anyone can take Hunter's finisher—the brainbuster—it's Chop Top.

Hunter starts a chant. "Ap–a–la–chee!" and holds his jacket high. A cheap pop. And exactly what the fans need.

ACKNOWLEDGMENTS

Thanks to Hunter and Billy Ray, who opened up their lives to me. Thanks to the wrestlers, promoters, families, and fans who shared their experience and insight with a notepad-wielding stranger, especially Matt Hankins, Todd Sexton, Crystal Rose, Azrael, Chop Top, Slim J, Nick Halen, Judais, Triston Michaels, Bill Behrens, Jamie Holmes, Justin Legend, and Sarah and Robert Noblett.

The mentors and students of the University of Georgia's narrative nonfiction MFA program nurtured this work long before it became a book. John T. Edge's all-capped notes [in brackets] continue to make me a better writer. I'm grateful to Valerie Boyd for creating the program. Thanks to Vicki Michaelis for sharpening my focus. Beth Burch and Diana Keough for the lunches. Jarrett Van Meter and Mikeie Honda Reiland for the check-ins. Martin Padgett for hopping on the phone. And Tommy Tomlinson for a formative guest lecture that taught me to search for subtext.

The Hambidge Center for the Creative Arts and Sciences in Rabun Gap, Georgia, and the Virginia Center for the Creative Arts in Amherst, Virginia, afforded me the comfortable solitude I needed to write this book and its proposal. Thanks to all who support residencies like these for creatives in search of time and space.

Thanks to Margot Guralnick, who taught me the economy of words. To Ted Conover, whose work inspired this. Katie Carter King, who kept *Rough House* in line. Mrs. Ridgway, my high school English teacher, for making me into a writer. Emily Kimbro for friendship and photo editing. David Black, who saw what this could be before I did. Dan Gerstle at Norton for saying yes. And Zeba Arora for shepherding me.

Thanks to Alfred Konuwa and Brandon Thurston for sharing their wrestling knowledge and to Larry Goodman for being the unofficial historian of professional wrestling in Georgia. To the writers of *Georgia Wrestling History*, a critical source in my reporting.

Thanks to Judith Winfrey for hosting me at the farm and to Matt Hankins, Najasism, Rose Gold, Bryce Cannon, and my friends and family for showing up and listening.

Thanks to my husband, Dan, who never questioned my need to spend Saturday nights in locker rooms populated mostly by men in sparkly underwear. And thanks to my daughter and occasional reporting partner, Avery, who is always ready to rumble. I love you both so much.

RECOMMENDED READING

Roland Barthes, *Mythologies* (Hill and Wang, 1972).

Scott Beekman, *Ringside: A History of Professional Wrestling in America* (Bloomsbury Publishing, 2006).

Aaron Feigenbaum and Shawn Michaels, *Heartbreak & Triumph: The Shawn Michaels Story* (Pocket Books, 2005).

Marcus Griffin, annotated by Steve Yohe and Scott Teal, *The Annotated Fall Guys: Barnums of Bounce* (Crowbar Press, 2019).

John D. Hollis, Lex Luger, and Steve "Sting" Borden, *Wrestling with the Devil: The True Story of a World Champion Professional Wrestler—His Reign, Ruin, and Redemption* (Tyndale House Publishers, 2013).

Sharon Mazer, *Professional Wrestling: Sport and Spectacle* (University Press of Mississippi, 1998).

Josephine Riesman, *Ringmaster: Vince McMahon and the Unmaking of America* (Atria Books, 2023).

Nicholas Sammond (ed.), *Steel Chair to the Head: The Pleasure and Pain of Professional Wrestling* (Duke University Press, 2005).

David Shoemaker, *The Squared Circle: Life, Death, and Professional Wrestling* (Penguin Publishing Group, 2013).

R. Tyson Smith, *Fighting for Recognition: Identity, Masculinity, and the Act of Violence in Professional Wrestling* (Duke University Press, 2014).

Ray Tennenbaum, "Sleeper Hold: How Professional Wrestling Worked" (http://www.ray-field.com/SleeperHold).

IMAGE CREDITS

9	Chris Nelms
17	Alison Lyn Miller
40	Amanda Dutton
56	Peter Sigmund
69	Alison Lyn Miller
83	Alison Lyn Miller
88	Alison Lyn Miller
109	Bob McAteer
120	Terry Hallman
157	Hunter James
172	Bob McAteer
194	Alison Lyn Miller
226	Xander Seabolt
234	Alison Lyn Miller
241	Allie McPhetridge
245	Alison Lyn Miller